DEGREES OF SEPARATION

Schneur Zalman Newfield

DEGREES
OF SEPARATION

Identity Formation While Leaving
Ultra-Orthodox Judaism

TEMPLE UNIVERSITY PRESS
Philadelphia • *Rome* • *Tokyo*

TEMPLE UNIVERSITY PRESS
Philadelphia, Pennsylvania 19122
tupress.temple.edu

Library of Congress Cataloging-in-Publication Data

Names: Newfield, Schneur Zalman, 1982– author.
Title: Degrees of separation : identity formation while leaving ultra-Orthodox Judaism /
    Schneur Zalman Newfield.
Description: Philadelphia : Temple University Press, [2020] | Includes bibliographical
    references and index. | Summary: "This book uses interviews with people who have left
    the Lubavitch and Satmar sects of Judaism to explore how people build a new identity
    after being raised in an ultra-orthodox worldview. The transition is an ongoing process
    where exiters navigate many links to their old life"—Provided by publisher.
Identifiers: LCCN 2019030091 (print) | LCCN 2019030092 (ebook) | ISBN 9781439918951
    (cloth) | ISBN 9781439918968 (paperback) | ISBN 9781439918975 (pdf)
Subjects: LCSH: Orthodox Judaism—Relations—Nontraditional Jews. | Ex-Orthodox
    Jews. | Habad—United States. | Satmar Hasidim—United States. | Judaism and
    secularism.
Classification: LCC BM197.6 .N49 2020 (print) | LCC BM197.6 (ebook) |
    DDC 296.8/332—dc23
LC record available at https://lccn.loc.gov/2019030091
LC ebook record available at https://lccn.loc.gov/2019030092

Printed in the United States of America

9 8 7 6 5 4 3 2 1

To my uncle, Jeff Janus,
a true lover of books, knowledge, and culture,
and
to my daughter Maya Esther,
an eager learner with an inquisitive mind

Contents

Acknowledgments

In researching and writing this book I have incurred many debts of gratitude. I thank Kathleen Gerson, my dissertation chair in the Sociology Department at New York University (NYU), who stuck by me and remained warm and positive throughout the long, twisted process of my research. She encouraged me to embrace data that ran counter to expectations. She also provided me with invaluable insights regarding the theory and practice of qualitative research, in-depth interviews, and data analysis, as well as guided me through the process of publishing this book.

Iddo Tavory read my work closely and provided deep insights based on his expert knowledge of the ultra-Orthodox world. He challenged me to think beyond my personal experiences inside the community, which I have sought to do throughout this process. The other dissertation committee members, Steven Lukes, Lynne Haney, and Ruth Horowitz, also deserve my humble thanks for their commitment to me and my work. I am grateful for all of their support and teaching both during the dissertation process and throughout my graduate career.

I will always treasure the time I spent exploring the social theories of religion with Steven in preparation for my comprehensive exam on the subject and the cappuccinos he warmly treated me to. It was particularly thrilling to explore E. E. Evans-Pritchard with someone who was a personal student of the celebrated anthropologist. I felt that I was participating in a chain of tradition.

I also remember with great fondness Lynne's course on sex and gender. She inspired me to think about the role that gender plays, often hidden or overlooked, in many aspects of our society. Throughout this work I have tried to remember the lessons I learned in her course and apply them to my research. While working as Ruth's teaching assistant for her senior thesis writing course, I learned an immeasurable amount about the research process.

Vivek Chibber, also of the Sociology Department at NYU, was an invaluable support, especially in the early stages of this project and of my graduate training more generally, providing all manner of guidance and assistance. Throughout my time at NYU, Vivek challenged me to think clearly and rigorously. I am a better scholar and a better person because of him. I also thank the following faculty members of the NYU Sociology Department for making themselves available to me to discuss aspects of my research throughout my time in the department: David Greenberg, Deirdre Royster, and the late Gerald Marwell. I also thank Professor Colin Jerolmack, who read a paper of mine connected to this research and provided useful feedback.

Among the many friends I made in graduate school, two stand out for special recognition. It is rare to find a colleague whom you also think of as a mentor. I am privileged to have found exactly that in my dear friend and cohort member Jeremy Cohan. Since the day I met him, he has been expanding my thinking about religion, politics, and culture. I am honored to call him my friend and mentor. I also owe a tremendous debt of gratitude to Stacy Torres, another cohort member and a dear friend. We connected early in our first semester in the program, and our friendship only grew deeper with time. I will never forget the late-night pep talks on the phone and all the moral support she showered on me. It meant the world to me and certainly contributed to finishing my dissertation.

I thank the following institutions for their financial support: New York University for providing me with a McCracken Fellowship for the first five years of my stay at NYU, the Feinstein Center at Temple University for awarding me the Kevy Kaiserman Memorial Summer Fellow in 2013, Targum Shlishi for awarding me a Dissertation Grant in 2013, and Footsteps for awarding me an Ignite Microgrant in 2018 to cover the expenses of hiring a indexer for this book.

I am especially grateful to the seventy-four Lubavitch and Satmar men and women who agreed to be interviewed for my research. They trusted me with their life stories and inner thoughts. I would not have been able to conduct this research without them. I greatly appreciate their trust and have strived to produce a work that honestly reflects their experiences and does justice to the quiet heroism of their life journeys.

I also acknowledge Deborah Tambor and Faigy Mayer, two ultra-Orthodox exiters who committed suicide during the time this study was conducted. Neither of them was interviewed for this study, but they are part of the ultra-Orthodox exiter community, which was deeply pained by their loss. Perhaps shedding light on the struggles that ultra-Orthodox exiters face and explaining their reality to outsiders will lighten the incredible burden they carry. I also thank Lani Santo, executive director of Footsteps, and the staff of Footsteps for providing basic demographic data about their membership and allowing me to use their organization to seek subjects for my research.

I thank Gennady Estraikh of the Skirball Department of Hebrew and Judaic Studies at NYU for the countless hours we spent together speaking Yiddish and discussing Jewish history and culture. Our discussions encouraged me to think about the parallels in Jewish history that exist between the lives of my subjects and the lives of other Jews in different historical periods who went through similar transitions. I hope he will not be too disappointed that I did not use formal transliteration of the Yiddish that appears in the quotations from interviewees throughout the book.

In addition to those faculty members at NYU, numerous other scholars took the time to meet with me or talk on the phone and give feedback on my ideas or early drafts of my work. These include Benjamin Zablocki, Todd Clear, Jody E. Myers, and Ayala Fader. Such acts of kindness are the hallmark of intellectual communities and the very best of academia. I also thank Rabbi Robert Scheinberg, a scholar in his own right, for his support and insights.

In addition to those who guided and inspired me while in graduate school, I acknowledge those academic mentors I was lucky enough to have as an undergraduate at Brooklyn College, City University of New York (CUNY). To begin with, I thank Joseph Varga. I wrote my first major paper in his course on socialism, communism, and anarchism, and he provided me with wonderful feedback that challenged me to clarify my thinking and helped me learn the art of doing research.

Similarly, Curtis Hardin and Lee Quinby were my senior thesis advisers, back when I first tried to analyze the Lubavitch community from a social-scientific perspective. Their caring and dedication to me were deeply felt and greatly appreciated. They convinced me that I could get into graduate school and that I might actually enjoy scholarly work. Many thanks go to Michael Magee, who was my teaching assistant for the experimental psychology course I took. He was truly committed to improving my academic writing, and although I gave him a hard time when he first returned one of my papers covered in red ink, the truth is that he challenged me to become a better writer. I hope some of that shows in this book. I also thank Carolina Bank-Munoz, who believed in me and supported and encouraged me both while I was her student and afterward, when I was deciding if I should to apply to Ph.D. programs in sociology.

Special thanks go to Rabbi Dr. Rachel Safman, whom I met in 2002 while I was a Lubavitch rabbinical student doing a year of outreach work for the

Jewish community in Singapore and she was a sociology professor at the National University of Singapore. She had a huge effect on my life. She was the first sociologist I had ever met and the first professor I had ever befriended. I still remember with great affection our conversations during Saturday-afternoon lunches following synagogue services. They were wide ranging, covering literature, philosophy, and history, but mostly focused on her passion at the time and what was quickly becoming my passion as well—the social sciences. I remember her trying to explain the basics of research methodology and the fact that sociology could say a great deal about people in the aggregate but that it was almost impossible to predict what any given individual would do in a particular situation. From those early conversations developed a deep friendship that I still cherish dearly. I could not have asked for a better, or better-informed, first teacher of the social sciences.

I also thank Dr. Michael Klein, who provided me with much-needed emotional support and perspective during the last two years of graduate school. I am not sure where I would be without him. He also provided me with a forum to freely exchange ideas, and he offered critical insights into some of the psychological issues discussed in the book.

In January 2018, I joined the Social Sciences, Human Services, and Criminal Justice Department at Borough of Manhattan Community College (CUNY) and immediately felt at home. I especially thank my officemates, Geoffrey Kurtz, Jacob Kramer, Yana Durmysheva, and Melissa Brown, for welcoming me and fostering a warm and collegial atmosphere in which to complete the final research for this book and prepare it for publication. I also thank my colleagues Rifat Salam, Lisa Rose, and Shenique Davis for encouraging my research and providing me with insights and guidance in the last stage of this book's development. I also benefited from CUNY's program of course reductions offered to untenured faculty so I could pursue my research while teaching.

I am also very grateful to Temple University Press, especially my editor, Ryan Mulligan, for his professionalism and dedication to this book. I am particularly thankful for his patient and detailed feedback on this book's introductory and concluding chapters. Special thanks also go to my copyeditor, Cynthia Lindlof, for her meticulous job preparing the book for publication. In addition, I thank the two anonymous reviewers for their careful reading of the book and their many helpful suggestions.

This book is dedicated to my dear uncle Jeff Janus. He is a major part of why I ever went to college in the first place and ever dreamed of going to graduate school. For years while I attended yeshiva high school and rabbinical school, he encouraged me to learn to read English and explore the world beyond the walls of my yeshiva. His love of learning and his passion for culture, particularly Shakespeare, Dickens, and Molière, were and are infectious.

I remember with great fondness the time we spent together in the basement of his New York apartment taking turns reading out loud *The Merchant of Venice*, *Hamlet*, and *King Lear*, consulting the Signet Classic notes at the bottom of the page when we encountered obscure words or phrases. I learned much more than just "what doth trouble" Hamlet's mind. I learned about the beauty of language, about the joy books can offer a diligent reader, and that I had an uncle who cared a great deal about me and my future. He was a faithful guide to a world I knew nothing about, and I will be forever grateful for his many kindnesses.

I also thank my late grandmother, Ruth Newfield, whom I knew simply as Bubby Ruth, as well as Drs. Phillipa and Philip Gordon and Marta and Martin White for their love, encouragement, and financial support, without which it would have been impossible to ever finish this book. Thanks go to my entire family for their love, support, and encouragement throughout my graduate school experience. Special thanks go to my older brother, Rabbi Yossi Newfield, for graciously assisting me with locating numerous Lubavitch and other rabbinic sources.

This book is also dedicated to my daughter Maya Esther, whose bright smile, along with that of my other daughter, Liba Pearl (whose mother's first book is dedicated to her), warmed my heart at the beginning and end of every day that I worked on this book. And last, but surely not least, I thank my dear wife and true companion, Dr. Jenny Labendz. Her love and acceptance mean the world to me. I am deeply grateful to have her not only as my life partner but as an intellectual partner, and I cherish our discussions. Her generous feedback on this work has made it immeasurably stronger, clearer, and more beautiful.

Degrees of Separation

You Can Check Out,
but You Can Never Leave

Just when I thought I was out, they pull me back in!

—**Michael Corleone,** *The Godfather, Part III*

The superstition in which we grew up, though we may
recognize it, does not lose its power over us. Not all are free
who make mock of their chains.

—**Gotthold Ephraim Lessing,** *Nathan the Wise*

I was raised in the ultra-Orthodox Hasidic community known as
Lubavitch. I spent my childhood and young adulthood in Lubavitch yeshivas and summer camps studying religious texts, praying, and
strengthening my bond with the spiritual leader of the community, Rabbi
Menachem Mendel Schneerson. Although the community forbade the
teaching of secular subjects such as English reading and writing and mathematics in its schools, I learned to read English on my own and at twenty-one
sat for the GED high school equivalency exam. I eventually enrolled in
Brooklyn College, and by the time I graduated from college, I had shaved my
beard, had stopped wearing a skullcap (yarmulke), and no longer believed in
God, let alone the spiritual powers of Rabbi Schneerson.

In graduate school at New York University, I read Karl Marx, Émile Durkheim, and Max Weber and eventually found myself poring over contemporary scholarship on political economy, social movement theory, and the sociology of religion. It was not long before I found myself reading sociological
literature on religious exiters like myself. That was what stopped me in my
tracks and ultimately led to this book.

Despite my enthusiasm to better contextualize and theorize my exit, I
was surprised to find that the existing literature offered me few tools to help
make sense of my story. I was searching in particular for scholarly literature
on individuals who leave religion and on where they end up once they do.
Most of this existing literature relates to the boom in new religious movements (NRMs), popularly known as "cults," in the 1960s through the 1980s.
Within this area of study in particular, sociologists have been much more

interested in why and how young, educated adults from middle-class backgrounds *join* fringe religious communities than why and how they *leave* them (Albrecht, Cornwall, and Cunningham 1988; Richardson 2009). The scholarship I found on religious exiters—for example, David G. Bromley (1988, 1998), Janet Liebman Jacobs (1987, 1989), and Stuart A. Wright (1984, 1987)—tended to look at people who were raised in mainstream society and then decided as adults to join the NRMs, only to leave those groups afterward. That population is different on many levels from the population of individuals who leave the religious communities they were born into.

Such stories of joining and then exiting religious movements have much to tell us about what people look for from these religious movements, how their leaders cultivate a following in their particular context, and how these movements succeed or fail in retaining converts. But it does not tell us about the habits and perspective instilled by a life raised within a totalizing point of view, how those unique circumstances transition to life beyond the community, how exiters must invent new ways of being that their upbringings had not prepared them for, and what these particular individuals lose and retain in the exit process. I was confident that individuals born into totalizing religious groups had something new and valuable to offer to the work done thus far on religious exit. And perhaps the experience of these particular individuals might reveal new insights into the nature of identity and the transition between identities more broadly.

The dominant focus on NRMs in the literature on religious exit leads to what my research concludes is an incomplete picture of religious exit. The narrative of an individual falling in and out of a "cult" might lead one to assume a binary, "in or out," nature of leaving a religion. The possibility of a prolonged in-between state might not suggest itself to researchers within the limits of existing studies and merits further consideration. Wright suggests that if an individual goes through an extensive process of transition, including adopting an alternative plausibility structure from the one held by the group one is leaving, it is possible for this individual to "put the past behind him/her" (1987, 79). Wright also states that for individuals who go through this process of transition, "defection is complete. The old life is history. The individual begins a new life" (81).

Similarly, Susan Rothbaum tells us, "Two or three years after leaving, they may go for months without recalling [their experience in the religious movement]" (1988, 228). These quotations show a binary in the literature that maintains that nothing remains of former identity post-exit. Although this may be the case for Wright's or Rothbaum's interviewees, who joined a religious movement for only several months or years, the same cannot be said about me or people like me who were born into their religion and lived within it for decades. This book dives into the alternative possibility that for individuals raised within certain religious worldviews, the old life is very much bound up in the new. Further, it explores how this binding of old and new lives plays out in the lived experience of exiters.

One can find evidence of the power of the binary transition narrative even in studies of exiters who were born into the religious communities they eventually left (A. Mauss 1969; Caplovitz and Sherrow 1977; Hoge, McGuire, and Stratman 1981; Streib et al. 2009; Zuckerman 2012; Bengtson, Putney, and Harris 2013), as well as the literature specifically on ex–Orthodox Jews (Shaffir and Rockaway 1987; Shaffir 1998; Winston 2005; Topel 2012).[1] This assumption is embedded in the language used to describe the behavior of these individuals: "leaving," "exiting," "apostasy," "deconversion," "disidentification," "disaffiliation," and so on. All these terms describe a process that is unidirectional and appears permanent. At stake in this characterization is what we can learn from taking the exit process seriously as its own inquiry, with its own fruitful complexities and contradictions. When we learn how the exit process is ongoing, we learn which aspects and pieces of a totalizing identity lived in since birth can be rejected, which linger, which come and go, which haunt an individual in the process of building a new identity, and which take new forms. Such an understanding brings us closer to fundamental questions of how religion functions in social life and the process of identity construction more generally.

There are exceptions to this narrative pattern that do show greater attention to the continued process of exit. Among scholars who study religious communities, several have noted the long-term effects of religious exit, such as Benjamin Zablocki (1980) and Stephanie Levine (2003). Similarly, within the literature on religious exit, several scholars have discussed this fact. Norman Skonovd uses the term "floating" to describe the confusion, doubt, fear, and guilt associated with the decision to leave a religion, although even he seems to believe that after a while this subsides (1981, 133). Similarly, Eileen Barker challenges the "clear-cut distinction between members and nonmembers of movements which are in tension with their social environment" (1998, 83). Although Barker expands the view of the literature by introducing the idea of marginal and peripheral members of religious communities,

---

1. An extreme example of this binary view of religious group membership is found in the dispute between Samuel Heilman and Menachem Friedman (2010) and Chaim Rapoport (2011) regarding the biography of Rabbi Menachem Mendel Schneerson, the last leader of the Lubavitch community, known simply as "the Rebbe." They all assume that before the Rebbe arrived in America from Europe in 1940, he was either Orthodox and committed to Hasidic life or he was non-Orthodox, ignorant of Hasidic life, and wanted only to be a professional and assimilate into secular Parisian society. Why is it not possible that the Rebbe wanted to do both, that he had multiple desires and conflicting goals? There were many people in Berlin and Paris at the time who came from deeply Orthodox homes and felt very connected to them but also wanted to be part of the larger European cultural milieu (for an analysis of six such transitional Eastern European Jewish figures, see Goldberg 1989).

she too ultimately assumes that once a member ventures out from the movement to join the broader society, the individual has left his or her community
of origin behind for good.

Another exception is Lucinda SanGiovanni, who studied ex-nuns and
coined the term "passage lag" to describe "the appearance in the new passage
of specific values, self-images, preferences, and behaviors derived and carried over from the prior passage." SanGiovanni notes that some of her respondents missed the sense of community and purpose they shared in the
convent, still spoke softly because of their training as a nun, felt guilty for
spending money and being "materialistic," and struggled with an inability
to make small talk, since as nuns they were taught not to discuss "trivia"
(1978, 114–115). This all highlights the extent to which it may be difficult to
jettison the socialization one undergoes within a religious environment.

This book presents for the first time a detailed portrait of the exit process
for those exiting ultra-Orthodoxy. I interviewed seventy-four exiters from
two ultra-Orthodox Hasidic communities, Lubavitch and Satmar. My research explores the features and implications of the prolonged state of being
in between that characterizes exiters from both communities, including the
significant traits and practices from their upbringing that remain and transform in their new lives as exiters.

To remain consistent with the scholarship, I do not introduce a new term
to describe the phenomenon of distancing oneself from a religious community while remaining in an in-between state. Instead, I adopt the term "exit,"
introduced by Helen Rose Fuchs Ebaugh (1988a, 1–2) and used by numerous
scholars. But this book shows, first, that the journey of those who were raised
in strict religious communities and deviate from them is not completely unidirectional and, second, that these individuals are not completely disconnected from their roots once they "arrive" at their new destination. Therefore, I describe interviewees as "exiting" rather than as "having exited,"
allowing for the possibility that they feel pushed to move outside their community, but they may also feel pulled to remain connected to it. Exiting is an
ongoing process of becoming. One of the main contributions of this book is
to complicate the assumed binary in much of the scholarly literature on religious exiting and detail the prolonged in-between state that many exiters
experience.

Beyond the NRMs, most scholarship on religious exiters focuses either
on exiters from liberal or mainline religions rather than from strict ones or
on a combination of individuals from various religious backgrounds. A good
example is the large-scale work of Heinz Streib and colleagues (2009). Because of the design of the study, the researchers combined data from conservative exiters and liberal exiters (only approximately half of their 126 interviewees who "deconverted" came from religions in "high tension" with their
surrounding society that may be called strict religions). Thus, although the

authors acknowledge this and try to incorporate this difference into their analysis, the most they can do is outline six types of "destinations" that various exiters might choose among. The study leaves open for future research the question of why an individual from a particular religious background will choose a particular destination or, more important, describe what that choosing process entails. This book begins to address these issues.

Furthermore, this study emphasizes the distinctiveness of the outcomes for those exiting from strict religious communities, attending especially to the type of social institutions or environments from which people are exiting in the understanding that a strict worldview will have particular effects on the nature and trajectory of the exit. This opportunity informed both my choice of which religious exiters to study and my inclusion of contextual information about the religious communities from which they were exiting.

The broader scholarly literature on personal transformations also stands to benefit from a deeper understanding of the effects of different types of social institutions or environments being abandoned. For example, when Ebaugh develops a general model to be applied to all personal transformations to explain the "generic social processes" involved (1988a, 32), major traumatic experiences (such as exiting a religious order) are grouped in with other types of experiences (such as the retirement of a physician). Might not some of these experiences have more long-term effects than others? This book addresses this question by identifying the aspects of ultraconservative religious identities that prove resilient and those that prove more fungible for individuals in the process of transition, as well as what factors lead these characteristics to vary from exiter to exiter. The book embraces the opportunity to deepen our understanding of how personal transformations may differ depending on the nature of the identity from which an individual is transitioning.

The foundational principle from which this book seeks to launch its inquiry is that people born into strict religions who decide to exit them remain in an in-between state even years later because of the internalization of the totalizing institutions in which they were raised (Goffman 1961). This argument builds on Ebaugh's idea of "role residuals," which helps us think about the long-term effects of major life transitions (1988a, 173–174). From there, the book explores the patterns among the experiences of exiters, including the ways that the old life continues within the new. For the individuals in this study, the transition in identities goes beyond what would be in play for other Americans changing religions, even religions they were born into. This study addresses a form of detachment and reinvention from a cultural and social world much more enveloping than the word "religion" may ordinarily connote.

This is not simply a case of individuals suddenly deciding to completely disconnect themselves from their religious upbringing. Nor is it about them choosing to stay connected to some vague "symbolic ethnicity" or "symbolic religiosity" (Gans 1979, 1994) or some kind of "ethnic option" (Waters 1990), transitions with which many people exiting less orthodox forms of Judaism might identify. However, this study explores how those who were raised in "total institutions" (Goffman 1961, 4) and "greedy institutions" (Coser 1974) that focus on rigid conformity and are encompassing of all aspects of its members' lives internalize elements of their upbringing such that they are unable to disengage completely from them, even after years of trying. Instead, they transform themselves over an extensive period and blend aspects of their past with aspects of the broader society to shape a new future for themselves.

To use Charles Taylor's language, this is not a "subtraction story" in which individuals abandon their religious past to reveal a completely modern or secular identity (2007, 253). It is about the tension between continuity and discontinuity that manifests in the identities they shape.[2] I explore how the form and substance of their exiting directly relates to their upbringing. This exploration yields tools with which future research might interrogate other transitions from similarly or even less totalizing identities.

Although there are significant aspects of discontinuity in the lives of exiters from the Lubavitch and Satmar communities of Hasidic ultra-Orthodox Judaism, there are also many aspects of continuity with their religious upbringing, some of which they are aware and some of which they may not be aware. Clear examples of discontinuity are the radical changes in dress, abandoning the traditional religious garb for more modern clothing. Often men shave off their religiously mandated beards and (for Satmars) cut off the long side curls, the *paiyyes*.[3] Women often begin wearing pants rather than skirts as well as more revealing clothing, and married women uncover their hair instead of wearing the wig (*sheitel*) required by the religious community. Discontinuity could also include discarding one's Yiddish or Hebrew name for a more Americanized name and physically moving out of the community to live in a different neighborhood not surrounded by other ultra-Orthodox Jews.

Other less visible aspects of discontinuity include eating habits; exiters begin to eat nonkosher food. Religious beliefs are also affected by the exiting. Exiters often stop believing in the divine authorship of the Torah, a central

---

2. As Isaac Deutscher observes, "The Jewish heretic who transcends Jewry belongs to a Jewish tradition" (1968, 26). This contention supports David Biale's broad claim that secular Jews are directly linked to the tradition that they are rejecting. Referring to Baruch Spinoza, Heinrich Heine, Sigmund Freud, and others, Biale observes, "They were all heretics, yet their heresy might be understood as a rejection that grew out of the Jewish tradition itself" (2010, 1).

3. I am transliterating here according to the Satmar pronunciation. Other religious groups within Judaism may pronounce the term differently.

dogma of the religious community. Some doubt the very existence of God or of the supernatural powers ascribed to the religious leaders of their community. Although discontinuity has been the focus of most prior scholarship on religious exiters, this book focuses on the other side of the coin: aspects of continuity in the life of religious exiters as seen in their habits of thought as well as habits of action.

One important aspect of discontinuity, however, needs to be clarified. Exiting is not the same as relinquishing faith in God. Exiting a religious community is a public act, while relinquishing one's belief in God is a private, and potentially completely secret, feeling or thought. Furthermore, exiting and relinquishing faith are not necessarily even linked. It is possible to stay in the community without believing, and it is possible to leave the community while still believing in God and the basic veracity of the Bible. This study focuses on the consequences of actually exiting the religious community. What actually happens to those who do exit? What residual effects remain of their upbringing, and how do they negotiate their new identity, both within themselves and with their families and communities?

The individuals in this study retain elements of continuity and discontinuity with their upbringing, but the focus here is on interrogating the elements of continuity, in part because thus far the literature on religious exiting focuses largely on the elements of discontinuity. In addition, there is a philosophical perspective that drives my interest in continuity. This study challenges the basic Enlightenment idea about the power of reason to transform individuals and society. This idea leads observers to overestimate the power of personal choice in identity transformation. This study illustrates the limits of personal transformation by noting that although people can change much about their appearance, attitudes, and behaviors, there are aspects of the self that are highly resistant to change and may never be totally transformed. This study proposes to probe some of the boundaries of what individuals can construct in their identity and what a particular context is capable of constructing for them.

To describe the in-between state of people who exit strict religion, I adopt a variant of Victor Turner's (1967, 1969) usage of the term "liminality." Liminality describes the position of exiters in the world once they distance themselves from their religion but before they enter fully into the broader society (if indeed they ever do so). Turner calls the ambiguous and paradoxical period in between two states "the liminal" and describes it as being caught "betwixt and between": "Liminality is the realm of primitive hypothesis, where there is a certain freedom to juggle with the factors of existence," and when in the liminal period individuals "are at once no longer classified and not yet classified" (1967, 93–110).

This description of liminality captures essential aspects of the individuals' plight. They are in the process of exiting from strict religion, but because of their unfamiliarity with their new surroundings and of the internalization of their religious upbringing, they are still struggling with forging their new selves. There is a crucial difference, however, between Turner's original usage of the term "liminality," for which he is remembered, and the way I use it here.

Whereas Turner views the liminal as a temporary situation, I use it to refer to a long-term or even permanent condition.[4] It is of course possible that the individuals will at some future time emerge from this liminal state to be completely disconnected from their religious backgrounds, but my research shows that this state of liminality is more than the temporary situation Turner describes. But even according to Turner there are instances of the "institutionalization of liminality," where it becomes a permanent condition, such as in various monastic and millenarian religions (1969, 107, 111). Robert D. Putnam and David E. Campbell (2012) also use the term "liminal" to refer to a long-term condition rather than a temporary state. My use of the term "liminal" to describe a long-lasting or permanent in-between state is somewhat unusual but warranted and helpful.

My divergence from Turner does not relate merely to whether liminality is temporary or permanent. More significantly, we have a fundamentally different view of the nature of liminality. Turner sees it as liberating, assisting individuals in moving from one state to the next, becoming ever more integrated into their original society. I emphasize the way that individuals' capacity for change is fundamentally circumscribed and limited. People are not completely able to reinvent themselves. They can make great strides, but they will forever be connected to their past.

I open this chapter with my personal story for two reasons. First, my background is not incidental to my research. Having been raised in the Lubavitch community, I have intimate knowledge of its symbols and language, its practices and beliefs, and its educational system. This not only made it possible for me to understand various dynamics and realities, but it also helped me gain the trust of my Lubavitch interviewees and eased communication with them. This knowledge also helped with my Satmar interviewees, who share much in common with the Lubavitchers, including their use of the Yiddish language. Likewise, Ebaugh (1988a) argues that being an ex-nun was essential for gaining access to other nuns in cloistered convents and for interpreting the information gathered.

---

4. The idea of liminality as it is being used here is similar to Georg Simmel's (1908) idea of the stranger and to Robert E. Park's idea of the "marginal man." As Park notes, "There are no doubt periods of transition and crisis in the lives of most of us that are comparable with those which the immigrant experiences when he leaves home to seek his fortune in a strange country. But in the case of the marginal man the period of crisis is relatively permanent. ... [He] is one who lives in two worlds, in both of which he is more or less of a stranger" (1928, 893).

But the second reason I begin with my own background is that I want to lay my cards on the table. My personal relationship to this topic, in addition to aiding my research, also poses a danger that I project my personal experiences onto the interviewees. I take seriously Janja Lalich's (2001) warnings about reflexivity bias when someone studies the group of which he or she was formerly a member. Lalich argues that former members have an advantage in knowing the language of the group, but they must be open about their former membership and experiences and use rigorous research methods, especially triangulation of sources, to prevent their own biases from entering the research. I have taken all these precautions for this study.

I went through the exit process and developed my own perspective on the issues that shaped my own experiences. At the same time, when I began this research, I did not have an agenda, and I have strived to allow the evidence to lead wherever it may. The fact that I grew up ultra-Orthodox and exited helped, in the sense that it made the interviewees feel a connection with me that encouraged them to join my study and to speak freely without needing to translate the Yiddish and Hebrew words, ideas, and sources in their natural speech.

Nonetheless, there are possible drawbacks to studying something that one is very close to personally. As Alexis de Tocqueville observed, "The stranger often learns important truths in the home of his host that the latter would perhaps conceal from a friend; with a stranger one is relieved of obligatory silence; one does not fear his indiscretion because he is passing through" (2000, 14).

Although I found the interviewees quite open and willing to share their experiences, only the Satmars, who knew that I did not come from or know many people inside their community, felt comfortable speaking to me about their own sexual abuse inside their community. (There was one Lubavitch exception to this.) It is possible that few of the Lubavitchers had been abused, but it is also possible that their silence on this sensitive subject may have been in accordance with Tocqueville's observation. Indeed, some of the Satmars saw me as an outsider to their world and were, for example, completely surprised that I spoke Yiddish fluently. Several of them exclaimed, "Lubavitchers know Yiddish?! I never knew that!"

The Language of Exiting

As noted previously, scholars use many different terms to refer to the process of leaving a religious tradition, including "apostasy," "disaffiliation," "disidentification," "leaving," and "exiting"; I use the term "exiting" because it is value neutral and reflects an ongoing process. Within the ultra-Orthodox community there are several phrases in use to refer to exiting the religious community. One of the most popular is to go "off the *derech*," off the path, often referred to by community members as being OTD. This expression is certainly not neutral, since it assumes that there is a single path and those who deviate from it are off that path, and it negatively judges those who do so. Even though this phrase is problematic, some within the exiter community use it to refer to themselves, although others reject its use. One Satmar interviewee told me that for a long time he was not sure what OTD meant; he thought it stood for "out the door."

Inside the Lubavitch and Satmar communities, exiters are described with various epithets. There are several terms popular among Satmars for exiters: *shaygets* (a derogatory term for a non-Jew), *farforin* (a person who has veered off), and *mishches* (a person who is spoiled or rotten). Lubavitchers often call exiters "bums." Lubavitchers also often describe exiters as "going *frai*," a Yiddish word derived from German, meaning "free." This phrase may sound less judgmental, or possibly even value neutral, until the true meaning of the word "free" in this context is understood. "Free" is not associated with a free spirit or free as a bird but rather with someone who is free from "the yoke of the sovereignty of heaven" (*oil malchus shamayim*). The person exiting is devoid of the constraining force of Jewish law and tradition and is as depraved as an animal wholly at the mercy of its natural passions.[5]

Although the phrases "off the *derech*" and "going *frai*" have achieved a certain amount of popularity, even among exiters themselves, and thus lost some of their opprobrium—similar to how the terms "Puritan" and "Quaker" have entered mainstream use and lost much of their original sting—I refrain from using them except when quoting from interviewees or the work of other scholars who use the terms.

There are other terms in use that should similarly be eschewed in academic writing about this population. The Hebrew term *yotzim leshe'iela*, "leaving to question," used widely in Israel to describe Jewish religious exiting (riffing on the traditional term *chozrim bi-t'shuva*, "returning in repentance," which describes those who become religious) is never used in Lubavitch or Satmar in America, and it is undesirable from an academic perspective since it places all the focus on questions and thinking. The terms "ex" or "former" are likewise unsuitable, since they imply that the separation is complete and final, an implication this book challenges. "Exiters," al-

---

5. This meaning of freedom based on religious constraint recalls the Puritan leader John Winthrop's contrast between two kinds of liberty: "There is a liberty of corrupt nature, which is affected both by men and beasts, to do what they list; and this liberty is inconsistent with authority, impatient of all restraint. . . . 'Tis the grand enemy of truth and peace, and all the ordinances of God are bent against it. But there is a civil, a moral, a federal liberty, which is the proper end and object of authority; it is a liberty for that only which is just and good; for this liberty you are to stand with the hazards of your very lives" (quoted in Mather 1820, 116–117).

though somewhat clunky, may be the preferred term because it is value neutral and leaves open the question of when they exited and whether they exited completely.[6]

It is important also to distinguish these interviewees, who are genuine religious exiters, from rebellious teens, often referred to in the Orthodox world as "at-risk" teens and conflated with exiters. Although some of those teens may decide eventually to leave the community for good, many of them end up returning once they have had time to consider their situation. Almost none of the interviewees in this study are in their teens (the average age is twenty-five), and they have thus had many years to consider returning to the community but have not done so.

Similarly, the exiters in this study are distinct from both members of the ultra-Orthodox community who live slightly "modern" lives while still considering themselves full members of their community and those members of the ultra-Orthodox community who are secretly irreligious and are the focus of Hella Winston's (2005, 2006) work. Like rebellious teens, members of those populations might eventually actually exit publicly, but it is much more likely that most of them will not because of the high costs involved. As William Shaffir (1998) observed, many think about exiting but few do.

Concerning language and terminology, throughout this study, individuals who grew up Satmar or Lubavitch are referred to as "Satmar interviewees" and "Lubavitch interviewees," respectively, even though they may no longer identify themselves with their community of origin. This was done to avoid the need to resort to a different term that would either be cumbersome or inappropriately binary, such as "former Lubavitcher" or "interviewee who was raised Lubavitch." In fact, however, some interviewees still refer to themselves as Lubavitch or Satmar, even while talking about their exit process.

In regard to non-English usages in this study, throughout the book there are quotations that include Yiddish, Hebrew, and Aramaic words, which I explain in brackets in the text. These are not necessarily exact translations but rather English renderings intended to assist the reader who is unfamiliar with these terms and concepts. One of the difficulties with these translations is that certain words are used, often by the same individual, to refer to different things.

For example, the term *frum* can mean "religious," "pious," "Orthodox," or "ultra-Orthodox." I provide the most appropriate meaning based on the

---

6. Fishel Schneerson (1922), a relative of the Lubavitcher Rebbe, who became a physician and professor of psychology in Europe before World War II, wrote a semibiographical novel titled *Chaim Gravitzer* about a Lubavitch man who struggles with his faith. The author refers to his protagonist as "the fallen *Hasid*." However, I have never heard anyone use this appellation to describe contemporary exiters, and I am not sure if it was a common one at that time or merely the author's own literary flourish.

context. Transliterations always reflect the usage of the individual being quoted or, in my own descriptions of the community, the common usage of that community. Yiddish and Hebrew are pronounced differently in different communities—the Satmar community, which derives from Hungary, pronounces Yiddish and Hebrew differently than the Lubavitch community, which derives from Russia—and more progressive Jewish communities today often adopt an Americanized Israeli-Sephardic pronunciation. An individual may even vacillate between two different pronunciations, which is reflected as well in my transliterations. While I do not focus on this feature of their speech, those familiar with different pronunciations may note this aspect of liminality in the speech patterns of the interviewees.

The term "post-exit" is sometimes used. It does not refer to the end of a process but rather to the initiation of the visible stages of the process of exiting—the point at which an individual has made a visible break with his or her community of origin.

Typologies of Exiters

All the interviewees exhibit a range of degrees to which they have actually replaced, adapted, or harmonized old communal goals and means with newfound personal goals and means. I divide them into three categories: trapped, hybrid, and disconnected.

Those exiters who are trapped appear to be and believe themselves for the most part to be functioning members of secular society, albeit facing some challenges. On closer analysis, however, they are unable to substantially replace the goals and means of their community, despite having exited. Rather, they feel they are stuck, living in a no-man's-land, as it were, uncomfortable and constantly struggling with the alternative goals and means that they find in the outside world. In other words, they either retain elements of the means and goals from their original community or struggle to adopt new ones. Trapped exiters carry over many aspects of their upbringing, but the key factor in this classification is not the number of those holdovers but the level of doubt and uncertainty that they inspire.

Exiters who are hybrids adopt new goals and means while simultaneously incorporating a limited amount of their former community's means and/or goals into their new lives.[7] Again, while hybrids tend to carry over less from their former communities, the key factor in determining whether

---

7. Naomi Ragen (2013), in her recent novel *The Sisters Weiss*, dramatizes the concept of a hybrid exiter in the character of Rivka, who runs away from her ultra-Orthodox upbringing and promptly abandons almost all Jewish observances. Over the next three years, as a single parent, she realizes that there were many Jewish practices, such as keeping kosher and observing the Sabbath and Jewish festivals, that she cherishes. She reinstitutes them for her sake and for the education of her young son.

they are hybrid or trapped is how well-adjusted they are in their new lives. For instance, their classification does not depend on whether they still read the ultra-Orthodox press or visit their old neighborhood but on what effect such actions have on their lives. Hybrids may be curious to read the ultra-Orthodox press and may enjoy visiting friends or family still in the community. But trapped exiters feel a consuming need to keep up with all the goings on in the ultra-Orthodox world, and visits to the community can leave them in tremendous pain, tearing open deep wounds and causing them to relive their earlier internal debates and religious doubts.

Thus, for example, numerous people have managed to use aspects of their former life, potentially aspects they feel deeply attached to, as a way of making a living, such as a journalist who writes about his old community or someone who takes his rabbinic ordination and becomes a rabbi in a more liberal denomination of Judaism. These individuals have managed to take a part of their former life and use it constructively to assist them in their new life, and these continued attachments are not disturbing or anxiety inducing. Thus, they are hybrids. Hybrid exiters successfully incorporate aspects of their old lives into their new lives. A trapped exiter, by contrast, may find it too emotionally or psychologically unsettling to use his rabbinic ordination to work in a liberal synagogue.

Exiters who are disconnected appear on the surface to have replaced all of the goals and means of their former community with new ones, without any residual effects. On closer analysis, however, they still struggle with their attraction to the old goals and means. Disconnection may be thought of as a kind of "reaction formation" (Freud [1905] 1962, 44–45), which takes the appearance of complete separation while inspiring significant preoccupation with their upbringing. Although the hybrids may visibly incorporate aspects of their upbringing into their new life, this plays a smaller role and is less mentally consuming than the role that the community plays in the life of disconnected people who actively resist their upbringing and repress feelings and behaviors that express a connection to it. Disconnection, my research shows, is more taxing to maintain.

Within these three subcategories of exiters, there inevitably are further gradations. Among trapped and disconnected exiters, gradations are based on two factors: the exiter's self-awareness and the exiter's ability to control or change his or her situation. These do not necessarily go hand in hand. Among hybrids, gradations relate to how well-adjusted the exiter is and, on a more superficial level, the frequency of residual effects from the former communities incorporated into his or her new life; again, these two do not necessarily go hand in hand.

Since this study does not include longitudinal data, it is impossible to determine whether the categories of "trapped," "hybrid," and "disconnected" represent types of exiters or stages that exiters go through. In other words, it is impossible to address whether exiters move from one of these to another over time or whether these are essential types of exiters. Thus, these categories are presented here as "processes" or "modes of being," ways that exiters make sense of their experiences and handle the contradictions they contain rather than as types or stages. It is possible that particular exiters move from one to another, and it is also possible that they stay where they are, but the data can describe only where they are currently.

The vast majority are best described as hybrids. Several are best described as trapped, and several as disconnected. There are two methodological reasons that disconnected exiters are not well represented in my sample. First, twenty-four interviewees were recruited through Footsteps, a New York–based nonprofit organization that promotes the healthy engagement with one's past that is characteristic of hybrids rather than disconnected exiters. Second, disconnected exiters tend to cut ties to the very networks that allowed me access to a sample of exiters. Furthermore, part of their disconnection may be a disinclination to discuss their past.

There are also two possible reasons that trapped exiters may be underrepresented in my sample. First, though their ties to their former community tend to be stronger than those of hybrids, they may experience those ties both as more important to them and at greater risk of being lost. Therefore, they have a heightened fear of exposure through participation in a study of exiters. I encountered such fear several times while speaking with potential interviewees. Second, trapped exiters experience considerable suffering from being trapped. They know that an interview is not therapy, and they do not wish to talk about their suffering with someone who, from their perspective, is ill equipped to handle such a conversation. I also encountered this concern while speaking with potential interviewees.

I use the term "liminality" to refer to the position of all interviewees (i.e., "between two worlds" and not completely a part of either), whereas I use the term "hybrid" to refer to a subset of interviewees. Furthermore, the term "hybrid" is used to refer to interviewees who employ a particular approach for coping with their liminality (i.e., they incorporate elements of their upbringing with elements from the outside world). Chapter 5 explores the strategies that hybrids use.

Background

The Lubavitch and Satmar Communities

Ultra-Orthodox Judaism is composed of numerous communities, often profoundly different from one another. The most basic division among these communities is between Hasidic and non-Hasidic groups. This book deals with the Lubavitch and Satmar communities, both of which belong to the

Hasidic movement. Lubavitch, also known as Chabad,[8] and Satmar are two of the largest Hasidic communities, each with its own school systems, summer camps, synagogues, charitable organizations, publishing houses, kosher-certification organizations, and other community institutions, as well as community-mandated distinct dress codes and rigidly defined ways of life. Since there is no official membership roster or census, the precise numbers of Lubavitchers and Satmars throughout the world are unknown, but according to Marcin Wodzinski (2018, 198–199), on the basis of his analysis of the respective community phone books and an estimate that the average size of a Hasidic household is 5.5 persons, there are 16,376 Lubavitch households (with roughly 90,068 people) and 26,078 Satmar households (with roughly 143,429 people).[9]

Hasidic communities observe the strictures of Jewish law (*halacha*) while also maintaining distinct Hasidic beliefs and rituals. Hasidic communities revere a leader called a "rebbe" who is believed to possess great spiritual powers. In addition to fulfilling all the Jewish commandments (*mitzvos*), the central practice of being a Hasid is connecting to the rebbe, following his every directive scrupulously, and studying his teachings diligently.[10] Hasidim believe that rebbes have unique spiritual powers that separate them from the rest of humanity (a textbook case of what Max Weber [1978] labeled "charisma") and that these powers give rebbes the ability to provide blessings for physical, financial, and spiritual well-being (see *Wonders and Miracles* 1993).[11]

Within Lubavitch it is believed that a rebbe is "the essence of God clothed in a body" (M. Schneerson [1950] 1991, 511). Some Lubavitchers took this to mean that the Rebbe (that is, the last Lubavitcher Rebbe, who died in 1994 and is commonly referred to simply as "the Rebbe") was in fact God, but this does not seem to have been the original intent of the Rebbe's words when he wrote them about his father-in-law and predecessor. Its meaning seems to be that all

---

8. The term "Lubavitch," like the term "Satmar," refers to the city in Europe in which the community is understood to originate. "Chabad" is a transliteration of a Hebrew acronym *chochmah, binah, da'at,* which describes core values of the community. Lubavitch emissaries on college campuses and around the world commonly refer to their movement as "Chabad," but within the community itself, "Lubavitch" is the more common term in use. Occasionally the two terms are used together as "Chabad-Lubavitch."

9. Some scholars and journalists give much higher estimates for the number of Lubavitchers worldwide, but I believe these numbers are inflated. This may be due to the high visibility of Lubavitchers around the world, or the higher estimates may include those who attend Lubavitch synagogues and programs but are not actual members of the movement.

10. For an analysis of the status of the rebbe in Hasidic culture, see Green (1977); Dresner (1987); and Lamm (1999).

11. It is significant that contemporary Lubavitchers focus on the Rebbe's miraculous powers since historically miracles did not play a significant role in Lubavitch life. As Louis Jacobs notes, "It is . . . true that in some versions of Hasidism—Kotz and Habad [Lubavitch], for example—the miracles aspects of zaddikism [devotion to a saintly leader] are relegated to the background" (1990, 100).

humans have a spark of the divine inside them, but in the case of a rebbe this spark is not covered over by his physical existence. Maybe the best expression of how Lubavitchers feel about their Rebbe is that before his passing, and for a period afterward, many, if not all, believed he was the Messiah. Some continue to believe so to this day—more than two decades after his passing.[12]

One aspect of Lubavitch life that is not well known outside the community, and one that is shared with Satmar, is the ban on most secular pursuits, including secular books, television,[13] movies, and non-Hasidic music. This is not to say that all members of the community abide by such prohibitions. There are certainly some, if not many, in the community who quietly violate the rules and are still members in good standing. Nonetheless, the facts that there are rules against such behavior and that those who break the rules know that they are doing so influence the nature of the community.

Most interviewees grew up in homes that took these rules seriously, while several were raised in more permissive homes. However, even those raised in the permissive homes were well aware of the community's rules and the negative attitude toward secular pursuits embodied in these prohibitions.

The ban on secular pursuits includes discouraging Hasidic Jews from obtaining a secular education.[14] In practice, most elementary and high schools for girls do teach secular subjects such as English, mathematics, science, and social studies. However, many elementary and high schools for boys do not teach any of these subjects. The entire day is devoted to learning religious subjects, such as the Bible, the Talmud, Jewish law, and Jewish mysticism. In addition, yeshivas (rabbinical schools for men) and most seminaries (post–high school educational institutions for women) do not teach basic secular studies.

---

12. For a discussion of Lubavitch Messianism, see Shaffir 1993; S. Heilman 1994; Elior 1998; Berger 2001; Schochet 2001; Student 2002; Dalfin 2002; C. Rapoport 2002; Singer 2003; Kravel-Tovi and Bilu 2008; Wolfson 2009; and Dein 2012. This is by no means a complete bibliography but includes Lubavitch as well as other Orthodox perspectives, along with Jewish mystical and sociological scholarship on the subject.

13. One example of the Lubavitcher Rebbe warning his followers of the dangers of television is the following: "Today through television one brings inside the home the church, the priest, and the cross, Heaven forbid" (M. Schneerson [1982] 2006, 460). The first Satmar Rebbe viewed television as "Satan's domain" (see Rabinowicz 2000, 218). For details of how some in the Satmar Hasidic community of Williamsburg, Brooklyn, circumvented their community's ban on television, see Mintz 1994, 182–183.

14. Maristella Botticini and Zvi Eckstein (2014) argue that after the destruction of the Temple in Jerusalem in 70 C.E. the Jewish religion emphasized literacy, the reading of the Torah, and prayers, so Jews invested in literacy, which was expensive, and this literacy allowed them to obtain higher-paying urban jobs and move away from farming. If this argument is true, it is ironic that today in ultra-Orthodox communities, as a result of religious convictions opposing secular studies, they are unprepared to compete in the job market and often suffer economically.

Furthermore, even when secular subjects are taught in elementary and high school, teachers and parents often make it clear to students that such subjects are less important than religious ones. As a matter of principle, the Lubavitcher Rebbe was staunchly opposed to his followers attending university. This policy of opposition to secular education had a direct influence on the interviewees' knowledge of secular studies and hence their ability once they exited the community to attend college and pursue successful careers.

In most Satmar schools, both girls and boys ostensibly receive rudimentary instruction in secular subjects a few hours per day, but, generally speaking, it is completely ineffective. There is also a total lack of engagement in Satmar schools with aspects of life that are deemed secular. As one Satmar Hasid writing under the nom de plume Katla Kanya (the harvester of reeds, a rabbinic appellation connoting the everyman) lamented,

> What we forget is that when we speak about children not learning secular studies, this really means that entire subjects are not taught to them at all. Zero. Nada. I am referring to those sorts of subjects and activities that are learned and taught in normal schools and that are a fundamental aspect of elementary school training, even though they are not taught out of a textbook. I mean such things as shapes, colors, human anatomy, health, hygiene, germs, allergies, how to brush your teeth, communicating with others, the economy, the environment, sports, painting, cooking, baking, analyzing a picture, visiting museums and other interesting places, and other similar activities that young children learn and thereby broaden their minds through play and activities. (2018, 32–33)[15]

Several interviewees reported that their secular classes were "a complete joke," a time to unwind from the stressful day of religious instruction, and it seems that parents and administrators are aware of this situation and do nothing to improve it. This view is supported by the experience of Gerry Albarelli, a non-Jewish teacher who taught secular studies in Satmar for five years: "English [studies] was seen as a threat and therefore dismissed as a waste of time. Boys may have been told to respect their English teachers, but it was also conveyed to them at home and by the rabbis that the English teachers were not quite worthy of respect" (2000, 35).

The secular education provided in Hasidic schools is so poor that a New York–based grassroots organization called Young Advocates for Fair Education (YAFFED) is campaigning to raise the educational standards of these schools and is even pursuing legal action against the state agencies responsible

---

15. I thank my brother, Rabbi Yossi Newfield, for bringing this source to my attention and for translating it.

for overseeing nonpublic schools for failing to ensure that these schools provide the legally required "substantially equivalent" education offered in public schools (see Partlan et al. 2017, 7). YAFFED has composed a list of thirty-
nine ultra-Orthodox schools in Brooklyn that are the worst offenders. Four
Lubavitch schools are on the list, including Educational Institute Oholei
Torah, the flagship Lubavitch boys school in Crown Heights, and eight Satmar schools, six of which are named the United Talmudical Academy Torah
V'Yirah, located in the Williamsburg and Borough Park sections of Brooklyn (73–74). Many interviewees are the products of these schools.

YAFFED's activities have stirred up a great deal of opposition within
these communities, as can be seen in the more than sixty comments on
a Lubavitch website, *COLlive.com*, responding to a news article about
YAFFED's activities. The comments are highly instructive in terms of the
derision some members of the community feel toward secular education as
well as the fear it arouses in them. For example, numerous Lubavitchers,
whose ancestors emigrated from the Soviet Union and who were raised on
stories of the evils of communism, implausibly associated YAFFED with the
Yevsektzia, the Jewish Sections of the Communist Party of the Soviet Union,
remembered for trying to forcefully destroy all the institutions of organized
Jewish life in the Soviet Union.[16]

These policies discouraging secular education often lead to low economic
attainment and sometimes poverty. For example, as the journalist Sam Roberts (2011) reported, according to the U.S. Census Bureau, Kiryas Joel, one
of the two main locations of the Satmar community, has the highest percent-
age of poverty among the thirty-seven hundred villages, towns, or cities in
the United States that have more than ten thousand people.[17]

Global Lubavitch and Shtetl Satmar

As Wright (1984) points out, the nature of the community one is exiting and
the relationship it has to the broader society have a profound effect on the
exit process itself. Although it is beyond the scope of this work to give a de-

---

16. As one Lubavitcher commented on the *COLlive* website, "Education???? People, do
you realize that our forefathers in Russia went on real Messirus Nefesh [self-sacrifice] to be
spared from a few hours of secular education? The public education system needs to be examined for producing a generation of savages who have no respect for human life. I can't
believe people are falling for this Yevsektzia Yaffed!!" (Anonymous 2015). For a detailed
analysis of the history of the Yevsektzia, see Gitelman 1972.

17. These statistics are based on per capita income. Given that Hasidim tend to have very
large families, larger incomes appear far smaller. As Frieda Vizel (2018) has argued and many
Hasidim have asserted in private conversation, this statistic is questionable because it relies
on Hasidim's self-reported income, and informal Hasidic social networks allow them to
flourish economically despite their lack of secular education. Further study is needed to
verify the impact of the lack of secular education on Hasidic household incomes.

tailed analysis comparing these two communities, I briefly note several significant areas of difference. This aids in explaining why the two communities respond somewhat differently to exiters. In many ways the two are very similar: They are both Hasidic and believe in the essential importance of a rebbe for their spiritual fulfillment; they both place great stress on the importance of religious conformity for spiritual fulfillment and community acceptance; and they both minimize secular educational and recreational pursuits. Nonetheless, there are significant differences.

Lubavitch and Satmar both mandate explicit codes of "modest" dress for both men and women, although the Satmar requirements are significantly more extensive and restrictive. Men in both communities are required to wear a yarmulke at all times, as well as ritual fringes (tzitzis). They also tend to wear conservative clothes, such as white dress shirts and dark slacks, rather than jeans and T-shirts. Furthermore, the men in these communities are prohibited from shaving or even trimming their beards.[18] Lubavitch men wear black fedoras and dark sport coats when in public; Satmar men similarly wear distinctive hats and long, black coats. Women in both communities are prohibited from wearing pants, skirts above the knees, sleeves that are short enough to reveal the elbows, and blouses that expose the collarbone. Married women are required to cover their heads with a *sheitel*.

Satmar has many more rules. In addition to these general requirements, Satmar demands that girls and women wear only dark, usually gray or black, clothing, well tailored but never tight fitting. Sheer or clinging fabrics are prohibited. Women are also required to wear thick, opaque, seamed stockings (known as Palm stockings).[19] Girls and single women wear short hairstyles. Married women are required to shave their heads after their wedding and wear not only a wig but also a hat or some other kind of covering on top of it. The Satmar community of Kiryas Joel banned girls from wearing makeup, even at weddings, on pain of being expelled from school (see Rosenberg 2014 for a reproduction of the public notice of this ban).[20]

---

18. For an extensive discussion of the Jewish legal requirement for men to maintain a full beard and for its mystical significance and its association with divine blessings, see Wiener 2006.

19. According to Dovid Meisels (2011), a committed Satmar Hasid, Reb Yoel Teitelbaum was personally involved in designing the stockings to ensure that they were completely opaque. Reb Yoel personally tested the potential fabrics by placing them on his arm and stretching them to see if the hair on his arm was visible. He settled on a fabric that was ninety denier. ("Reb" is a colloquial Yiddish diminutive honorific for rabbi.)

20. From 2004 to 2016, Shmarya Rosenberg published FailedMessiah.com, a website that focused on scandals and alleged wrongdoings within ultra-Orthodox communities. I use this website as a reference several times in this book, but only for its digital presentation of primary sources that are not otherwise easily accessible, such as scanned versions of a local Yiddish newspaper or of a leaflet distributed in the community. These references are not meant to refer to his comments or analysis but to the sources alone.

Both communities maintain strict gender segregation, but Satmar's is much more severe. Both communities separate boys and girls and men and women in schools, summer camps, and prayer services. Men and women are forbidden to socialize in public or at home. Even casual conversation between the sexes is strongly discouraged. But Satmar goes further. For example, the Central Rabbinical Congress of the United States and Canada (CRC), a rabbinic organization founded by Reb Yoel Teitelbaum, the first Satmar Rebbe, and largely run by Satmars today, issued a ruling that all buses used by community members must be gender segregated with men on one side and women on the other with a divider (*mechitza*) between them; if that is not possible, the men should sit in the front, and the women, in the back.

The additional stringency on the part of Satmar with regard to the mixing of the sexes can also be seen in the rules for dating in both communities. Lubavitch permits young men and women to date for a brief period of time, usually a few weeks to a few months before getting engaged, going out together in public areas such as hotel lobbies or bowling alleys; all physical contact is strictly forbidden, but the prospective couple is encouraged to talk and spend time together. In Satmar the prospective bride and groom meet once, perhaps twice, in the home of one of their parents, for an hour or so of "private" conversation, with the parents in the other room waiting for the good news that "It's a match!"[21]

A similar reflection of Satmar's pattern of greater restrictiveness can be seen in the curriculum of religious instruction of girls at the community-run schools. Although Lubavitch girls do not study the same classical rabbinic source, the Talmud, that boys do, the girls are taught a strong curriculum of Bible, Hasidic philosophy, Jewish law, and some rabbinic texts, because the Lubavitcher Rebbe believed it was important to teach these subjects to girls.

In Satmar, the girls are taught far less. They are not given an actual Bible in Hebrew and learn instead from photocopies of Yiddish paraphrases of the Bible. They also spend a great deal of time learning how to cook and sew. This discrepancy in female education is based on the different beliefs of the Lubavitcher Rebbe and Reb Yoel Teitelbaum of Satmar regarding teaching Judaism to girls. The Lubavitcher Rebbe believed that it was essential for women to have a strong Jewish education to fulfill their roles as homemakers, teachers of young children, and future emissaries throughout the world dedicated to Jewish outreach. Reb Yoel Teitelbaum believed it was very dangerous to teach girls Torah and that the Torah needed to be protected from them (see Fuchs 2014).

---

21. According to Meisels, Reb Yoel Teitelbaum was opposed to "the *chosson* [groom] spend[ing] time with the *kallah* [bride] before and after the engagement" (2011, 364).

Furthermore, women in Satmar play a much less visible public role than in Lubavitch.[22] This is especially true when you consider the prominent role that *rebbetzins*, the wives of rabbis, play in Lubavitch outreach work around the world (even though secondary to their husbands).[23] The diminished public role of women in Satmar is mirrored in their absence from Satmar-owned print media. That is, images of women are routinely edited out of photos because their presence is deemed immodest. For example, one Satmar Yiddish newspaper, *Di Tzeitung* (The Newspaper), cropped Hillary Clinton out of the iconic picture of President Barack Obama and his staff huddled together awaiting news of the killing of Osama bin Laden. Likewise, two Satmar-owned Yiddish newspapers, *Di Tzeitung* and *Der Blatt* (The Page), edited out Raizy Glauber from her own wedding picture after she and her husband were tragically killed in a car accident (for photos reproduced in all three newspapers, as well as the originals, see Rosenberg 2011, 2013b).[24] Most Lubavitch print and digital media do not have a rule against showing images of women.

My comments about the relative public role for women in Lubavitch should not be taken to mean that in Lubavitch communities themselves women and men have equal standing. This is hardly the case. A relatively minor example is that in Crown Heights, Brooklyn, the central headquarters of the Lubavitch community, elections are held for the community's own representative body, the Crown Heights Jewish Community Council (CHJCC), but only men are allowed to stand for office and vote.

Another area of significant disagreement between Lubavitch and Satmar is the issue of Zionism and the state of Israel. The Satmar community is famous for its anti-Zionist stance. Reb Yoel Teitelbaum was a fierce opponent of Zionism before the creation of the state of Israel and maintained his opposition to the state until his death in 1979 (see Keren-Kratz 2015). From his understanding of Jewish sources, particularly one passage in the Talmud (Ketubot 111a), he argued that it was the obligation of religious Jews to wait for the Jewish Messiah to bring them to the land of Israel.[25] He believed that

22. According to Ada Rapoport-Albert (2013), the Lubavitcher Rebbe elevated the status of women in the community by reframing the theology of the community to position women as a source of divine blessings.

23. Women play a somewhat less public role than their husbands in outreach work; for example, rabbis' wives almost never lecture to men in the community but only to other women, whereas the rabbis themselves lecture to the entire community.

24. For a discussion of the practice of ultra-Orthodox publications, including the Satmar ones, to edit out female images, see Shapiro 2015; and Goldberger 2013.

25. Aviezer Ravitzky (1996) studied the discourse around this passage in the Talmud from antiquity to the modern era and found that many Jewish authorities agreed that Jews were prohibited from conquering (and according to some, even settling) in the land of Israel before the coming of the Messiah.

for secular Jews to create a state before the arrival of the Messiah was a heretical act of impatience and that the Holocaust was a punishment for Zionist activities. He encouraged his followers who lived in the state of Israel not to have any official dealings with the state. He also believed the existence of the state of Israel was actually preventing the coming of the Messiah (Teitelbaum 1961).

This anti-Zionist stance has remained a distinct part of contemporary Satmar life. Nowadays Satmars can be seen in Israel and in America burning Israeli flags and participating in rallies against the state of Israel. Furthermore, Reb Aaron Teitelbaum said that those who instituted the draft of the ultra-Orthodox in Israel are worse than those who killed us (referring to the Nazis) (quoted in Nahshoni 2013a), and his brother, Reb Zalman Teitelbaum, called them "Amalek," the traditional enemy of the Jews harking back to biblical times (quoted in Nahshoni 2013b). (Rabbis Aaron and Zalman Teitelbaum are the two contenders for the leadership of the Satmar community since the passing of their father, Reb Moshe Teitelbaum, in 2006.)

In stark contrast, the Lubavitch community is considered strongly "pro-Israel" in the sense that this term is commonly used in contemporary political discourse. That is, Rabbi Schneerson, based on his own reading of Jewish law (*Shulhan Arukh*, OH 329), strongly supported all of the Israeli government's military operations and was strongly opposed to any "land for peace" settlement with the Palestinians (see Schneerson 2001, 2018). Many Lubavitchers in Israel serve in the Israeli military.

Lubavitch has historically and continues to be opposed to the *secular* ideology of Zionism that maintains that the essence of the Jewish people is nationalism—a land, a language, and a history—rather than religion, God, and Torah. Even today Lubavitch does not sing "Hatikvah" (Israel's national anthem), does not display the Israeli flag, and does not celebrate the Israeli national holidays of Yom HaShoah (Holocaust Remembrance Day), Yom HaZikaron (Israeli Memorial Day), and Yom Ha-Atzmaut (Israeli Independence Day), which are celebrated by many Jews all around the world. Notwithstanding its disagreements with the secular ideology of Zionism, Lubavitch is often seen by others as, and also claims that it is, Zionist. A clear statement of this was made by a Lubavitch spokesman in Israel, Rabbi Menachem Brod:

> When the average Israeli citizen says "Zionism," he is referring to love of the land, strengthening the state, and being close to the nation and the land, to military service. If all this is Zionism, then Chabad is super Zionist! But there is also another kind of Zionism, an ideological Zionism, as referred to by the founders of Zionism. This kind of Zionism is, in other words, simply secularism, so why is it surprising that Chabad is opposed to this?! (Quoted in "Radio Clash" 2011)

As can be seen from Brod's comment regarding the colloquial use of the term "Zionist," it is indeed proper for Lubavitch to be called Zionist.

In addition to their positions on gender and Zionism, possibly the greatest point of divergence is in the basic orientation of these two communities: Lubavitch, as a result of its commitment to outreach among the broader Jewish community, has an outward-looking orientation.[26] For this reason, one of the biographers of the Lubavitcher Rebbe, Chaim Miller (2014), titled his work on the Rebbe *Turning Judaism Outwards*. Lubavitch sends young people around the world to interact with Jews of different backgrounds and tries to convince these people to alter their lifestyle and become more religiously observant.[27] They also need to fund-raise great sums of money to finance this huge global operation. Thus, it is vital that Lubavitch appear to be in touch with and maintain a positive image in the world. The idea of "making a *kiddush* Lubavitch," of maintaining Lubavitch's good name, has become a significant priority.

This need to present Lubavitch in a way that is palatable to the outside world has been in tension with the deeply conservative religious ideas and values at the heart of the community. For this reason, when the Lubavitcher Rebbe had his *farbrengens*, his public gatherings, broadcast live on the radio, there were certain things that he would speak about only once the broadcast ended and he was alone with his followers. These comments would not be published in the official proceedings of the gatherings.

Furthermore, there has been an effort since the Rebbe's passing in 1994 to soften his public image and revise or bury his opinions that are not appealing to outsiders or that make him seem too extreme a figure. Possibly the most concrete example of this effort is the recent biography of the Rebbe written by Joseph Telushkin (2014). Lubavitch assisted in the research for the book, provided financial support to its author, and publicized it widely on social media. It was especially promoted to non-Lubavitch outsiders, such as secular and liberal Jews.

The book avoids entirely certain socially significant and controversial issues. In a far-reaching work of over five hundred pages, Telushkin never discusses the basic fact that the followers of the Rebbe believed that he had supernatural powers to heal the sick and foretell the future. He also never

---

26. This outward-looking orientation of Lubavitch seems to go back at least to the times of Reb Dov Ber, the second Lubavitch leader, in the early nineteenth century, when Lubavitch Hasidism was envisioned as a means to motivate the masses of the Jewish people (Loewenthal 1990).

27. For a sympathetic journalistic review of the growth of Lubavitch organizational infrastructure around the world after Rabbi Schneerson's passing, see Fishkoff 2003. For an analysis of how Lubavitch harnesses its visual culture, in particular its public lighting of large menorahs during the holiday of Hanukkah, to engage in American civic life, see Katz 2010.

mentions the Rebbe's strong views against homosexuality, in an effort to make the Rebbe appear more like a sagacious liberal rabbi than a charismatic and militant Hasidic grand master.[28]

In stark contrast to that of Lubavitch, Satmar's basic orientation is inward looking. Although the community has small pockets of followers in Canada, Israel, Europe, and South America, the vast majority of the community is located in two places, Williamsburg in Brooklyn and Kiryas Joel in Orange County, New York. They have no outreach agenda and are primarily concerned with maintaining their traditions and preserving their Hasidic lifestyle brought over from Europe.

In fact, when the establishment of the second community of Satmar in America—Kiryas Joel—was being considered, it was explicitly discussed as intended to be a "shtetl," removed from the impurity of American life.[29] Furthermore, Reb Yoel explicitly repudiated the outward-looking orientation characteristic of Lubavitch when he declared: "Why was I more successful in planting Torah in America than all the other *gedolim* [Orthodox leaders] who tried? Because they took in too much, they wanted to make the whole America good. In order to reach people, they had to make compromises. But I realized that *Yiddishkeit* [Orthodox Judaism] can only grow if you plant perfect seeds. It doesn't grow from compromises" (quoted in Meisels 2011, 150). The difference in the two communities' orientations can be seen in the fact that unlike Lubavitchers, who for the most part speak English at home, Satmar families speak Yiddish as a means of preserving their Eastern European culture and keeping the outside world at arm's length.

This difference can also be seen in each community's position on the internet. Satmar bans internet use—Reb Aaron Teitelbaum (2012) speaks of it as a "plague" that is a mortal danger to the community—and threatens to expel children from school if parents do not comply (for the official text of the internet ban, see Rosenberg 2012b). Lubavitch seeks to use the internet to further its outreach activities; Lubavitch has numerous highly successful websites, including Chabad.org—and in general the Lubavitcher Rebbe sup-

---

28. The Rebbe spoke cryptically but unmistakably about homosexuality as a disorder (see M. Schneerson 1986). The Rebbe argued that people are born with homosexual inclinations (*tchunas, netiyas*), but these can and must be overcome because they are dysfunctional, as are kleptomania, trichotillomania (the persistent urge to pull out one's hair), or the urge to bang one's head against a wall. Furthermore, the Rebbe maintained with certainty that it is possible to correct these inclinations since they go against human nature and are dangerous to one's health. The Rebbe also stated that homosexuals are ill, and the more they insist otherwise, the deeper their illness. Telushkin never mentions the Rebbe's views on homosexuality, even in his section on the Rebbe's "controversial views."

29. A shtetl is a small town with a large Jewish population in Central or Eastern Europe as it existed before the Holocaust.

ported technology as a tool to promote godliness.[30] Thus, for example, starting in 1989 the Rebbe eagerly embraced the new technology of satellite broadcasts (known inside the community as "hookups") that allowed live, simultaneous video feeds of Hanukkah celebrations on all six continents to be viewed at numerous locations around the world. The Rebbe personally participated in this program.

Although Lubavitch is more outward looking than Satmar, this must be understood in context. That is, because of its outreach work Lubavitch is perceived by scholars and the general public as open to the world and moderate in comparison to other Hasidic groups, such as Satmar. As Ayala Fader notes, "Lubavitchers interact most often with other kinds of Jews because they do the most outreach. This has made them the most fluent in North American popular culture" (2009, 224n42), and "ethnographies of Lubavitchers, who are the most open to outsiders, are the most common in the literature [on Hasidim]" (223n25).

Although, strictly speaking, when comparing Lubavitch to other Hasidic groups, both these statements are certainly true, these statements and their associations can give the false impression that Lubavitch is in general fluent in pop culture or open to outside ideas and lifestyles. This is certainly not the case. One can simply refer back to the previous comments about Lubavitch opposition to secular pursuits. Many interviewees reported that they were overwhelmed with how much they did not know about the outside world when they began exiting.

How Common Is Ultra-Orthodox Exiting?

The short answer is that it is not very common, but there is not a lot of data on this question. In the rich extant scholarly literature on ultra-Orthodoxy, the subgroup most often overlooked consists of exiters. That is, most of the literature on ultra-Orthodox Jewish communities (Poll 1969; Shaffir 1974; Helmreich 1986; Belcove-Shalin et al. 1995; Rubin 1997; Heilman 2000; Feldman 2003; Stadler 2009) tends to focus on those members who stay and largely ignores those who exit.

According to Steven M. Cohen's (2014) analysis of the data collected by the 2013 Pew Research Center study of American Jewish demographics, only 6.5 percent of those raised ultra-Orthodox exit their communities. The problem with this statistic is that it does not distinguish among the various ultra-

---

30. For example, this is what the Rebbe had to say about the radio: "In radio, there is reflected a sublime spiritual matter," a "tremendous power implemented by the Creator within nature so that, by means of an appropriate instrument, the voice of the speaker may be heard from one corner of the world to the other" (quoted in Ravitzky 1994, 307).

Orthodox communities, and it does not single out Lubavitch and Satmar respondents. Given the particular dynamics within each ultra-Orthodox community, it is conceivable that the numbers may vary greatly.

Regarding Lubavitch, Avrum Ehrlich (2005) states as a fact that after the passing of the Lubavitcher Rebbe in 1994 there was a huge exodus from the community. Given the tremendous impact the charisma of the Rebbe had on maintaining group membership as analyzed by Sydelle Brooks Levy (1973) decades before the Rebbe's passing, it stands to reason that his absence might trigger a major exodus, but Ehrlich does not provide any substantial evidence for this claim.

Mark Trencher, a nonacademic market researcher, whose 2016 survey of 655 ultra-Orthodox exiters is the largest such study to date, estimates that there are at present approximately ten thousand exiters from ultra-Orthodox Judaism. As of this writing, a single closed Facebook group for Orthodox exiters called "Off the *Derech*," whose members have to be vetted as genuinely ex-ultra-Orthodox before being admitted, has 3,036 members. There are more than thirty such Facebook groups, although it is difficult to know how many members have joined numerous groups.

Another possible measure of the prevalence of ultra-Orthodox exiting is membership data from Footsteps, an organization founded in 2003 that provides educational, vocational, and social support for individuals transitioning out of ultra-Orthodox and Orthodox communities.[31] As of 2019, Footsteps had over 1,700 members (Footsteps 2019), and among the 134 new Footsteps members in 2018, 21 percent were Lubavitch and 20 percent were Satmar (Footsteps 2018).

However, these numbers are only a fraction of the total number of exiters, since many exiters do not join Footsteps. This is especially the case with Lubavitchers, who are relatively more prepared than Satmars or other Hasidic exiters for the outside world; almost all Lubavitch girls and some Lubavitch boys learn secular studies in their community, and most Lubavitchers grow up in families that speak English. Furthermore, most Lubavitchers have traveled abroad during their teen years in the course of their outreach activities.

Certainly the number of exiters from ultra-Orthodoxy is significant enough to attract attention within the Orthodox Jewish world. One Lubavitcher, Binyamin Tanny, who considers himself an expert on the subject and wrote a book aimed at helping parents and teachers prevent such exiting from occurring, had this to say about the "problem": "The 'going off

---

31. There are organizations with goals similar to those of Footsteps in other countries, although I do not have membership data on them: Forward in Montreal, Mavar in the United Kingdom, GesherEU in the United Kingdom and Europe, Jouw Leven Jouw Keuze in Belgium, and Hillel in Israel.

the derech' issue today is an epidemic. It is one of the biggest issues facing observant Judaism" (2012, 15). In fact, ultra-Orthodox exiting has become so common that numerous rabbis and others in the Modern Orthodox community have appealed to ultra-Orthodox exiters to join their community rather than leave Orthodox Judaism entirely.[32] One such appeal was made by Rabbi Nathaniel Helfgot (2013) in the *Jewish Press*, a popular Orthodox newspaper. Helfgot ends his appeal to would-be exiters thus: "You don't have to write yourself out of that grand Jewish story, and you have so much to add and contribute. Welcome, and let us grow together."

Within the Lubavitch community, which is more comfortable discussing such issues publicly than is the Satmar community, the issue of exiters has become a hotly debated topic, and many articles have been published on it. For example, some have posited that the blame should be placed at the doorsteps of the yeshivas and girls' schools, which fail to provide the necessary religious supervision throughout the year. Others criticize the parents for not instilling in their children the proper religious values. Yehuda Kaplan (2015) rejects the idea that the school system or parents are to blame and instead sees the problem as the inevitable result of the Lubavitch summer camps, which do not provide enough religious supervision. Kaplan claims that counselors and head counselors are only interested in being "cool" and giving the campers a fun time rather than acting as role models and imparting Hasidic values.

Possibly the two most high-profile acknowledgments of this phenomenon are the public statement by one of the leaders of the Satmar community, Reb Aaron Teitelbaum, in a tearful Yom Kippur speech in 2013 about the "lost *neshumas*," the lost souls, who are leaving the community, and two statements by thirty-three prominent Lubavitch rabbis from around the world proposing that community members get married earlier to ensure that members stay faithful to the community (see "Rabbis Urge to Marry Young" 2012).[33] These statements illustrate that both communities are well aware that members are exiting and are trying to respond to this situation as they see fit.

There are also some other practical steps being taken by both communities to address this issue. A synagogue in Crown Heights was created to serve "modern" Lubavitchers and either prevent them from leaving or help get

---

32. Modern Orthodoxy is a stream of Judaism that adheres to traditional Jewish law but does not isolate itself socially and culturally from secular society as ultra-Orthodoxy does. It also tolerates television, accepts social dating, and encourages college education.

33. There was some disagreement among the Satmars I interviewed over what exactly Reb Aaron Teitelbaum said on Yom Kippur. One reported that he said that the Satmar community should treat the exiters with special kindness, while others thought that he simply bemoaned the fact that they were exiting but never stated anything about treating them kindly.

them back. In addition, Lubavitch has several yeshivas designated to deal with teens who are at risk and might exit, such as Bais Menachem in Wilkes-Barre, Pennsylvania, described by journalist Uriel Heilman (2014). Similarly, in Williamsburg the Satmar community set up an organization called Williamsburg Kollel for teens and married people who were starting to exit. This organization provides large *kiddushes*, afternoon lunches on the Sabbath following prayer services, and offers special lectures for them during the week with speakers from outside Satmar, such as from the ultra-Orthodox (though non-Hasidic) outreach organization Aish HaTorah.

One important factor that may mitigate the number of exiters from the community is the high cost of exiting. That is, the mental and emotional costs of exiting Lubavitch and Satmar are profound. The experience of needing to figure out who one is and develop one's own identity is totally foreign to the ultra-Orthodox community. Anthony Giddens argues that "the self has to be reflexively made" (1991, 3). In contrast, ultra-Orthodox society emphasizes conformity. Giddens's concept of self-discovery would be anathema to the ultra-Orthodox community.

This need to find one's own way, often against the background of intense pressure from family and community to conform, along with precious little support from the outside world, causes tremendous psychic distress. In many cases this can lead to suicidal ideation and occasionally even suicide. Leah Vincent (2013), an ultra-Orthodox exiter who is now an activist and author, writes about her own suicidal ideation and notes that this is common among many exiters: "To be a former ultra-Orthodox Jew too often means to exist in a tug-of-war with destruction." Indeed, according to Footsteps (2013), 26 percent of its members experienced suicidal ideation.

Historical Perspective

Norbert Elias (1987) urged sociologists not to retreat into the present and instead to seek to understand contemporary society through connecting it with other historical cases. There is a sense in which the focus of this study—the tension between maintaining a deeply religious and Jewish communal life and engaging in the world outside that community—is a central theme of all Jewish history, from antiquity to the Middle Ages, and especially throughout modernity. But this tension has looked different in each particular historical period and geographic location. The options available to exiters and the surrounding societies in which they live inform their actions and our understanding of those actions, as John Simpson (1997) notes. Furthermore, in different historical periods people can exit for different reasons.

For example, according to Ezra Mendelsohn (1970), in imperial Russia, some Jews left their traditional communities after becoming radicalized into a socialist milieu. Similarly, Mendelsohn (1983) notes that in the period between the world wars numerous Jews in the eastern part of Central Europe tried to join the broader political culture in their society and were rebuffed; as a result, many of these Jews turned to Zionism. In addition, in the nineteenth century in countries where being Jewish carried severe penalties in terms of economic and social advancement, some Jews converted to Christianity. As Todd Endelman (2015) argues, this was seldom due to conviction but rather pragmatism. All this highlights how the historical period in which the exiting occurs and the options available in that environment have a significant impact on exiters' motivations and destinations.

Even in the contemporary context, depending on the decades under discussion, the outcomes can be significantly different. Specifically, Lynn Davidman (2014) argues that nearly half of her female respondents and several male respondents who left ultra-Orthodoxy complained about gender inequality in the ultra-Orthodox community and that they exited to seek an environment in which women had equal status.

This perspective was almost completely absent from my findings. On the contrary, whenever I asked female interviewees if they felt upset because they were not taught the Talmud, most said that they had learned enough and did not need to study the Talmud. Only two Lubavitch female interviewees reported that they were envious of the depth of learning of the boys and that they wanted to be more involved in the ritual activity in the synagogue, but their being female prevented them from doing so.

Davidman's respondents were between the ages of twenty-five and forty-five in 2005 and for the most part left at least ten years before being interviewed, which means they were coming of age in the 1970s or early 1980s. It is possible that developments within the feminist movement and its prominence in American society between that time and the more recent years relevant to my study contributed to the discrepancy between our findings.

The interviewees in this book are largely millennials who were coming of age in a post-9/11 America awash in Islamophobia and politically conservative voices on the airwaves and in print. They take for granted the ubiquity of social media and cell phones. The Lubavitchers were coming of age in a Lubavitch bereft of its charismatic leader, Rabbi Menachem Mendel Schneerson, who died in 1994, and still struggling to redefine its mission in the shadow of this leader. The Satmars were coming of age during a rift over the leadership succession between Rabbi Aaron Teitelbaum and his brother, Rabbi Zalman Teitelbaum, neither of whom inspired the kind of loyalty and commitment that guided the followers of their great-uncle (and the founder of the Satmar dynasty) Rabbi Yoel Teitelbaum.

In addition, it is relevant to this study that Brooklyn, home to Lubavitch headquarters in Crown Heights and to the main Satmar community of

Williamsburg, has experienced a tremendous amount of gentrification over the past decade. Crown Heights and Williamsburg have both seen huge numbers of white middle-class gentrifiers moving into neighborhoods in which the only neighbors the Hasidim had for decades were poor people of color. Gentrification makes it much more difficult for these communities to maintain clear boundaries between themselves and the non-Jews around them. Suddenly the outside world seems more desirable, and race can no longer be used as an obvious line of separation.

This study is about these two communities in this particular moment. It must be remembered that these communities are themselves constantly evolving as a result of external and internal pressures. For example, although Lubavitch has a general policy, based on the Lubavitcher Rebbe's views, to refrain from teaching secular studies to boys, lately there are some parents in Crown Heights advocating such instruction for their sons. Whether the main Lubavitch yeshiva will change its policy of exclusive religious instruction remains to be seen. But what is certain is that attitudes in the community are changing on all sorts of issues. In ten or twenty years, these communities may look very different and may produce very different outcomes.

These interviewees are exiting their communities in a historical period in which Jews in general have a great deal of freedom. Jews have economic, political, and cultural power. The acceptance and integration of Jews into mainstream society allow religious exiters to aspire to be fully integrated into society.

Despite the historical contingency of these interviewees' experience, this study is relevant to the larger phenomenon of religious exiting irrespective of these contingencies. My goal is not to establish why exiters choose to leave their communities of origin or to delineate the range of destinations at which they arrive. Rather, my goal is to explore the dynamic process of establishing and residing in a liminal state for a prolonged period of time. This liminality will likely look different for exiters in another generation, but my contention is that the liminality itself is a consistent and essential feature of religious exiting that must be taken into account in all future studies of religious exiting.

Overview of the Book

This introductory chapter includes a review of how this study diverges from and builds on existing scholarship and a discussion of this study's aims, as well as some background regarding the exiters in this study. Chapter 2 turns to the Satmar and Lubavitch communities, with particular attention to these communities' relationships with outsiders and with exiters. It is easy to focus solely on the experience of the exiter, but as discussed previously, the context can make a great deal of difference. Understanding why and how liminality functions in the lives of these exiters relies in part on understanding where they came from.

Chapter 3 turns to the exit narratives the interviewees construct to make sense of their experiences and their processes of leaving the community. Chapter 4 then describes the "habits of action" and "habits of thought" that characterize these exiters and define, in large measure, their liminality. Chapter 5, in turn, explores the lives of the interviewees after their transition out of the community is, from their perspective, technically complete. Once they could be described as "formerly ultra-Orthodox," what did their lives look like? However, since the major finding is that the process of exiting is ongoing, the focus is not on the final destination of religious exiters but on the various strategies exiters employ to help them manage their liminal status, "betwixt and between" the two worlds, for the long term.

The concluding chapter summarizes the book's findings and elaborates on its contributions to the relevant scholarly literature. It also looks at the relevance of the study of religious exit to other types of exit by exploring how the concepts and tools gained from exploring religious exit might tell us more about other sorts of identity transition, such as divorce, exit from prison, and immigration.

Permeable Boundaries

He that troubleth his own house shall inherit the wind.
—Proverbs 11:29

To understand how the Lubavitch and Satmar communities deal with religious exiters, it is necessary to first understand the nature of the boundary these communities try to maintain between themselves and the outside world. This chapter begins by describing how they create distance between their communities and non-Jews by denigrating the non-Jews. After discussing the treatment of non-Jews, I explore the boundaries between these communities and other Jews, including other Orthodox Jewish communities. I describe how these boundaries are maintained in the case of Lubavitch even when members are traveling, often abroad and without much community infrastructure or scrutiny. I also describe how these boundaries, although socially profoundly significant, are transcended under certain conditions on a regular basis.

With this information, it is possible to move on to the central issue: how these communities respond to religious exiters. The most significant empirical finding, which contradicts previous scholarship, is that as a rule neither Lubavitch nor Satmar families cut ties to exiters. Their relationships may not be easy, but exiters are not navigating black-and-white terrain. In addition, Satmar exiters tend to be treated worse than their Lubavitch counterparts by friends and community members. For this reason, many Satmar interviewees do not feel comfortable attending synagogue in their community when they visit family. I also found that Satmars say that they were treated decently by family because their family is not typical Satmar and that exiters are treated better in Satmar these days than was previously the case. I bring evidence to challenge both of these claims.

Moving beyond the response of individual families to their exiter children, I explore the differences between how the Lubavitch and Satmar communities respond to religious deviation generally. Although neither community formally excommunicates members, Satmar is much harsher in its response, by expelling from school the children of parents who show signs of nonconformity and by attempting to help the parent who remains in the community to receive full custody of his or her children—potentially totally cutting off the exiting parent from his or her child forever. Yet both communities pathologize dissent as the primary means of preventing religious exiting.

Communal Boundaries within Lubavitch and Satmar

Denigrating Goyim

Lubavitch and Satmar deal with their exiters by using the same mechanisms that maintain boundaries between their and other communities, both Jewish and non-Jewish. These two communities denigrate and shame their exiters and try to portray them within the community as "other," the same way that they denigrate and make an "other" out of non-Jews and Jews from outside their communities. Thus, to understand the Lubavitch and Satmar responses to exiters, it is necessary to first describe the boundaries that these communities erect between themselves and the non-Jewish world as well as between themselves and other Jewish communities.

There is also a direct linguistic connection between how Satmar and Lubavitch maintain their boundaries with non-Jews and how they deal with exiters, since they sometimes use two derogatory Yiddish terms for non-Jews—*goyim* and *shkotsim*—to refer to exiters. This association between non-Jews and exiters is meant to be deeply insulting, because these communities view non-Jews unfavorably. The connection between how these communities view non-Jews and exiters was made by Hershy, a Satmar man in his mid-twenties:

The *haredi* [ultra-Orthodox] world didn't just invent what it means to be a Jew; they also invented what it means to be a non-Jew—how a goy looks. They also give you an image of that when you're a child, and I think both are wrong. They're wrong about what it means to be a Jew, and they're wrong about what it means to be a non-Jew. And for a while I rejected their idea about what it means to be a Jew, but I didn't realize that I still held on to their idea about what it means to be a non-Jew. And for them it meant how they defined "bums" and how they defined "dropouts," and I was very afraid of that description.

But that description was just as wrong, or at least I feel it is just as wrong.[1]

It is a central tenet of Orthodox Judaism that the Jewish people are a chosen people and are special and separate from the rest of the world. For the Lubavitch and Satmar communities this is an extremely important precept, and they make a great effort to distinguish themselves from non-Jews and nonreligious Jews and even from other ultra-Orthodox Jewish communities. The boundaries these communities maintain between themselves and the outside are not primarily objective "social boundaries" that cause unequal access to resources and social opportunities but rather subjective "symbolic boundaries" that create a sense of distance and separation between those on the inside and those on the outside (Lamont 1992, 9).

From the Lubavitch perspective, this idea of separation between Jews and non-Jews has its roots in the founding text of the community, the *Tanya*, first published in 1797, which states that Jews have two souls, an animalistic soul and a divine soul, whereas non-Jews have only the animalistic soul. The most neutral interpretation of this principle is that non-Jews are a part of nature, no better or worse than an animal in the field. Non-Jews are thus subject to the laws of nature, whose control they cannot escape. Jews, however, because they have a divine soul, are able to transcend the laws of nature; for instance, when they fulfill a religious obligation with a physical object, they actually imbue themselves and that object with divinity. Non-Jews have no such power according to the *Tanya*.[2] The idea that Jews are fundamentally different from non-Jews was also a regular theme in the public discourse of the last Lubavitcher Rebbe, Rabbi Menachem Mendel Schneerson. He stated many times that Jews are like oil, which always remains separate from and higher than water (the non-Jews), and that these differences are unalterable. He also stated that non-Jews are fundamentally opposed to and hate Jews (for these sources and many similar ones, see Seligson 2011, 179–180, 464–468).

This idea of non-Jews being part of nature while Jews are able to transcend it is often understood to mean that non-Jews have no free will. As Yehuda, a Lubavitcher in his mid-twenties, remembered, "I was taught that non-Jews have no choice; they have no free will. My teachers went as far as to say that non-Jews were robots." He added, "I think Lubavitchers think

---

1. This and all other unattributed quotations in the book come from my interviews with exiters conducted in the New York metropolitan area or via phone or Skype between 2010 and 2014. All interviewee names in the book are pseudonyms.

2. Ariel Evan Mayse, a scholar motivated to "find *Tanya*'s relevant voice for the twenty-first-century Jewish world," acknowledges that "*Tanya*'s unwavering pro-Jewish and equally strong anti-gentile sentiments . . . drift very close to xenophobia and perhaps even outright racism" (2017, 149).

there's something wrong with non-Jews." Mordy, another Lubavitcher in his mid-twenties, elaborated on this point:

> We were told that the outside world is full of people who have no reason to be alive. It's surprising that they don't all commit suicide every day, because they really have no reason to be alive. We are the only ones who get it, who know what the universe is really all about— and aren't we lucky? I felt, "Aw, *nebech* [how tragic] for them; they just don't know what's going on, oh well."[3]

Lubavitchers within the community commonly tell outsiders that this belief that non-Jews have only an animal soul is not intended to denigrate non-Jews. The Lubavitcher Rebbe expressed this point in a letter:

> Judging by your letter, it is surely unnecessary for me to emphasize to you what has already been indicated above, namely, that *our belief in the chosenness of the Jewish people is not a matter of chauvinism or fanaticism*, but rather the deep-felt realization that this uniqueness carries with it great responsibilities and special obligations. This is why, for example, Jews have to fulfill "Taryag (613) mitzvoth" [commandments], whereas Gentiles are not obligated to observe kashrut [Jewish dietary laws] and various other restrictions connected with the idea of holiness, holiness being the essential aspect of the Jewish soul. (Quoted in Kirschenbaum 2009; emphasis added)[4]

The belief that Jews are fundamentally different from non-Jews is not unique to Lubavitchers.[5] As Ayala Fader notes regarding another Hasidic sect, Bobov, they also believe that Jewish souls are "just different" from non-Jewish ones and that Jews master their physical urges while non-Jews cannot (2009, 14, 38). Satmar holds a view similar to the Bobov's with regard to the

---

3. This idea that non-Jewish lives are worthless or meaningless is highlighted in a story the Rebbe told, the punch line of which is that Jews eat in order to live and non-Jews live in order to eat (see Chabad.org, n.d.).

4. This passage is from a letter of the Lubavitcher Rebbe, possibly from 1966, that has not been published and possibly may never have been sent. It occasionally happened that the Rebbe would have his secretaries compose a letter, but he would later decide not to send it, usually because of its controversial nature. However, among Lubavitchers, these letters are considered authentic representations of the Rebbe's views and are therefore cherished. Another of his letters from 1984, regarding whether Jews should assist Ethiopians who claimed to be Jewish, was never sent but was published twenty years later in a Lubavitch magazine (*Kfar Chabad*). For the text of this letter, see M. Schneerson (2004).

5. As Jody Myers (2011) points out, there persists even among otherwise relatively progressive schools of kabbalistic thought today the idea that there is a separation between Jews and non-Jews and that the non-Jews have only an animalistic soul while the Jews have a divine soul as well.

inferior status of non-Jews. In fact, Reb Yoel Teitelbaum is quoted in a 2013 issue of the Satmar-founded and -owned Yiddish newspaper *Der Blatt* as saying, "Ale goyim zenen shmutzik" (All non-Jews are dirty) (see Rosenberg 2013c for a facsimile of the newspaper article). Although it is almost impossible to determine if Reb Yoel actually said this, what is significant is that it was quoted in a Satmar newspaper without editorial disapproval or comment. In other words, for average Satmars today this alleged comment of Reb Yoel is perfectly acceptable and unsurprising.

In the case of Lubavitch in Crown Heights, Brooklyn, the idea that non-Jews have only an animalistic soul combines with their attitudes on race. Lubavitchers believe that their Afro-Caribbean neighbors are fundamentally different from them. Henry Goldschmidt (2006) argues that Lubavitchers view this difference as largely based on religion rather than race. However, Goldschmidt underemphasizes the role that race plays in Lubavitchers' perception of their black neighbors. For example, Lubavitchers refer to their neighbors as not just goyim (non-Jews) but more commonly as *shvartzes*, a derogatory Yiddish term for black people.

The combination of animosity toward outsiders with racial prejudice is not unique to Lubavitch. One Satmar interviewee of African American descent, Alter, who is in his late teens and joined the Satmar community with his family when he was five, recounted how he was mocked publicly for the color of his skin.[6] When I asked him if it ever came up that he looked different from other Satmars, he replied:

> Did it ever come up that I look different? It always came up! I was on the bus—it was twelve years ago. I remember where I was standing; I remember where he was standing. He said, "You're a *shvartze*." *Now* I'm laughing; it doesn't bother me. The truth is girls like the color, but then it bothered me so much. I was a seven-year-old kid. What do you want from me? I'm seven years old, and you tell me that I'm a *shvartze*, and you tell me that I'm different from everybody. There's a hundred kids on the bus, and you're the one dark one there. It's embarrassing. It's very embarrassing.

Recently Alter was working in the Hasidic community while wearing a small yarmulke, but he no longer had side curls or a beard. That is, he looked Orthodox, but the Hasidic women he encountered did not assume that he knew Yiddish. Since he grew up in Satmar, he actually speaks Yiddish flu-

---

6. This is one of only two interviewees whose families joined the Hasidic community after their birth. The other's family joined the Lubavitch community when she was seven. Both were raised in their respective Hasidic communities for the majority of their childhood and attended Hasidic schools as soon as they joined their community.

ently. He overheard one Satmar woman ask her friend in Yiddish about him, "Far vus iz er azoy shvartz?" (Why is he so black?). Possibly because he has heard these comments so often, he says that now they do not really bother him; they are like "a joke." But it is clear that he would prefer not to have to deal with this sort of "humor" at his expense.

Fader (2009) points out that from early childhood the ultra-Orthodox place a great emphasis on the importance of their communities and the denigration of non-Jews. She observed how often the teachers and principals in the ultra-Orthodox elementary schools she studied used "goy" as a derogatory term, such as, "If you act wild and misbehave, you're acting like a goy!" Technically speaking, goy simply means someone of a different nation, but it is not understood or used in such a neutral way in the ultra-Orthodox community. It is always infused with a derisive undertone.

The denigration and revulsion of non-Jews are well documented in my own research. For example, Naftuli, a Satmar exiter in his late twenties, recounted that as a child he was informed by his teacher that it was prohibited to ride a bicycle. The name used to refer to the prohibited object was not "bike" but "shaygets bike." The Yiddish word shaygets derives from the Hebrew word sheketz, meaning "abomination," and is used colloquially to mean "rascal" or "scoundrel" and a non-Jew. This association between the bicycle and the despised shaygets was intended to be sufficient reason to prevent any child from daring to ride one. (It did not work on Naftuli, who stubbornly refused to give up riding his bike.)

Another crucial source of data regarding how these communities really feel toward non-Jews, a subject that they are not eager to openly discuss with outsiders, are reports from individuals regarding the intense process they were required to undergo after exiting to unlearn the disgust and hatred they were socialized to feel toward non-Jews. That is, interviewees were aware that although they had separated themselves from their community of origin, they still sometimes had negative feelings toward non-Jews and were actively trying to change this part of their thinking.

For example, this is how Mendy, a Lubavitcher in his late twenties, expressed it:

> I think I had to unlearn the denigration of non-Jews. I think that the broader Orthodox community as well as Lubavitch—probably in order to insulate itself from non-Jews and secular culture—has a process of denigration on many, many levels of anybody not of the Jewish faith.

Mendy went on to report:

> Now I've become—to an extent—less judgmental of non-Jews and people of other belief systems and other lifestyles. I've come to realize

that what works for one person doesn't necessarily work for the other. And I don't really believe that one belief system is more true than another system. I believe it's more true for those that see it, but I believe it's a relative thing and not an absolute thing like I was taught growing up.

Similarly, Ruchy, a Satmar woman in her early twenties, recounted the horrible things she was taught about non-Jews:

I was taught that non-Jews are unclean; they never take showers, apparently. They're all out to kill us; we all know Amalek [the nation in the Bible that tried to destroy the ancient Israelites and is believed to be the source and model of all future anti-Semites]. They all want us dead. They weren't portrayed as caring, loving, family-minded people like us. We live for our families, for our kids; we love our kids. They don't love their kids; they hurt their kids all the time. There is so much abuse going on—even though there is so much abuse going on in our communities, but whatever.

Ruchy went on to describe spending Christmas at her non-Jewish girlfriend's family home, and what she saw contradicted the messages she got from her community about non-Jews:

I spent a Christmas with my girlfriend's family. It was so beautiful, and there was a lot of love in the room. And that's Christmas. There was amazing food, they were saying grace, whatever, and they went to church the day before, whatever. It was really beautiful, and it felt much like home. You know, like when I was a little kid and there were times that it felt like I was actually home; that's what it felt like. And this was all surprising because this is not how my community portrayed this life to be like. They told us that non-Jews, all they do is lie around and waste their time. That they are not as caring and as human as us. And it turns out that they are just like us. I'm dating this Italian girl, and Italian families are very intense. They are very passionate, and they are all about family. So someone got it wrong somewhere.

Thus, based on both the doctrines of these communities and the evidence from interviewees and other ethnographic sources, it is clear that non-Jews are denigrated and described as less than Jews and that this image of the non-Jew is maintained to protect the enclave of the community. Exiters being characterized as non-Jews communicates a profound and clear message to both the exiters and those who remain within the community. Naturally, by the time people begin exiting the community, they have often internalized these messages about exiting, which is one of the hurdles—emotional and psychological—that they must deal with as they transition.

Divisions within the Holy Citadel

The boundaries that the Lubavitch and Satmar communities erect are not meant merely to exclude non-Jews but also to create a separation between these communities and nonreligious Jews and even other religious Jewish communities.[7] These communities are like citadels with concentric circles of boundaries around them.[8] The innermost boundary separates Lubavitch or Satmar from other ultra-Orthodox communities, and the outermost boundary separates them from the non-Jewish world. The outermost boundaries have the thickest walls, and the innermost have the thinnest walls, but even this innermost boundary is highly significant. For example, the boundary between Lubavitch and Satmar is substantial, even though they are both Hasidic communities.

There is a decades-long history of animosity between the Lubavitch and Satmar communities (see Mintz 1994), which may partly be caused by their maintaining very different philosophies and modes of religious practice. It may also be the result of an incident that occurred some thirty-two years ago when a charismatic rabbi, Mendel Vechter, who was teaching in a Satmar yeshiva, secretly "converted" to Lubavitch after studying Hasidic thought with a Lubavitch rabbi named Pinchas Korf. Rabbi Vechter then proceeded to secretly convert some twenty of his students to Lubavitch as well.

When these conversions were discovered, they caused a huge outcry in Satmar, which viewed this "stealing of souls" as foul play and led to open hostilities between the two communities. Both Rabbis Vechter and Korf were brutally beaten by members of the Satmar community, and the latter's beard was cut off, which is a major violation of Jewish law and a huge personal humiliation. The Satmar community protected the attackers and apparently paid off witnesses to the attack on Rabbi Korf so they would not testify to the police.

---

7. Within Lubavitch there is also strong animosity toward the non-Hasidic ultra-Orthodox community, known as *misnagdim*, opponents of Hasidim, also referred to as the Litvish or Lithuanian tradition, also called the *yeshivish* community. The term *snag* is a derogatory term for this group and is used ubiquitously in Lubavitch. In fact, at the Detroit Zoo there was a dead tree with a sign that read, "Snag is a dead or dying tree," and among campers in the nearby Lubavitch summer camp it was a popular practice to take a picture of it when visiting the zoo. There was also a popular Lubavitch song with the refrain, "If you're a *misnaged*, your soul is gonna die!"

8. Related to this is the idea of making a wall or defensive boundary around the Jewish faithful, which has a basis in the classical Jewish tradition. In the first chapter of *Pirkei Avot*, the *Ethics of the Fathers*, a rabbinic text from the second century, readers are instructed to make a "s'yag la-Torah," a fence or wall around the Torah.

In response to the attack against Rabbi Korf, the Lubavitcher Rebbe publicly demanded that those who witnessed the attack go to the police and testify and that those in the Satmar community who were protecting the perpetrators cease doing so. The Lubavitcher Rebbe also declared that this attack was an outrage against the entire Jewish people and that it was a Jewish legal obligation to work with the police to punish the perpetrators (M. Schneerson 1983, 1800–1813). During the same period, a group of Satmars physically attacked a group of Lubavitchers as the latter attempted to travel through the Williamsburg neighborhood on their way to conduct outreach activities. The police intervened to rescue the outnumbered Lubavitchers. Lubavitch instituted a boycott against all Satmar-owned food companies and kosher-certification services, which is still followed by some Lubavitchers today.

Although only a small fraction of Satmars were actively involved in these hostilities, many were marginally involved. In fact, one Satmar interviewee, Nachman, who is in his late thirties, reported that his father was one such person, who in his own way participated in the struggle against Lubavitch and through this taught his son hostility toward Lubavitch. Nachman told me, "I was raised to hate your people [Lubavitchers]." He continued, "Back in the day my father would put eggs outside our house overnight so they would become rotten, and then he would throw them at your people as they passed our house on the Jewish holidays."

Although some in Lubavitch still maintain the boycott against Satmar and refuse to eat Satmar products, such as Golden Flow milk and meat products that carry the Satmar kosher certification (granted by the CRC), relations between the two communities have improved recently. In fact, one of the two rebbes currently feuding for control of the Satmar community, Aaron Teitelbaum, has actively tried to mend relations with the Lubavitch community. He even attends the religious services conducted in a Lubavitch synagogue in Palm Springs, California, when he travels there for his health.

David Landau (1992) and Jerome Mintz (1994) describe at great length the conflicts between the various ultra-Orthodox communities.[9] Adin Steinsaltz (2014), himself a committed Lubavitcher who tries whenever possible to present the Lubavitcher Rebbe in the most favorable light, notes the extent to which contemporary Lubavitch is far removed from other Orthodox communities. Although he frames this gulf as the result of "ideological disputes

---

9. Reb Yoel Teitelbaum had contempt for the non-Hasidic ultra-Orthodox style of learning Torah: "Their style is not more than three generations old. . . . It's a totally new *derech* [path]. We see that not one *halachic* [Jewish legal] authority came out from them. There is one of them who *paskens shailos* [decides Jewish legal matters], and he wreaks terrible destruction. It's a totally new *derech*, and it's not *Toras Emes* [the true Torah]" (quoted in Meisels 2011, 457).

and perhaps envy" on the part of the detractors of Lubavitch, he nonetheless observes the following: "Such opposition [to Lubavitch] did not break the Rebbe, or Chabad, but it had its influence in distancing them from the [Orthodox] mainstream. . . . The Rebbe lost both allies and partners who could have helped him in his mission" (Steinsaltz 2014, 160–161).

Although Steinsaltz places all the blame for the distance between Lubavitch and the rest of the Orthodox and ultra-Orthodox world at the feet of Lubavitch's detractors, for those who were raised in Lubavitch, the idea that Lubavitch is separate from and better than all other Orthodox and ultra-Orthodox communities was a basic principle and source of pride. As Dovid, a Lubavitcher in his late twenties, recounted,

> Lubavitch believe themselves to be in a separate universe within the Orthodox community. So they think of themselves as elite, and—the way I looked at it was—Chabad is the savior of the Jewish nation. And it is also the best place to be and the funnest place to be, and the place where the people are the most dedicated, and full of people whom everyone looked at and wanted to be like.

Dovid was constantly told these ideas, and he believed them entirely until the age of twenty-four, when he made a break with the community.

Akiva, in his mid-twenties, described the feeling of superiority among those in the Satmar community:

> Satmar tends to only respect their own. They don't respect anybody else. That's the main problem they have. People respect their rebbe [Reb Yoel Teitelbaum]; that's why they think they're better, but they don't respect anybody else—that's also why they think they're better. . . . It plays out in a lot of ways. Anyone who doesn't go their way [*pauses*]. They can be nice to you, but they think you are just a piece of rock out there. Just another guy, you're not worth anything. They act nice to you, but they don't think too highly of anyone who is out of their circle; they laugh everybody off—even within *Hasidish* [Hasidic] circles. Anyone who is not their own, for some reason they just laugh like they're nothing.

Yocheved, in her mid-thirties, from a Satmar-like Hungarian Hasidic sect, experienced the consequence of the superiority of Satmars firsthand:

> Once when I was a teenager, maybe thirteen or fourteen, I went to a family wedding and was looking forward to spending time with my Satmar cousins. We were a big family, and I didn't get a chance to see them often—we usually met at family weddings. I was really looking

forward to speaking to them. One of my Satmar cousins came over to me and said that her mother said she can't speak to me because I am a goy [non-Jew] since I'm not Satmar! That was it. We didn't speak for years. I was so hurt.

Among Satmars it is clear that nonreligious Jews are not really considered Jewish. Lubavitch on some level rejects this and claims that all Jews are equally Jewish and possess both an animalistic and divine soul. I have heard several Lubavitch rabbis proudly declare something to the effect that "all Jews, regardless of how religiously observant they are, are as Jewish as Moses."

Nonetheless, although Lubavitch accepts the Jewishness of any given individual Jew as an individual, it rejects the legitimacy of other Jewish denominations. That is, Lubavitchers do not believe, for example, that the Reform or Conservative movements represent an authentic form of Jewish expression. This is not merely a theoretical issue but has concrete consequences for how Lubavitch deals with other Jewish denominations. For example, Lubavitch will not formally join with other Jewish denominations to organize even social or cultural, let alone religious, programs.

Thus, in addition to the boundaries between Lubavitch and Satmar and non-Jews, there are also significant boundaries between these communities and nonreligious Jews, as well as between them and other ultra-Orthodox communities. Rhetoric and attitudes liken non-Lubavitch or non-Satmar Jews to non-Jews.

Traveling Boundaries

Given that Lubavitch is deeply involved in outreach work around the world and that many interviewees personally participated in this work, some of them committing years of their lives to this cause, it is reasonable to ask whether these symbolic boundaries are present at the outposts or whether they exist only in Brooklyn and other major Lubavitch centers. The answer is that Lubavitch has been so successful at inculcating this ideology of separation in its members that even when they travel in the outside world, they often remain in what one Lubavitcher, Dovid, called "the Lubavitch bubble."

Dovid explained that when doing outreach abroad,

you're traveling in like a "bubble," because you're putting on these glasses and seeing everything through a certain perspective, because that's how Lubavitch is. So you go to Milwaukee or Australia—you go to any other country—you're there to teach other people. So if you're there to teach other people, you're not really going to accept their culture or even be open-minded to it, because all you're there to do is teach it to them . . . for them to see things your way.[10] So, yeah, I interacted with people in communities—from different stations of life, but there was no—I didn't get anything from them. All it was was to teach them. Everything I looked at was through the bubble and through the glasses of Lubavitch and ultra-Orthodoxy.

Dovid went on to explain further:

Lubavitch doesn't only insulate their members [in their own communities], but they also teach their members to go out there and teach other people. But the brainwashing—in my opinion—goes so deep that, even if they go out and talk to people in other countries, they only see things through their own lenses. . . . Lubavitch wants you to reach out to the outside world, but they kind of make the outside world part of Lubavitch. So they'll send you to other countries, but, on the other hand, they're insulating you, telling you those other people do not have good lives.

Dovid also connects the idea of the "Lubavitch bubble" with the idea that non-Jews "do not have good lives." In other words, Lubavitch tries to use its general denigration of non-Jews as a way to ensure that those who are away from the community doing outreach work remain pure and are not influenced by the outside world with which they are forced to interact.

The boundary between Lubavitchers doing outreach work away from home and the other kinds of people they meet there, and the similar boundary between Satmars and all others, does not necessarily inoculate young Lubavitchers and Satmars from the more general impact of simply being away from home. Several interviewees, particularly Satmars, reported that traveling away from home was part of what helped them imagine breaking away from their communities and that they took advantage of this opportunity to look around at the world. But no Lubavitchers reported meeting individuals from outside their communities who influenced them while they were away from home doing outreach work. A useful contrast is described by Stuart Wright (1987), who notes that the people whom his interviewees in new religious movements (NRMs) met while they were away from home missionizing in small groups or by themselves were often a significant factor in their initial stages of doubt and reflection that ultimately led them away

---

10. Dovid's comments are remarkably similar to Richard Hofstadter's observation that certain political conservatives see themselves as "transmitters" of information and not as "receivers" of it (1964, 38), and this mind-set protects them from the need to change their beliefs when exposed to evidence that contradicts them.

from their NRMs. Given the number of non-Lubavitch individuals they meet during such work and the lack of supervision over these young Lubavitchers, the bubble is remarkably effective.

Transcending Boundaries

Even the elaborate boundaries just described are not completely impermeable or rigid. As Iddo Tavory correctly points out, these boundaries are "situationally circumscribed"; indeed, among members of these communities, "the boundaries between Jews and non-Jews are often transcended, usually on a daily basis" (2010, 146, 166). For example, even the greatest boundary, the one between the community and the non-Jewish world, continues to be transcended when members of the Lubavitch and Satmar communities go to work and interact with non-Jews and occasionally even become friends with their non-Jewish colleagues.

Lubavitch certainly transcends the boundary between itself and the non-Jewish world much more frequently and to a much greater extent than does Satmar. The reason in part is that Lubavitch has emissaries all around the world to conduct its outreach work who are constantly meeting with non-Jews. And the Lubavitch movement has a somewhat less rigid and isolationist mind-set, so even when Lubavitchers are in Crown Heights or other major Lubavitch neighborhoods, they are somewhat more open to talking with their non-Jewish neighbors and having interactions with the non-Jews around them.

It is important to remember that even though these moments or episodes of transcending the boundary have sociological significance and speak to the fact that the boundary is permeable, these walls are not any less socially significant. On the contrary, the reason it is significant that they sometimes are transcended is that they usually are *not* transcended. Generally the separation between the ultra-Orthodox Jew and the non-Jew is too great to overcome.

Guarding the Fence: Boundaries between the Community and the Exiter

The boundaries just discussed are outward facing: The Satmar and Lubavitch communities look out at the world around them and identify the groups they want to keep at a distance. But a different kind of boundary is necessary when looking inward at potential exiters. Such a boundary is erected and maintained not between two groups who are ostensibly already separate and have objective differences. This boundary must function somehow as a fence around the community designed to keep members inside.

Tactics to Prevent Exiting

Some strict religious communities employ formal systems of sanctions and excommunication for those who seriously deviate from the norms and expectations of the community. For example, the Old Order Amish (Hostetler 1993), the Bruderhof (Zablocki 1980), Seventh-day Adventists (Ballis 1999), Jehovah's Witnesses (Holden 2002), and the Church of Scientology (Wallis 1977), which all share with Lubavitch and Satmar an emphasis on obedience to a rigid system of religious belief and practice, make extensive use of such systems. Indeed, the practice of shunning is so severe among Jehovah's Witnesses that it is even forbidden for members to attend the funeral of someone who was shunned in life, on pain of the offender being excommunicated (Holden 2002). In stark contrast, however, neither Lubavitch nor Satmar has any formal system of sanctions for those who deviate. Instead, they both use informal methods of sanction to promote religious conformity. In this arena Satmar responds much more harshly than Lubavitch to religious deviance.

There are two key punitive measures Satmar uses to instill fear and obedience in its members, neither of which is used in Lubavitch. The first tactic is used on those members who the community feels are modernizing and becoming a "problem" and involves threatening to expel the children of the deviating parent from the community's school if the parent does not stop the deviant behavior and return to the norms and expectations of the community. This is no idle threat. If the parent or parents do not heed the warning, the children are in fact expelled from the school.[11]

The following is an official notice from the Vaad Hatznius, the Modesty Committee in the Satmar enclave of Kiryas Joel, which is similar to the notices that several interviewees received informing them that their children will not be accepted back to school if the parents do not change their behavior:

---

11. In addition to Lubavitch, various other ultra-Orthodox communities seem to refrain from using the threat of expulsion from religious school as a means to command religious obedience from parents. In fact, one of the most venerable ultra-Orthodox non-Hasidic (Litvish) rabbis in Israel, Rabbi Aharon Leib Shteinman (2017), responded to a questioner by stating that yeshivas must accept all students who seek entry. The questioner claimed that certain children "are not the type" for his school and that they come from an Orthodox but "open-minded" family and may have an adverse effect on the other students. Rabbi Shteinman insists that the school must accept them and that the proper arrangement is for the school to cater to all types of children. When pressed, he mockingly asks, "Where do you want the child to go to school, on the moon?!" Rabbi Shteinman also mentions that even children from the best families can go "bad," so there is no point in not allowing children from a questionable family to attend the school.

Modesty Committee
Dear Mr. _____
Since you are acting in an inappropriate manner and you are cutting
your beard, we want to inform you of our resolution that we cannot
keep your children in our institutions in the following semester.
The Administration[12]

Sheindy, a Satmar woman in her late twenties, described the sequence of
events that led to her daughter being expelled from the Satmar school she
was attending. It all began with a slight change in the mother's appearance:

I had modernized my dress a bit . . . changes that you would not have
noticed. . . . There are all different types of styles of head covering,
and the smaller the band around the *sheitel* [wig], the more modern
you are. I used to wear a short *sheitel* with a hat, and I started wearing a *sheitel* with a band. Over time the band got smaller. This was
not really an infraction; it's just seen as modernizing. My skirts grew
shorter, still way below the knee [the basic length required by the
community] but higher than the four to five inches below the knee
that Satmar demands. I wore more fashionable clothing. I wore more
colors, not only black and blue. I dabbled a little in eye shadow
maybe, stuff like that. I also stopped shaving my head [as is required
of married Satmar women]. . . . I think we got one warning in the
mail. Then they sent a letter asking us to come for a meeting.

Sheindy went on to describe the meeting she and her husband had with the
Modesty Committee:

The meeting took place in a side room of the main Satmar *bais medrish* [study hall] in Williamsburg. About eight middle-aged men
were sitting at a table. They listed all the problems they had with me,
all the while speaking only to my husband, and then they said that
they could not accept our daughter back into the school. That was it;
I wasn't willing to accept all of their requirements, so they weren't
willing to let my daughter stay in their school.

Expelling a child from school is a severe punishment because all the
Satmar and many other Hasidic schools in the New York area coordinate
and communicate with each other. That is, if a student is expelled from one
school, no other school will accept him or her. This means that if parents still

---

12. The original notice was written in Yiddish; the translation is mine. See Rosenberg
2012a for a facsimile of the letter.

want their child to attend a religious school, the family may need to move to a different neighborhood with a more liberal Jewish school, possibly quite far from their friends and family.

Thus, expelling a child from school is tantamount to expelling a family from the neighborhood. As Sheindy reflected,

> My daughter couldn't go to the school. We wanted to remain *Hasidish* [Hasidic]. We tried to. We tried to apply our daughter to other *Hasidish* schools, but they didn't accept us. There is this thinking that when you come out of Williamsburg, then you are on a slippery slope and deep in the bowels of secularism, so other schools don't want to accept you. They fear the influence that your children will have on the other children. . . . So in order to find a school that would take our daughter, we needed to move away from our community. We left the community because we were expelled.

The limitation of the school-expulsion tactic in terms of commanding obedience is that it has the potential to work only with those members who want to stay within the community and send their children to its schools. For those members who are eager to leave and send their children to a more liberal Jewish school or to public school, this is no threat at all.

For such individuals a second tactic is used. The community often makes a concerted effort to interfere in custody battles to ensure that the parent who stays in the community maintains full custody if the parents divorce. (It is often the case that if one parent wants to stop being Orthodox and the other wants to remain, they divorce. Furthermore, given that Satmars usually marry at a very young age, men as young as eighteen and women as young as seventeen, it is extremely common for individuals to already be married, often with children, by the time they decide to exit the community. Thus, for example, of the thirty-five Satmar and other Satmar-like Hungarian Hasidic interviewees, twenty-five were previously married in their community, and many of them had children from those marriages.)

Several interviewees reported that their community was helping their partner who stayed in the community to retain custody of their child or children. This was the experience of Malky, a Satmar woman in her late twenties: "I always felt that I would have to stay Satmar for 'them' not to take away my son. I thought this because that was the talk of the town, that was the way that they would talk: 'We'll take away your child if you're not *frum*.'" I asked Malky if anyone ever threatened her specifically like that. She responded:

> Yes, my ex. He told me if I become more modern, he would take away my child. And I kept on asking him, "How is that possible?!" . . . If

the couple is not together, then it's going to be a fight, and I would have to fight it. . . . So the talk in town is, "So she became more modern, so how come her kids are with her? She's probably going to go crazy, so how come her kids are with her? Can we trust her?" Then the community goes to the court and says that the kid will have a lot of problems if he stays with the mother.

I asked Malky if anyone in her community had gone to court against her. She responded, "Yes, there are people in the community that are defending my ex and helping him get custody. He has a bunch of friends in the community that lie about me to the court and are helping him. They say that I'm crazy and a bad mother."

Gitty, a Satmar woman in her mid-thirties, spoke of her knowledge of exiters who, because of the support of the community, lost all custody of their children:

> I know stories of women with children who become OTD [who exit], and the community claims that the women are crazy and the man gets complete custody. These women get completely cut off from their children; they can never see them, nothing! The fact is the community conspires along with certain judges to prevent these women from getting their children back. It is a fact, and anyone who doesn't believe it is naïve.

Evidence that the community interferes in custody battles is not limited to reports by exiters. I also interviewed the parents of a Satmar exiter, and they readily defended this policy. That these parents agreed to be interviewed means that they are relatively open-minded, yet they wholeheartedly endorsed this policy. The mother, Mrs. Grossbaum, who is in her mid-sixties, explained:

> You know that when a person goes off the *dayrech* [proper path], the person that stays doesn't want the children to also go off the *dayrech*. So whether it's a husband or a wife, they're the party that will fight to keep their children *frim* [ultra-Orthodox]. Of course, the other side, the one that's going off, wants to drag the children with them. There is this terrible fight, more than in any other divorce. Because now both sides are fighting for the *oosid* [future] of the children. It's not just that you're fighting because you want your child; you're fighting for your child's future, which means everything.

She went on to explain why it was impossible for the Hasidic community to compromise or be "democratic" about the issue of child custody:

We don't live just for this world; we live for eternity, for the next world. So of course there is this vicious, vicious fight going on. And the community will always back the parent that stays *frim*. We're not democratic enough to say, "Oh, you're the mother and you want to take your children with you; you have a right to go off the *dayrech* with your children." No, we don't see it like that. We're fighting for the *oosid* [future] of the child. . . . This is a very serious thing we're talking about. It's not like, let's be democratic; you take half the children and I'll take half the children, and we'll exchange. . . . Your wife wants to go off the *dayrech*; your husband wants to go off the *dayrech*—you can't stop them. He's an adult. But to lose the children to this!

When I asked if the community uses the claim that the one who exited is crazy, Mrs. Grossbaum responded:

If the case ends up in court, not in *bez din* [religious court], you can't explain to the judge that I'm fighting for my child's future. Which judge is going to buy it—the judge is a secular person! So the next best thing is to say that the other side has mental issues and the children can't live with that person. We're forced into such a situation. . . . Go tell the judge that "ich vil mayne kinder zol blaybin erlicher yidden" [I want my children to remain pious Jews]. The judge is not going to buy it; a jury is not going to buy it. Nobody is going to buy it! Too bad. They chose to be not religious. . . . No one can understand how desperately we want our children to be *erlicher yiddin* [pious Jews]. It's like a fight to the death, almost.

When I asked if she heard of the idea of saying that the exiter suffers from mental illness even if he or she does not, she responded:

They're considered mentally ill if they want to leave. Also, in all custody cases, even by the *frier* [nonreligious], they make up stories about each other. . . . Sometimes there is an amicable divorce. It is never an amicable divorce when a person goes off the *dayrech* and the one who stays is fighting for the children. It cannot be amicable.

Several Satmar interviewees believe that the reason the courts favor the parent who remains in the community is that the judges side with the community in an effort to win its bloc vote to help with their reelection. As Leib, who is in his early twenties, explained it,

The community uses the power of bloc voting to get their way in child custody battles. The judges know that they can get thirty thousand votes from the Satmar community if they follow what the community wants by granting custody to the partner that is still inside the community, regardless of whether it's the mother or the father.

Several others felt strongly that the judges are *not* necessarily inclined to favor the parent staying inside the community to get the community's bloc vote. Instead, these individuals thought that exiters lost custody because they made mistakes along the way. As Etty, a Satmar woman in her mid-twenties and herself a mother, explained,

> I think that if a woman gets dragged into court over custody, she messed up; she did something wrong. You can't show weakness to the other side, and you have to be responsible. If the community tries to say lies about you, that will not work unless there is some truth to it. If you are not stable, you go out and party a lot; sure, you might have problems. But that's your fault because you are a mother, and you need to be responsible. . . . I don't believe that the courts are out to get us, and I don't believe in this bloc vote business.

Etty went on to say that sometimes exiting parents lose custody because unknowingly they "screwed up" in ways that make themselves look bad in court:

> I mean they act hasty or erratically without knowing the relevant laws. Like because they are scared or frustrated, they take their child away from the community without notifying the other parent. I get that they are a loving and desperate parent, but to the court this is kidnapping, and it puts the parent in a very bad legal position for the custody.

Ruchy, who got full custody of her child, also rejected the idea that judges side with the parent who stays in the community to get its bloc vote. She explained some of the variables potentially involved in these cases and how some of them worked to her favor in her case:

> There were a lot of factors. My child was so young, so it was hard for them to argue that my child was already set in one way. Also, I wasn't married for a very long time. It was a very short marriage. The longer you are in the community, it's like you were making a commitment to staying in that community. It's like you were happy with your life and decided to set up shop there. Even though it's not true. . . . The

earlier you leave, the greater chance you have of making it out with your child. . . . I also benefited from having friends who knew about the custody process and warned me not to do things that would be detrimental to my custody case.

Although several interviewees do not believe that election politics plays a role in the court's child custody decisions, it seems reasonable to assume that the judge may look favorably on leaving the child in the custody of the parent remaining in the community. This would preserve the community environment the child is accustomed to along with the religious way of life the child has known all his or her life.

In addition, the family of the parent who remains in the community, and sometimes even the family of the exiter, come forward to the court and submit evidence—whether true, false, or exaggerated—that the exiter is an unsuitable parent. It is therefore not difficult to see why the judge would rule against the exiter, even without the incentive of a bloc vote. Given these dynamics, it is understandable how the threat of the community coming to the assistance of the parent who remains in the community—attempting to completely cut off the exiter from his or her children—can act as a very strong disincentive for Satmars with children to attempt to exit.

Pathologizing Dissent

As noted, the Satmar community responds more harshly to potential exiters than Lubavitch does. Nonetheless, neither Lubavitch nor Satmar makes formal public denunciations of religious exiters. This is highly significant because according to Kai T. Erikson (1966) deviance performs its vital social function by being repudiated *publicly*.[13] That is, deviant acts help a community maintain its boundaries by giving it an opportunity to state publicly what is inside and what is outside the bounds of accepted community behavior. As Erikson notes, "Each time the community moves to censure some act of deviation, and *convenes a formal ceremony to deal with the responsible offender*, it sharpens the authority of the violated norm and restates where the boundaries of the group are located" (1966, 13; emphasis added).

This raises the following related questions: Why do these two communities not publicly denounce religious deviants? And what other tactics do these communities employ to accomplish the same goals of signaling the boundaries of accepted behavior and protecting those boundaries from additional violators? In brief, these communities do not engage in formal

---

13. The idea that social conflict leads to a strengthening of the group by clearly defining its boundaries has a long history in sociology. See Durkheim 1960; Mead 1918; Simmel 1955; and Coser 1956.

public denunciations because the exiters reflect poorly on the community. Instead, the communities engage in informal shaming of exiters (explained later).

The fact that these two communities do not engage in any formal acts of denunciation is understandable in light of Mary Jackman's (1994) analysis of the limits of overt forms of force. Jackman rejects Pierre Bourdieu's assertion that force represents the most complete form of control. She argues that in regard to dominant and subordinate groups or individuals, subtly shaming people is a much safer route to achieving obedience. More overt demonstrations of force are an acknowledgment of failure on the part of the dominant to keep the subordinate in line. This revelation itself undermines the power relationship.

Furthermore, such demonstrations of force sharpen the rift between the two groups or individuals.[14] The last thing the Lubavitch and Satmar communities want to do is stand up in the synagogue or issue a formal reprimand every time someone exits—especially if such exits are on the rise, as some believe they are. This would only draw attention to the problem and potentially cause some to wonder if something was lacking in their community and whether they should likewise exit.

Mary Douglas ([1996] 2002) argues that societies organize the complexity of the world by classifying things into neat groupings. Those things that do not fall neatly into the categories created are considered a threat to the consistency of the society and must be neutralized. Exiters pose just such a threat.

In a sense, ultra-Orthodox Jewish communities try to maintain a neat separation, at least conceptually, between themselves and the non-Jewish and secular world. From the ultra-Orthodox perspective, those who are inside the community are pious, godly, and virtuous, while those on the outside are secular, selfish, and without merit. Those who grew up in ultra-Orthodox communities and then decide to leave pose a serious threat to this neat view of the world. Such exiters are the brothers and sisters or friends and neighbors of community members and cannot be discounted automatically as good-for-nothings, and their acts of rebelliousness may serve as a model for others to emulate. Both Satmar and Lubavitch project the binary categories of Jew and non-Jew even onto Jewish groups other than their own. This reflects a highly categorized and divided world, which the phenomenon of exiting radically upsets.

These communities attack anything located in the interstices of the established categories. The logic of this sort of tactic is highlighted by Shragy,

---

14. Lewis A. Coser (1956) makes a similar argument. He notes that in-group conflicts are often much more intense than conflicts with outsiders and that these conflicts can cause group fragmentation rather than integration. For this reason they are often suppressed rather than acted on.

a Satmar interviewee in his mid-forties, who reflected on the need of the Satmar community to attack people who were considered in the middle of the road, people who occupied an ambiguous position:

> In Satmar it's much less problematic if someone leaves and leaves completely so the community can say, "This is what happens if you start dabbling in Haskalah [Jewish Enlightenment], if you start reading secular books! You'll become a *shaygets* [derogatory term for non-Jew], *loy alayni* [Heaven forbid]!" But if you can go and be modern and still have a beard and *paiyyes* [sidelocks] and still have the *l'vish* [traditional Hasidic garb], I think it's much more challenging; it's much more frustrating to the community.

Shragy went on to recount a famous story about the ancestor of the founder of the Satmar community that made this point powerfully:

> There is a story of Reb Yoel Teitelbaum's grandfather, the Yismach Moshe, in Sighet [in Transylvania], who had a *hoosid* [a follower] who became a doctor but remained very *frum* [religious], and the Rebbe said, "I wake up every morning and *daven* [pray] to the *Reboyne shel oylem* [God], *halevay* [if only] this *hoosid* would *shmad* [convert to Christianity]!"

This story expresses the idea that the community would prefer that its errant members go completely to the other side, including converting to Christianity, than stay closer to the community and potentially convince others to similarly deviate from the strictures of the community.

Given this mind-set, it is not sufficient to simply maintain that exiters are wrong or misguided. Their actions must be completely delegitimized, and rumors are spread around the community about the exiters to accomplish this goal. The function of the ultra-Orthodox communities' gossip regarding exiters fits with Max Gluckman's (1963) argument that gossip is a social phenomenon intended to exert social control and maintain the values and unity of the group.[15]

As Leib explained,

> Once people leave, the community right away makes up stories about why they left to explain why the person that left wasn't really normal. The stories could also contradict each other. They said about me that

---

15. See also Rosnow and Fine 1976. The authors see gossip as an economic transaction for profit based on mutual interest and argue that it has numerous functions, but one of those functions is moralizing.

I was always irreligious and that I was too holy. My rebbe said that I
left because I learned kabbalah, the Jewish mystical tradition, and
that the *sitra acher*, the forces of darkness, got hold of me because I
wasn't ready to learn these things.

It is not surprising that the community's narratives about individuals or
about the phenomenon of exiting are self-contradictory. As Albert Hirschman (1991) points out regarding reactionary rhetoric, it is common for defenders of the status quo, sometimes even one and the same critic, to switch
from one criticism of change to another even if these criticisms contradict
each other.

Yitty, a Lubavitcher in her early twenties, reported that she makes sure
to wear a skirt rather than pants while in Crown Heights to keep her name
out of the rumor mill:

People recognize my face, even though they may not know my name.
They'll look at me and recognize me and try to figure it out—who is
that face?—because I went to Bais Rivkah [the main Lubavitch girls'
school]. . . . I don't want to be talked about; I don't want people talking about me behind my back.

I asked Yitty what kinds of things she thought they would say, and she responded, "It's the same thing. . . . I've heard the conversation about other
girls: 'Oh my God, have you seen her?! She's wearing pants?! She's probably
on drugs, and she's probably a huge slut; she's probably dancing like a whore!
Oh my God, she's wearing pants!'" I asked Yitty if she personally heard such
things said about other women, and she responded:

Yes, because they were wearing pants or they are holding hands with
a boy, they are for sure off the deep end. They don't have their life in
order. They're crazy; they're just unstable; they're not healthy. Being
not religious comes along with a billion other things. They're also x,
y, and z. There is a reason why they are not religious.

In addition to the basic assumption that all who exit are completely given
over to temptation and base instincts, the rumors and denunciation that the
ultra-Orthodox community engages in to respond to religious deviance and
exiters take three forms: It is claimed that to deviate religiously is unnatural,
that those who exit all come from dysfunctional families or had horrible life
experiences, and that those who exit are mentally ill or in some way "crazy."

Since members of the community assume that the life they are living is
the natural and only way to live, it follows that those who decide to do otherwise are committing themselves to acting and living in an unnatural man-

ner. A clear illustration of this point comes from Simcha, a Lubavitcher in his mid-twenties who violated the regulations of the community and trimmed his beard even while in rabbinical school and was caught several times in the act.

The head rabbi of the school tried to understand why he was doing it and inquired, "Was it because your beard grew in faster than the other students' and you feel uncomfortable?" The rabbi kept pressing him, "Explain to me why you are doing this thing." Simcha remarked, "It was always assumed that there was something not normal about what I was doing, and if he could only figure out its cause, he could fix it. He never thought maybe I just don't like to have a beard and that it's a perfectly normal thing to do to shave my beard."

These communities also claim that all exiters had horrible life experiences inside the community or that they come from dysfunctional families, and that is why they exited rather than because of any deficiencies in the community itself.[16] This point comes out clearly in the work of Faranak Margolese (2005), an Orthodox woman who wrote a guidebook from the perspective of the Orthodox community on how to prevent religious exiting. She also conducted online surveys of exiters for her book. She argues that for the most part all those who exit Orthodoxy do so for emotional rather than intellectual reasons.

In addition, based on the data she collected from her online survey, she notes that more than 50 percent of her respondents were verbally or physically abused by someone in the community, but it is left unclear whether this was a one-time event or they were consistently abused their entire life. She also leaves completely unexplored what role, if any, this had on people deciding to exit. Presumably there are many people who remain who also suffered in this way.

A telling example of how community members create narratives about exiters that place all the "blame" for the exit on a horrible life experience of the exiter rather than some "legitimate" cause, comes from Naftuli, who was sexually abused inside the community when he was a young boy:

My family has made my leaving the community all about my abuse. My mother "knows" that I left the community because of my abuse. I

16. Although the community is quick to label exiters as abuse victims, the community also often belittles those who come forward as abuse victims to tell their story. A chilling example of this dismissive attitude can be seen in a lecture by Rabbi Manis Friedman, one of the major intellectuals of Lubavitch (quoted in Rosenberg 2013a). Friedman belittles the effects of sexual abuse and rape and claims that it may be talking about it that causes the negative consequences of the rape rather than the abuse itself. Friedman's remarks caused widespread outrage, and he eventually apologized, but his original remarks are illustrative of the common attitude among many in the ultra-Orthodox community.

don't completely agree with that, obviously. My extended family are also understanding, and they feel "Oy nebech! [What a tragedy!]. This is the guy who was wronged in such a terrible way by our community. We failed him!" Whatever they think of me, if they see me, they'll come over to me with a smile, shake my hand, and be civil to me.

Although in this case the person was indeed abused as a child, according to Naftuli that was not the sole or possibly even the main reason for his exiting. Nonetheless, from the perspective of community members, including his own family, that is the only reason imaginable for his exiting.

As a last tactic to delegitimize and denigrate exiters and their decision to exit, these communities claim that all those who exit are "meshuga," mentally ill (see Shaffir and Rockaway 1987; Winston 2006). That is, these communities perpetuate a narrative about why individuals exit that rejects out of hand the claim on the part of exiters that they have legitimate reasons for leaving. These communities posit that the only possible reason a person would leave is mental illness.

Furthermore, at least in the Lubavitch community, there is a doctrinal basis for the claim that all who exit are crazy. According to the *Tanya*, without *nichnas bo ruach shtus*, temporary insanity, no Jew would ever sin. Logically, if someone decided to establish his or her entire life on "sin," it follows that the individual is insane.

This tactic of ultra-Orthodox communities was clearly visible in their response to the tragic suicide in 2015 of Faigy Mayer, a young woman who was born to a Hasidic family but decided to exit her community as a young adult. It appears that Faigy struggled with mental health issues for years and that these issues continued to plague her after she exited the community. Instead of allowing that there may have been other reasons for her exit, many within the ultra-Orthodox community focused exclusively on this issue, as if there could be no other possible explanation for her actions. For example, Rabbi Avi Shafran, a spokesman for Agudath Israel of America, a major ultra-Orthodox umbrella organization, claimed that Faigy's mental health issues were a reason why she exited the community:

> By her own account, Faigy faced deep internal adversity from her early youth, and her letter, read carefully, only corroborates the clouded lens through which she viewed her environment. Her psychological challenges were not the result of her leaving her home and community, but arguably a cause of it. (Quoted in Sokol 2015)

Rabbi Raphael Aron (2015), a Lubavitch self-described "expert on cults," made the point explicit:

In a similar vein, I do not believe that the decision of many people to leave their faith is simply the product of a philosophical or theological crisis; more often it is related to other deep-seated personal and emotional issues which the individual is confronting. Some of those issues are of a mental health nature.

Many individuals reported to me that they were considered meshuga by their family and community for exiting. As Shifra, a Satmar woman in her mid-twenties, noted, "Initially my siblings tried to convince me to come back. Then they decided that I was 'mentally ill' and should see a shrink, and they gave up their efforts to bring me back." Ruchy described the way that mental illness and sexual promiscuity are sometimes conflated in the community's rumors about exiters:

I'm apparently mentally ill. I went crazy; I started sleeping with all the women; then I slept with all the men. People in the community said, "This woman is crazy! Her poor husband, he's such a good guy! He was such a good yeshiva student, and she's just fucked up. She's not religious at all either."

Sheindy also noted the link between sexual promiscuity and mental illness in the rumors about her:

I moved to a community near where I grew up, and this community is Modern Orthodox. This Modern Orthodox community is well known in my old community, and it has a very bad reputation. There are all these rumors about our community, like that it's full of crazy people who are swingers. . . . I'm still waiting for someone to invite me to the swingers' party.

The evidence that the community tries to label all exiters as crazy is not limited to reports of exiters themselves. I received corroboration of this from the interview I conducted with the Satmar parents of one exiter. The parents are still proud members of the Satmar community, and the mother, Mrs. Grossbaum, confirmed that it is common for exiters to be labeled as "*mishige*," crazy. When I asked her what is meant by calling an exiter crazy, this is how she responded:

It could mean many things. It could mean mentally ill—that does happen sometimes—or it could mean he became crazy, *iz aran a juk in kup; a mishigas in kup* [he got a bug in his head; he got a crazy idea in his head]. . . . I'll give you an analogy. I have a friend who went to this very famous doctor in Washington, D.C. She needed pituitary surgery. . . . He was a very famous endocrinologist who worked for the National Institutes of Health. The next time my friend goes back, it's a lady! He just wanted to let my friend know that he decided to become a woman.

For her it was "crazy" that a man would want to become a woman, and it was equally "crazy" that a religious Jew would want to leave his community.

Iz aran a juk in kup, er hut gevolt veren a froy [He got a crazy idea in his head he wanted to become a woman]. *Hashem* [God] made him a man, and now he wants to be a woman. *Du bizt geboyren a yid; bizt geshtanen bay har Sinai* [You were born a Jew; you stood at Mount Sinai],[17] *itst vilst du es altz avekvarfen* [now you want to throw it all away]. . . . It could mean either a person lost his mind and as part of his illness he decided to leave, or a person is a normal person, continues to be a normal person, but he got this crazy idea in his head that he is a woman instead of a man.

Regardless of the precise meaning of the term "crazy" when used to describe exiters, it is a clear indication that from the perspective of the community there is no room for dispassionate religious disagreement. One either abides by the norms and expectations of the community, or one is completely discredited as no longer a person of sound mind governed by free will.

The potential to prevent further exits by claiming that exiters are crazy is not lost on interviewees. As Ruchy explained,

So I'll tell you the reason they have to say these things. If you say that a person that left out of his own decision because he came to the conclusion that this no longer works for him and that he has a different lifestyle in mind and he wants to lead a different life, he wants to raise a different family, people might think, "So hold on a second. So there's a different option out there like that, and it's okay?" And that could weaken their system. You've got to say, "That person is crazy!" in order to strengthen your system.

As Gary Alan Fine and Irfan Khawaja (2005) point out, one of the key elements that determine if gossip will be accepted is the "politics of plausibility," meaning whether it fits with basic assumptions and understandings of the audience of the gossip. For outsiders it may appear that the basic

---

17. This is a reference to the belief that all Jews who will ever be born in the future stood together at Mount Sinai when God gave the Torah to the Jewish people thousands of years ago.

assumptions underlying the rumors spread by these communities about exiters—that they are self-absorbed shallow people or that they have a mental illness—may seem implausible. But for the intended audience of this gossip, other members of the community, this view is perfectly plausible because the alternative, that there is nothing wrong with the exiters and their choice is a perfectly legitimate one, is simply unimaginable. (The other key factor is the "politics of credibility," the authority of the people who are spreading the rumors, and in this case, it is coming from parents, teachers, and respected members of the community, so the rumors have high credibility.)

To grasp the logical necessity, from the perspective of the communities involved, to pathologize exiters, it is helpful to relate this to Glenn Greenwald's (2014) analysis of why political elites respond to whistleblowers by attacking them personally, psychologizing them, and claiming they are mentally ill. Given the strong connection between these two cases (and the clarity and straightforwardness of Greenwald's explanation), I quote at length from Greenwald:

> There are obvious reasons for launching personal attacks on critics of the status quo. . . . One is to render the critic less effective: few people want to align themselves with someone crazy or weird. Another is deterrence: when dissidents are cast out of society and demeaned as emotionally imbalanced, others are given the strong incentive not to become one. But the key motive is logical necessity. For guardians of the status quo, there is nothing genuinely or fundamentally wrong with the prevailing order and its dominant institutions, which are viewed as just. Therefore, anyone claiming otherwise . . . must, by definition, be emotionally unstable and psychologically disabled.
>
> There are, broadly speaking, two choices: obedience to institutional authority or radical dissent from it. The first is a sane and valid choice only if the second is crazy and illegitimate. For defenders of the status quo, mere correlation between mental illness and radical opposition to prevailing orthodoxy is insufficient. Radical dissent is evidence, even proof, of a severe personality disorder. At the heart of this formulation is an essential deceit: that dissent from institutional authority involves a moral or ideological choice but obedience does not. . . . Obedience to authority is implicitly deemed the natural state. (2014, 227–228)

Greenwald explains here what it means for obedience to be the status quo. It is considered simply the natural way to be, and it is decidedly *not* the result of a rational, moral, or ideological choice. Choice—whether to remain inside the community or to leave it—has no place within this system. Those who remain in the community are not viewed as choosing to do so any more than one chooses to eat, shower, or sleep; this is simply how to live a normal life. Doing otherwise, therefore, cannot be viewed as a choice either but as a symptom of mental illness.

There is ambiguity within the reports from interviewees about whether these communities' use of terms such as "crazy" or "mentally ill" is meant literally or merely as a derisive way to belittle exiters. But its ubiquity and usage in other similar contexts indicate that this is not merely a put-down but reflects specific views about both exiters and those who remain within the community.

Still, "mental illness" may serve as a metaphor when used in this way. Susan Sontag (1978) argues that illness—in her case physical—is often used as a metaphor to describe a threat whose origin is mysterious and whose spread is little understood. In this case it seems that the label "mentally ill" is being used by the ultra-Orthodox community to describe an internal moral threat whose origin is misunderstood by its members that is greatly feared and its treatment or resolution unknown. Furthermore, the language of contagion, obviously not actually relevant to mental illness, seems very appropriate here because the community fears that if one member "goes bad" and exits the community, that member could influence others to do so. For this reason, a great effort is made to try to isolate the contagion, so to speak, and prevent it from infecting other members.

In this sense, exiters are not ostracized because they have adopted the ways of non-Jews but because they are a threat to the "health" of the community. This explains why Lubavitch can welcome outsiders (which occurs regularly as part of the group's outreach work) but still treat its own members who deviate with harsh ridicule and rebuke. Outsiders are not seen as a threat to the cohesiveness of the community since they have never practiced the proper Lubavitch way of life, so they cannot be judged for failing to live up to it.[18] However, the insiders who were raised in the community and decided to deviate from the accepted path are seen as mentally ill, a threat to the community's moral claims, and a negative influence on others within the community.

---

18. In Jewish legal terms, Lubavitch views a secular or liberal Jew as a "captive child" raised among the gentiles (*tinok shenishbah bein ha'akum*) who is not responsible for his or her sins because they are performed in ignorance of Jewish law. Maimonides (Mishneh Torah, Hilchot Mamrim 3:3) first applied this concept of the captive child to the children of Jewish heretics who were not technically captured but simply lacked proper Jewish education. Following his lead, the Lubavitcher Rebbe applied this concept to secular and liberal Jews today lacking Orthodox Jewish instruction. For further discussion of the captive child concept in contemporary Lubavitch thought, see Dubov 1999, 77–100.

Furthermore, even parents of Lubavitch exiters who are Lubavitch emissaries, people with decades of experience interacting with and attracting non-Orthodox Jews to their outreach programs, are not always capable of understanding or responding with compassion to their own children's exiting. This point was made clear by Dina, a Lubavitcher in her late twenties whose parents are Lubavitch emissaries:

> They are very open if it's other people, if it's not their kid. "Oh those goyim, those non-*frum* [non-Orthodox] Jews. Of course they are immoral, but our child, we raised her better." They didn't think I would be immoral enough to like boys, or immoral enough to smoke pot, or immoral enough to be interested in anything besides being a *frum* Jew. I mean, we had all different types of people over at our house— women in pants and people from many different lifestyles—but they were outraged by me! I think they see them as subhuman and me more like their daughter. I think it's typical that people are open to different walks of life, but if it's their own kid, they beat the shit out of them. . . . It's just they're hypocrites.

Of course, this "hypocrisy" can be explained if viewed in the context of the community's interest in guarding the fence around itself and maintaining its claim that it presents its members with the only natural way to live.

Lived Experiences and Permeable Boundaries

While the boundaries this chapter describes have profound and concrete consequences for the lives of those affected by them, these boundaries are permeable, as evidenced by the lived experience of exiters. The combination of this permeability and elaborate mechanisms of separation contributes significantly to the liminality of those who attempt to cross over the boundaries. This section explores the nature of this permeability in the experience of interviewees.

Families Do Not Cut Ties to Exiters

The popular perception among outsiders is that Lubavitch is an extremely progressive form of ultra-Orthodoxy and therefore does not excommunicate its exiters but allows them to make their own religious choices in relative peace. The popular perception of Satmar, however, is that it excommunicates its exiters. Scholars of ultra-Orthodoxy perpetuate this assumption as well (see, e.g., Winston 2005, 2006; and Topel 2012). My research has found that the situation is far more complex. Lubavitch is neither as tolerant nor Satmar as punitive as is generally imagined. The bottom line is that neither Lubavitch nor Satmar formally excommunicates or shuns those who exit the community.[19]

Of all the Lubavitch and Satmar interviewees, none were explicitly told by their families, "Because of what you did, you may never come back home to visit us." On the contrary, even though relations are often strained between exiters and their families, all the interviewees reported that their families and certainly their parents were willing to try to maintain some kind of relationship with them, however tenuous.[20] Although eventually parents and families agreed to maintain relations with exiters, this is not to say that they initially responded to the exit in a conciliatory manner. In fact, often families responded quite harshly, even threatening to cut off all ties. It was only later, once the dust settled, that things were able to be patched up somewhat.

The precise relationship with family varied considerably among exiters. Several reported that they had "wonderful" relations with their parents and family post-exit, but these were the exceptions (approximately five to ten individuals). One such exception is Binyomin, a Lubavitcher in his early thirties, who reflected:

I have a wonderful relationship with my parents and siblings. My parents were always accepting me for who I was. They always wanted me to be Orthodox, but they accepted me no matter what. They never argued with me about my observance level, and I even felt comfort-

---

19. The image that emerges from memoirs written by exiters from the ultra-Orthodox community may conflict with my findings. These memoirists may give the impression of being completely cut off post-exit. Assuming the veracity of their claims, there is a simple explanation for the discrepancies. Specifically, these personal memoirs represent the narratives of a marginal group who are indeed so disconnected from their family and community that they feel free to write about it and tell the whole world their personal story. However, the majority of ultra-Orthodox exiters who still have some connections with their family or community are loath to publicly discuss their disagreements with the community for fear of causing offense and jeopardizing those relationships.

20. Three interviewees were not from the Lubavitch or Satmar communities but from other Hungarian Hasidic communities who were kicked out of their houses for an extended period. One of them was essentially completely shunned for eight years, after which he was allowed to reconnect with his family. The other two had parents who considered them dead and mourned for them, going as far as to sit shiva. However, the latter two cases are extreme in the sense that not only did the exiters stop being religious, but they married non-Jews, which is something that almost none of the others have done. Furthermore, one of those two who were mourned over said that he thinks that his parents responded that way because their grand rabbi told them to. And the reason the grand rabbi told them to do so was not simply that the exiter married a non-Jew but that previously he had raised the issue of sexual abuse in the community (privately to the grand rabbi) and the grand rabbi was punishing him for raising this taboo subject.

able not wearing a yarmulke in front of them. They always stressed that the main thing is to be a good person. They gave us the space to make decisions for ourselves and to live with the consequences.

In addition to this exiter's parents being *baal teshuvas* (individuals who joined the Lubavitch community), they are of Sephardic, Middle Eastern Jewish descent. These parents may demonstrate comfort with various levels of religious observance partly because modern denominationalism within Judaism derives mainly from nineteenth-century Europe and did not penetrate Sephardic Jewish culture. Rather, Sephardic Jews regularly mingle with those of other observance levels.

Most interviewees (approximately fifty-five to sixty-five individuals) reported that they maintained relationships with their parents and families, but exiting caused a significant rupture in the fabric of the family. As Elisheva, a Lubavitcher in her late twenties and the child of *baal teshuvas*, reflected:

> My relationship with my family is very superficial, very very superficial. I'm not close with them. . . . They have a problem [that] I live with my nonreligious boyfriend and that I'm not married. . . . It's complicated with my parents. We definitely are not close, and we have a superficial relationship. They are very disappointed in my life, in the choices I've made. I don't think they are disappointed. I think they are sad.

Sheindy is a typical example of a Satmar interviewee who has a relationship with her parents and family and spoke honestly of the complexity of maintaining this relationship:

> I have a "cordial" relationship with my family. I speak to my mother once every three weeks and visit my parents several times a year, usually on holidays such as Hanukkah and Purim. I also go to family weddings. . . . However, I don't feel like my relationship is especially warm, and I don't have much to talk about with them. They are not interested in what is going on in my life. . . . I'm not sure if they really want me to come over to visit them, but they allow me to come, so I do. When I go to visit my parents, I wear a long skirt past my knees and a matronly shirt and maybe a sweater, so at least they won't be outraged by how I'm dressed. I also wear a *sheitel* [wig].

Clearly there are questions about the nature of the relationship, and she feels obligated to dress differently than she usually would. But her parents allow her to visit, and she obviously thinks it is ultimately worth it for her and her children to maintain a relationship with her family.

Benzion, a typical Lubavitcher, is a gay man in his early thirties who maintains a relationship with his family even though his homosexuality is a source of tension with his father:

> I have a good relationship with my family. My mother truly accepts me for who I am. My father says the "right things" about accepting me, but I feel my father has deeply homophobic feelings. My father loves me and understands that I am gay but would prefer if I were celibate. He has told me that "being gay is your *nisoyon* [challenge in life], and you have to deal with it as best as you can by not having sex." My mother has argued with my father: "Do you want our son to be alone and miserable?!" My father doesn't seem moved by this argument. My father also doesn't seem okay with having my non-Jewish partner over for Shabbos [the Sabbath]. My father also said that it's better that the partner is non-Jewish because "now only one person is committing a sin. If you were both Jewish, then two people would be sinning." We are welcome to come and visit during the week and on holidays such as Purim. My siblings and their husbands, including the religious ones, are very accepting of us. We were both invited to my sister's wedding and were both included in the family photos at the wedding.

Although most Lubavitch interviewees are not gay, the experience of Benzion is typical in the sense that most of the family accepts him, but there is either an individual, in his case, his father, or an area of life, such as his homosexuality, that can be a source of deep tension in the relationship.

As another Lubavitcher, Shoshana, who is in her early thirties and tries hard to maintain relationships with those family members who are not emotionally abusive to her, observed, "It's hard to separate religion from the other stuff in terms of my relationship with my family. I mean, emotional or psychological issues often show up as fights over religion or criticizing my religious choices."

The fact that interviewees, especially Satmars, reported that they now have a relationship with their family should not be taken to mean that this was always the case or that a modus vivendi was immediately reached after the individual began exiting. Not at all. Often a painful "cold war" of sorts was in effect for a period, sometimes even as long as a year or more, until gradually the two sides came together and reconnected.

Etty recalled, "My mother physically blocked me from coming into her house once because I was no longer *frum* [Orthodox] [*pauses*], so we didn't see each other for a year. Then she missed me and her grandson, so she called me and I came to visit. Now we see each other every once in a while."

For a small number (approximately thirteen individuals), it is clear from their interviews that they came from particularly unstable or dysfunctional families. By this I mean that while they were children or teens, they experienced trauma or abuse, including sexual abuse, neglect, or chaotic and unpredictable home environments. When such individuals deal with their families, there is more than just the religious separation that must be overcome. Malky is one such person. Understandably, she doesn't want to have a relationship with her family:

> After everything I've been through growing up, I don't want to have a relationship with my parents or my siblings. I haven't been in touch with my father for a long time, but it's not that my family doesn't want to have a relationship with me. I just don't want to have anything to do with them.

Another such individual is Perel, a Satmar woman in her early twenties who came from a dysfunctional family but still tries to stay in touch:

> I feel close to my father and try to have a relationship with him. But because we were disconnected for so long, it's very hard to suddenly build a relationship. I know that my father is very sorry that he wasn't around and that he really wants to have a relationship with me. . . . Recently after a wedding he hugged me and kissed me on the cheek and on my hand. It made me feel very strange. Like who was this stranger that was kissing me, and why does he want to have a relationship with me? . . . Personally I don't care about marrying a Jew, but I couldn't marry a non-Jew because of my father; it would just be too much for him. . . . I'm not close to my mother—she's not a smart person—but I try to have a relationship with her. I'm also desperate to have a relationship with all of my siblings. I go to visit them when I can, but I feel that it is very difficult to have such a relationship because they are living such different lives. I also feel close to my Satmar grandmother and uncle. They are both very religious but open-minded.

Although the quality of the relationship that interviewees have with their family post-exit varies, in part because of the extent to which their family life was healthy and loving prior to their exit, it is clear that none of them were prevented from maintaining at least a superficial relationship with their family post-exit. In several instances the exiters decided that they would prefer not to have a relationship with any or most of their family members, but this was their wish and not their family's demand. Furthermore, for most, although there were significant emotional obstacles to overcome in maintaining a relationship, they and their families were willing to attempt to do so.

Gitty believed that there were indeed Satmar exiters who were completely cut off from their family post-exit, and she told me that if I had not found any such individuals, I had not looked hard enough. I spent a lot of time trying to track down such individuals but was unable to locate any. It is of course possible that they do exist and that the pain and suffering of their traumatic ordeal of being completely cut off from their families make them unwilling to discuss it with an interviewer.

Sometimes, among the Satmar interviewees, there were instances when the immediate family maintained close relations with the exiter, but members of the extended family were cold or even hostile. One such case is Hershy, who reported that some of his uncles are not welcoming and that at a family wedding he was talking to a younger cousin when one of his uncles came over and grabbed the cousin away, scolding him for speaking to Hershy and threatening him: "Farvus retst mit der opikoyres? Vest du fargesen der lernen!" (Why are you talking to this heretic? You will forget your learning!) After this interaction Hershy tried to speak with the uncle and reason with him, but to avoid having to talk, the uncle ran away when he saw Hershy coming.

Satmars Are Fair-Weather Friends

Although the parents and usually the immediate family members of both Lubavitch and Satmar interviewees were willing to remain connected to exiters, there is an important distinction between how Lubavitch and Satmar former friends and community members respond to exiters. Specifically, many Lubavitch interviewees had a relationship with at least a few of their friends from their community. In stark contrast, many Satmars reported feeling completely cut off from their former friends and neighbors.

Hindy, a Satmar woman in her early twenties, described her lack of a relationship with former friends and the way that her clothing choices accentuated the gulf between them:

> I don't have any connection with friends still inside the community. And if my old friends saw me walking down the street, they wouldn't recognize me. I look like a shiksa [derogatory term for non-Jewish woman]! I walk down the street; I'm wearing headphones; I'm wearing my pull-on hat—nobody looks like that! I'm wearing a blue coat. Who wears a blue coat? They wear black coats, not blue. . . . Recently I was at my parents' house on Shabbos—they weren't home—and I'm wearing a tank top and sweat pants, and I went out to meet a friend and bumped into a neighbor. She looks at me and is like, Wow! She hasn't seen me like that. Not in sweats and a tank.

When I asked Hindy if she talked to the old friend she bumped into, she responded:

> Yes, I talked to her, and the only thing she had to say to me was like, "Did you hear this person died of cancer?" And she just looks at me, and you know, they play that guilt trip on you. She's just looking at me with this face that says, "It's so sad." . . . If I would meet a friend from school and they would see me now, they would have a heart attack; they wouldn't believe it. I don't think they would come over and talk to me. They would probably try to avert their eyes. They would look down or pretend to look at their kids.

Other Satmars reported that they were still in touch with some of their former friends but that there were serious limitations to these friendships. The experience of Alter, who is still Orthodox but no longer ultra-Orthodox, makes this clear. He shaves his beard, no longer has the long side curls, and no longer wears the Satmar attire of the long black coat and ritual fringes on top of his shirt; but he still wears a small leather yarmulke and is thus easily identifiable as Orthodox by community members. Some of his Satmar friends have completely severed their relationship with him and will not talk to him, and even those friends who are in communication with him treat him differently now. For example, he describes how one such friend responded to Alter's desire to find an apartment in the Hasidic community in which he was raised. Notice that in Alter's case, as in Hindy's, the issue of clothing is central:

> I told a friend I [have] know[n] for a long time that I'm looking for an apartment. He told me, "Very good. I have an apartment, but I can't rent it to you." I asked him why not. He told me, "Your clothes are no good. Your clothes are not right." And he told me, "Me personally, I like you, and I don't mind how you dress; it doesn't make a difference, but neighbors will see a guy dressed like you, and they'll start making problems." And it might be that he gave the excuse of the neighbors, but he was really the one upset about my clothing.

This distinction between the response of former friends and community members within Lubavitch and Satmar may occur because Lubavitchers are more accustomed to dealing with nonobservant Jews through their outreach activities and are therefore less uncomfortable being around the non-Orthodox behavior or dress of the exiters. This more accepting response by Lubavitchers may be motivated by a desire "to be *mekarev*," meaning to missionize the exiters and help them see the error of their ways. Certainly, numerous Lubavitchers reported that they thought that some of their former friends were speaking to them out of a desire to lead them back into the fold.[21]

Not All Feel Welcome in a Synagogue

Another difference between Lubavitch and Satmar exiters is that Lubavitch exiters tend to feel comfortable visiting their old synagogues and attending community functions when they are in the neighborhood, whereas at least some of the Satmar exiters are decidedly uncomfortable doing so. It is certainly possible that a friend or relative of the Lubavitch exiters will hassle them about their religious observance level—taking the form of "friendly" barbs—but none of the Lubavitchers ever mentioned that they feared going to a Lubavitch synagogue or community event.

In stark contrast, numerous Satmars mentioned that they did not feel comfortable doing so. Naftuli was one such example. He reflected:

> Part of why I haven't been bothered by Satmar people is because I haven't ever tried to go to a shul [synagogue]. If I did, I can only imagine that someone would say something or throw something at me. Probably not face-to-face—that's just the way they operate—but someone would do something. I could only imagine that. And I know things. . . . I go back to the community, and I see people standing and pointing at me and nudging each other. So it's not like nothing is happening; it's just [*pauses*]. To go into a shul—I can't even imagine doing that. I do go to family weddings, and people do look and point and stare. Some people come over and shake my hand, but most people just look. But at a wedding, I don't think they want to offend the person who is throwing the wedding.

The experience of Naftuli and other Satmar interviewees who felt unwelcome in Satmar synagogues is quite different from the experience of Lubavitchers who may not feel completely comfortable in a Lubavitch synagogue but know that they may attend without the threat of being accosted or seriously harassed.

"My Parents Are Not Hardcore Satmar"

Although no Satmar exiters were shunned by their families, there is a widespread belief within the Satmar community that this is the consequence of

---

21. Interestingly, several Satmars reported that now that they had exited their community, they are involved in Lubavitch outreach activities and do not feel that the Lubavitch rabbis are trying to "get them" to be more religious.

exiting. In fact, although not one of the twenty-four Satmar exiters was completely shunned by his or her family, several reported that they were not shunned because their family is "modern" or more "understanding" (and unique for that reason), but the "average" Satmar family would certainly shun one of its members who exited.

Ruchy is a good example of this phenomenon. When I commented that her parents seemed to be pretty accepting of her, this was her response:

> I don't like to use my parents as an example because they are more liberal than the average Satmar parents. My parents are not hardcore Satmar. They sent me to hardcore Satmar schools and raised me in a hardcore Satmar community, but their belief system was not hardcore; it was all over the place. My parents had their own doubts growing up. They just weren't smart enough or didn't have enough of a community on the outside to help them leave. . . . I don't feel that my parents' response to my lifestyle choices is the real picture. If any of my Satmar friends in high school would have tried the same journey, it would not have been the same. It would have been a lot harder.

I asked her if she knew Satmars who were not allowed to come home. She replied:

> Yes, absolutely. I know people who grew up in even less strict communities than Satmar, in Monsey [New York]. I know that their parents clearly sided with their ex [spouse]. . . . I'm not saying other people's parents don't come around; I'm saying it usually takes years to repair the damage. It takes years. I was very lucky. I move fast, and things move fast for me. . . . My parents came around a lot faster than I expected. And I believe this is unusual for Satmar families.

Although several Satmar interviewees may indeed come from families that are more modern and ideologically lax, many others come from strict families who are well regarded in the Satmar community, and none of them severed all ties to their children who exited.

Things Have Changed in Satmar

Another caveat that several Satmar interviewees raised is that maybe now Satmar families stay connected to their family members who exit, but this is a new development. They claim that this openness was not previously the case. As Shifra expressed it, "I think things are changing. Satmars are now more open to being in contact with family members who are OTD [no longer ultra-Orthodox]. They don't want to lose them. It didn't used to be like that. I know people who were told [to] get out and never come back."

Without any substantive empirical record of the past to go on, it is very difficult to determine exactly how Satmar treated its exiters previously. To shed some light on this issue, I interviewed three Satmar exiters ages forty-four, fifty-five, and sixty-five. None of them were completely cut off from their families after they exited several decades ago. One was involved with only several family members, by her own choice, but the other two were actively involved with their large families.

Pinchis, in his mid-fifties, recounted:

> After I left the community, I moved far away to start a new life. My mother made many attempts to reach out to me. Eventually, because I broke up with my girlfriend of many years, I decided to move back closer to home. It was at this point that I reconnected with my family. I still maintain a relationship with my family today, all these years later, although God knows it is not always easy.

Shragy, in his mid-forties, talked about staying connected to his family and the effort involved to make it a reality:

> My relationship to my Satmar family is stellar. It is probably nothing to do with me and everything to do with them [laughs]. This of course is a little of an overstatement. I think that both of us have made up our minds that we are going to do our utmost, to do our best, so that we have a healthy, good relationship. My wife and I decided that it is important to have parents and grandparents in our lives, and they from their perspective decided the same in the other direction. I would lie to you if I said that it was an easy process. It was an incredibly difficult process, because each of us challenge[s] the other person's fundamental assumptions and norms and behaviors from the small things to the big things.

Shragy went on to describe some of the practical steps he and his family took to ensure that they maintained a relationship:

> We keep the kosher level of our home way above our natural standard, so it's appropriate for my family to come and eat in it and feel comfortable. And they do the same as well. . . . They are accommodating to us. . . . It was a big issue whether my wife would have to cover her hair. We are still debating this, but we are able to come without her covering her hair. . . . I wouldn't say that I had the same process with my entire family. Some of my siblings took longer;

some, shorter. . . . It has been incredible, and it took a lot of effort and hard work.

In addition to the evidence about individual families, Shia, a Satmar exiter in his mid-forties, reported that at least one prominent Hasidic rebbe in Williamsburg in the mid-1980s encouraged parents to remain connected to their children who were exiting the community:

> About thirty-five years ago there was a whole class of *bocherim* [yeshiva students] in Williamsburg who went *frai* [exited], and it was a major scandal in the community. Parents didn't know what to do. Reb Hershel Horowitz, the Spinka Rebbe of Williamsburg, counseled these parents not to cut them off and instead should try to remain connected to them.

Although this is a rather small sample, it demonstrates that at least some Satmar families and some Hasidic authorities, even thirty or forty years ago, maintained and encouraged parents to maintain contact with their children who exited.

Two scholars encountered different data regarding ultra-Orthodox exiters' reception by their families. Marta Topel claims that exiters in Israel are all ostracized by their families, and "only in some cases (after periods that may last years) do the [exiters] succeed in reestablishing ties to parents and siblings" (2012, 95). It is indeed possible that in Israel the wall between the ultra-Orthodox and the secular society is much "thicker" than it is in America, where even the ultra-Orthodox must go to work and interact (at least occasionally) with non-Jews and nonreligious Jews.

Hella Winston (2006), who conducted her research in the United States, also found that several of her respondents were completely cut off from their family post-exit (although she notes that this was not the case for her Lubavitch respondents). It is possible that she spoke mainly to people who were in the initial stages of exiting and were ostracized, but in the later stages, the families would become more welcoming after learning to deal with the reality of the exiters' new lifestyle.

Conclusion

This chapter begins by describing the boundaries that ultra-Orthodox communities erect between themselves and non-Jews, as well as between themselves and nonreligious Jews and even other Orthodox and ultra-Orthodox communities, to maintain the integrity of their community. The key element of the messages regarding non-Jews is to denigrate them and call them *shkotzim* and shiksas, derogatory terms that are often associated with exiters as well. (These denigrating messages about non-Jews are shared with other members of the community and not with non-Jews, who are intentionally left unaware of them.)

Lacking formal procedures of excommunication or shunning, both communities use the informal system of rumors and denigration to isolate, punish, and delegitimize the actions of exiters. These rumors are based on the following three points: Exiting is unnatural; all exiters had horrible life experiences and come from dysfunctional families; and all exiters are mentally ill.

How did Lubavitch and Satmar families respond to exiters? Contrary to previous research, in neither case were exiters completely cut off from their families, although in Satmar it was more likely that some family members, and especially former friends and neighbors, might be unfriendly and even hostile to exiters. The Satmar community was willing to use severe punitive measures against exiters, including expelling children of parents who modernized and threatening to help the parent who remains in the community win full custody of the children after a divorce, thereby completely disconnecting the exiting parent from his or her children.

Despite the boundaries that separate Lubavitch and Satmar from everything outside their respective communities, and despite the vigorous methods of maintaining those boundaries, exiters traverse them. But traversing the boundaries does not erase them. The permeability of the boundaries and the subjectivity of some of the boundaries (for example, boundaries based on the claim that the ultra-Orthodox lifestyle is the only reasonable and natural lifestyle) allow their shape to change and their roles to shift in the lives of exiters. One of the results of this dynamic is an exiter's liminality.

Liminality is not the result of permeable and subjective boundaries alone. In communities in which the boundaries are more rigid, liminality may still result from the socialization process; people cannot shed all remnants of their upbringing as easily as some might assume. But the form of liminality in a given case will always be informed by the nature of the boundaries traversed.

Exit Narratives

> We knew their names because even though Troy didn't like
> Greenville [Michigan], he liked his friends, and other than
> shoot rifles the thing grunts spend most of their time doing
> is telling stories about the civilian world they left behind,
> even though they should be forgetting it.
>
> —Anthony Swofford, *Jarhead*

T he explanations that the Lubavitch and Satmar communities tell themselves, exiters, and the courts about exiters from their community, as Chapter 2 describes, are a form of what I call "exit narratives." Exit narratives are composed, consciously and unconsciously, by various parties related to the exiting. They make sense of the rupture, each party from its own perspective. The exit narratives of the communities from which people exit are designed to delegitimize the exiters and their decisions and simultaneously to maintain the authority, legitimacy, and boundaries of their own communities.

Those exit narratives are part and parcel of those communities' communal boundary construction and maintenance that in part define the exit itself. In turn, the exit narratives of the exiters themselves are part and parcel of the new identity construction toward which exiters labor. The narratives of the exiters implicitly refute the claims of the communities and argue for the legitimacy of exiting.[1] These narratives emerged throughout the interviews; they were not given in response to particular questions.

Two clearly defined groups of exit narratives emerged from the interviews, which I call the "intellectual" and the "social-emotional." Approximately one-third of the exiters described intellectual narratives, one-third

---

1. As Lynn Davidman and Arthur L. Greil (2007) argue, those leaving the Hasidic community face the daunting existential task of creating a new identity, a new "script" or "narrative" for themselves that explains who they are and justifies their act of leaving, especially since there is little structure in the outside world to ground their identity. In stark contrast, those joining these communities (*baal teshuvahs*) are provided a script and an entire identity, including a set of gender roles, behavioral norms, and religious beliefs.

described social-emotional narratives, and one-third did not discuss this issue in their interviews. Only five interviewees presented mixed narratives consisting of elements of the intellectual and the social-emotional narratives, and two reported switching from a purely intellectual narrative to one that included emotional elements, but these mixed or evolving narratives were clear exceptions that only proved the rule of the monolithic nature of most of the narratives. However, all interviewees possess a combination of intellectual and emotional elements. The designation "intellectual" or "social-emotional" refers merely to the majority or emphasis of exiters' narratives, but these are not strict categories.

Although both men and women employed social-emotional narratives, and several women used mixed intellectual and social-emotional narratives, only men employed exclusively intellectual narratives,[2] perhaps because boys and men are exposed to the lion's share of both communities' intellectualism in the first place. The corollary to the emphasis on intellectual exit narratives among the men is that only women talked about feeling resentful about clothing restrictions (informing their social-emotional exit narrative).

While men are also subject to strict requirements to wear distinctive clothing—including bulky woolen garments shaped like a poncho with ritual fringes attached to the corners and distinctive hats that mark them as members of a Hasidic community, preventing them from even temporarily blending into the broader society—the ideology of modesty and sexual purity plays a far more central role in the education and lives of girls and women than it does in those of boys and men.

The intellectual group consists of those who attributed their exit to intellectual disagreements with their community, based either on internal contradictions they perceived within its beliefs and practices or on external critiques of those beliefs and practices. The social-emotional group consists of those who attributed their exit to emotional suffering in the community, usually as the result of a feeling of alienation or persecution while they were members of the community. Moreover, each group was aware of the narratives of the other group within the exiter community, and each group vigorously rejected the other group's narratives, just as they rejected their community's narratives about themselves. This chapter explores the interviewees' exit narratives and their rejection of alternative exit narratives.

An important aspect of understanding these explanations as exit narratives rather than straightforward explanations for why someone exited is that

2. Hella Winston found a similar gender effect among her respondents: "I met fewer women than men whose critiques dealt explicitly with issues of the interpretation of the religion" (2006, 134). Interestingly, Lynn Davidman (2014) reports that some of her female respondents described intellectual narratives. Nonetheless, Davidman also emphasizes that her male respondents use the cultural skills they acquired in the community to study and analyze things intellectually as a means of exiting.

no explanation—neither the religious communities' explanations nor those of the exiters themselves—represents scientific or "real" reasons that individuals exit their communities. To the extent that accurate, historical reasons (as it were) can ever be determined for this kind of human behavior, they do not lie in exit narratives. These narratives were not composed as dispassionate, biographical accounts. They function, rather, in various ways in the lives and communities of those who compose them, as Chapter 2 describes.

Each type of narrative has its own functional advantage from the perspective of the exiter. The intellectual narrative is clear-cut and impersonal: One identifies a problem with the community's beliefs or practices and responds rationally. There is nothing "wrong" with the exiter. There is a certain self-congratulation in these narratives. They portray exiters as smarter than their parents, teachers, and classmates or, at any rate, more courageous.

In a sense the intellectual exit narrative comports with the values of the community; it focuses on the central texts and ideas of the community, objective answers, and logical decision-making rather than instinct or emotions. The Lubavitch community in particular emphasizes the idea that *moyach shalit al halev*—the mind should dominate the heart and its passions. The intellectual exit narrative not only embraces this principle but uses it against the social-emotional exit narrative. This is a form of liminality: These exiters retain the intellectualism of the community (such as it is), even as they use it to separate themselves from the community.

In contrast, the social-emotional narrative is highly personal, and it leaves the exiter exposed and vulnerable. It flouts the values of the community, which prioritize religion over personal needs. The social-emotional exit narrative ignores the community's charge that those who exit do so to follow their own *taivas* (temptations and physical desires). Instead, it places a premium on an individual's personal experiences and interests. This is not to say that it is more accurate or yields a more complete exit. But it may explain why this sort of narrative appeals to those eager to distance themselves from the community's intellectualism and appears implausible to those who retain the intellectual priorities of their upbringing.

Why "Why" Is a Bad Question

Exit narratives do not actually answer the question of *why* exiters exit their communities of origin. But why not address that question? To begin with, as scholars have noted (e.g., Streib et al. 2009), exiting religion is a gradual process related to transformations of deeply held beliefs and deeply ingrained practices rather than an acute moment of crisis. It is therefore extremely difficult to pinpoint exactly when or why it occurred.

In addition, the reasons that interviewees provide may suffer from hindsight bias (Tversky and Kahneman 1973), representing what exiters think about the facts after reflection rather than what was most important to them at the time of exit. Furthermore, individuals' exit narratives tend to be more coherent than real life because people try to compose narratives that are congruent and show logical connections between events, even if at the time no such logical pattern exists (see Lofland 1969). And as Diane Vaughan (1990) points out about divorce, people often do not know the actual reason that they leave a religion. It is the culmination of a long process of disengagement from their community and upbringing, the origin of which is murky at best, even to them.

Another point to consider is that the reasons some scholars posit for why people exit religion often merely describe aspects of their community that exiters disliked. Although it is perfectly believable that they disliked those aspects of their upbringing, it is by no means clear that those were the actual motivators that caused them to exit. These scholars are not really addressing the web of motivation and action, cognition and emotion, that lies beneath the decision to exit.

Notwithstanding these formidable challenges, I believe it is possible to answer why people exit religion, but it is necessary to combine a sociological understanding of the structural elements involved with a psychological understanding of personality traits that contribute to this phenomenon. It is also necessary to study both those who exit and those who stay. Without such an interdisciplinary and comparative approach, it is not possible to answer the question adequately.[3]

Heinz Streib and colleagues (2009) tried to answer the question by sampling both people who exit and people who stay within religious communities. They assessed their interviewees with a battery of psychological personality tests and determined that there are psychological personality traits that are stable throughout life (regardless of social circumstance) and pointed to these to explain the interviewees' behavior. Based on these data about personality traits, they claimed that ranking high on "openness to experience" is a major predictor of religious exit (92).

The trouble is that "openness to experience" is a tautological description of exiters from strict religious communities. The researchers provide no evidence for the inborn nature of that quality since they interview individuals only once they have made the decision either to exit or stay. It is entirely possible that this openness to experience is the result of exiting the community and being forced to learn to embrace new life situations rather than an innate proclivity that the exiters had their entire life. Since these scholars did not include a sociological analysis of the structural elements involved, their psychological findings were unable to fully address the question at hand.

---

3. Thus, Winston was half right when she observed that understanding the root causes of exit "seems a task better suited to psychologists" than sociologists (2006, 170).

Although findings are incomplete among studies that look at the question from a purely sociological perspective (including Caplovitz and Sherrow 1977; Hoge, McGuire, and Stratman 1981; Hostetler 1993; Holden 2002; and Zuckerman 2012), they have developed various instructive reasons for why people exit religion.[4] The main reason that my study does not seek to answer the question of why people exit is that this has already been explored in the sociological literature extensively, if incompletely. And many of the reasons explored in the literature show up in interviewees' narratives. These include feeling disappointed with religious leaders, having intellectual disagreement with religious principles and teachings, feeling alienated from the community and its culture, having suffered abuse in the community, having been raised in unstable homes, having a desire to explore the world and other cultures, and having a desire to escape the strict rules governing sexuality. (For a discussion of several key factors that enabled exiting, see Appendix A.)

Although the narratives of exiters are an incomplete means to answer the question of *why* people exit, they are invaluable for understanding *how* the exit process affects the exiter, and with this goal in mind we explore those narratives. In addition, toward the end of this chapter we see how conflict and competition between different exit narratives are an aspect of the exiters' liminality.

Intellectual Narratives

Background: Anti-intellectualism in Ultra-Orthodox Life

There is a common misconception regarding the life of the mind within ultra-Orthodox Judaism. In addition to the stereotype that all Jews are intellectuals and that everyone in the shtetl was a Talmudic scholar, outsiders assume that contemporary ultra-Orthodox men who spend their days poring over religious texts freely intellectualize and philosophize about their studies. They are thought of in a sense as pious graduate students.[5]

The following comments by the former Orthodox chief rabbi of the United Kingdom, Rabbi Jonathan Sacks (2013), written for the main Lubavitch website, Chabad.org, is a good modern example of the romantic view of Jews as intellectuals, a view that makes it difficult to understand how the

---

4. According to Rosabeth Moss Kanter, people base their commitment to a social system on an analysis of the "costs and rewards" of doing so along three dimensions: intellectual, emotional, and moral (1972, 68). What Kanter leaves unaddressed is how people assess these costs and benefits.

5. If Edward Grant (1996, 2001), among others, is to be believed, the idea of pious graduate students may be more accurately applied to Catholic thinkers, especially to the Jesuits in the Middle Ages, who combined a deep commitment to religious faith and intellectual, and even scientific, curiosity and exploration.

ultra-Orthodox could, in reality, stifle intellectual curiosity among their members. Sacks triumphantly proclaims:

> Judaism became the religion whose heroes were teachers and whose passion was study and the life of the mind. The Mesopotamians built ziggurats. The Egyptians built pyramids. The Greeks built the Parthenon. The Romans built the Coliseum. Jews built schools. That is why they alone, of all the civilizations of the ancient world, are still alive and strong, still continuing their ancestors' vocation, their heritage intact and undiminished.

Moving beyond the absurdity that all the ancient Greeks and Romans were interested in was buildings, as if they did not also produce Socrates, Plato, Aristotle, Lucretius, and Cicero, the point Sacks is making is that Judaism is all about "the life of the mind" and that this occupation continues to maintain center stage today, including in Lubavitch, for whose website he wrote his essay in the first place.[6]

The issue of the life of the mind is a particularly sensitive subject when talking about Lubavitch, which prides itself on being based on a long intellectual tradition of Hasidic thought and on being premised on the idea that Jews should serve God not only with their hearts but also with their minds, using the mind to try to understand God. This idea that Lubavitch was somehow distinct because of the pride of place it gave to the mind is even noted by no less a critic of Hasidism in general than the celebrated Eastern European Jewish historian Simon Dubnow, who remarked that the first Lubavitch Rebbe, Rabbi Schneur Zalman of Liadi, "succeeded in creating a remarkable system of thought, which may well be designated as 'rational Hasidism'" (1916, 234).

However, the facts on the ground tell a different story. In the ultra-Orthodox world, including Lubavitch and Satmar, although men, and to a much lesser extent women, spend a great deal of time studying religious texts and ideas, there are definite limits to such study. On the most basic level, all intellectual pursuits are limited by the need to accept the basic beliefs, practices, and institutions of the community unquestioningly.[7]

In fact, Ayala Fader (2009) found that the Bobover Hasidim believed that too much thinking could be dangerous to religious faith, and Fader does a

---

6. Rabbi Sacks's comments are particularly disturbing because he personally knows better than to characterize Greeks and Romans in this way. In addition to his rabbinic training he holds a doctorate in philosophy from Kings College London, and among his many academic distinctions, he delivered the 2008 Gifford Lectures (Edinburgh).

7. The fact that the Lubavitch and Satmar communities are able to study texts while curbing intellectual freedom is a substantiation of Richard Hofstadter's (1963) observation that even religious societies based on textual learning can be anti-intellectual.

remarkable job detailing the various beliefs and practices at work to prevent ultra-Orthodox children and teens from asking the "wrong" questions. These include the belief that parents and teachers have authority from God, so if someone questions them, he or she is actually challenging God's authority. One of the practices for dealing with "bad questions" is to mock them by labeling them as *goyishe*, "non-Jewish." In addition, once children became teenagers, they are considered "too old to ask" and are expected to simply fit in; asking questions is considered a sign of immaturity.

Furthermore, questions that seriously challenge authority are considered *khitspe*, "impudence," which is not tolerated. Teens come to understand that "certain questions and requests cannot even be asked," and when they are asked, conversations are shut down as quickly as possible (Fader 2009, 82–83). Although Fader was not speaking directly about Satmar or Lubavitch, this certainly describes Satmar as well, and it is not far from the reality in Lubavitch, its intellectual self-perception notwithstanding.[8]

The limits on intellectual curiosity are so profound that Fader wonders "how Hasidic boys in school learn the skills of Torah study, which are based on argumentation and questioning, while simultaneously learning not to question the authority of the texts themselves" (2009, 227n5). It is beyond the scope of this book to explore this important question in depth. But the answer lies in a clearer understanding of the ways in which "the skills of Torah study" are in fact based on questioning and a distinction between the role of questions in, for example, the research methods of a scientist or philosopher and the role of questions in the study skills of ultra-Orthodox boys and men.

When scientists or philosophers begin research with a question, they are using that question as a vehicle for intellectual discovery. The question is open-ended, and to the extent that its answer might unsettle prevailing theories, the researcher is all the more excited to pursue its answer. I do not mean to romanticize the work of scientists or philosophers. There is no question that academic thought is sometimes (perhaps often) constrained in practice by professional biases, regnant assumptions, and the authority of respected scholars (see Kuhn 1962; Lakatos 1970) and that politics and economics play a role in shaping the agenda as well as the content of academia (see Chomsky 1969). But there is also no question that students in those and other academic disciplines are trained to think of their questions as open-ended, motivational tools for inspiring the discovery of new and different ideas. Even if this form of pursuing research questions is only aspirational, it makes a profound impression on the life of a student.

---

8. Faranak Margolese, who is herself a committed Orthodox Jew, notes that among the Orthodox, questions are sometimes stifled because they are considered "heretical" (2005, 240).

This is all in stark contrast to the function of a question mark in the world of an ultra-Orthodox Torah student.[9] For him, questions are rhetorical devices. They frame the established ideas of the tradition in the same way a skilled public speaker might use a question to frame a speech. There may be multiple answers to a question such as, "What does the Talmud mean in this passage?," but in the ultra-Orthodox study house, including those of Lubavitch, there is a closed set of answers that excludes any entertainment of antinomian, iconoclastic, or otherwise heretical ideas.[10]

To take this one step further, if a teacher begins a discourse by asking whether or not the rebbe was correct when he claimed this or that, the answer will never be no, and it will never be maybe. Such a teacher is using the question only as a rhetorical device to frame his lesson, not as an invitation to truly question, as an open-minded scientist or philosopher would, whether or not the rebbe was correct. Ultra-Orthodox young men learn to understand and use this form of questioning, but they are never introduced to the art of the open-ended question. Some exiters have felt the pull of that "other" (wrong) kind of question.[11]

Intellectual Narratives

In a satirical essay titled "10 Prerequisites for Going OTD," Shragi (a nom de plume; 2014) proclaims:

> While frum [Orthodox] Jews often take pride in claiming to have emunah pshutah [simple faith], no self-respecting OTDer would admit to having kefirah pshutah [simple heresy]; s'possed nisht [it's unbecoming]. If you haven't read Richard Dawkins' The God Delusion or Christopher Hitchens' books, especially God is Not Great and done chazarah [review] on them, then you're not OTD, you're just an ignorant bum. . . . If you were molested by your rebbe, you're not allowed to admit it, because that makes the OTD cause look bad; a true OTDer went off the derech for pure ideological reasons.

---

9. To use Robert Merton's (1968) distinction, one can say that ultra-Orthodox yeshivas focus on erudition, while scientists and philosophers focus on originality.

10. Samuel Heilman makes a similar point about the subordinate role of Jewish learning in ultra-Orthodox society: "By itself, literacy has no value. Haredim [the ultra-Orthodox] do not learn to read so that they can explore the beauty of writing or revel in the pleasure house of literature. For these Yidn [Jews], literacy is an expression of, and a medium for, Jewish fidelity, a means of Jewish learning, a vehicle for plumbing the texts and getting at the essence of what God has revealed in the Torah, a ticket for entry in the house of study. It is a matter of faith" (2000, 215).

11. I am grateful to Jenny Labendz, author of Socratic Torah: Non-Jews in Rabbinic Intellectual Culture (who is also my wife), for helping me articulate this profound difference.

As with all good satire, there are important truths expressed in this passage. There is a strain of discourse among ultra-Orthodox exiters that frames their exiting as a result of intellectual disagreements with the community or as a desire to escape the intellectually stifling constraints of the community's regulations. Sometimes it is framed as a direct result of reading classical Jewish texts with open eyes (rather than with ultra-Orthodox goggles) and being shocked by their content.[12]

An intellectual narrative frames the reason for exiting as largely, if not entirely, the result of an attempt to move away from the intellectual constraints the community placed on the individual. A typical example is the view of Eliyahu, a Lubavitcher in his early thirties who explained why he exited the Lubavitch community:

> It wasn't that I just came to the point where I couldn't accept the tenets of Lubavitch anymore and I couldn't live with it. It was more that I just wanted to express myself more in different ways, and I felt that there were constraints, mostly I would say intellectual constraints, that were placed on me in Lubavitch and that bothered me a lot. Just the idea that I had intellectual constraints and I couldn't say what I wanted or that I wasn't supposed to think certain things, that bothered me a lot. . . . Basically I was looking for someplace where I could feel more comfortable intellectually.

When asked how precisely these constraints impacted him, Eliyahu responded:

> I felt that Lubavitch or any ultra-Orthodox community in some sense restricts not just what you believe but exploration of ideas. "You shouldn't read such a book because you shouldn't entertain the possibility that x, y, and z." I don't know whether that means that the

---

12. This phenomenon of coming to doubt through reading the central texts of a society is not unique to ultra-Orthodox Judaism. Mikhail Gorbachev describes in his memoirs a similar type of experience when he was at university in Soviet Russia and came to doubt aspects of the "truths" of Stalinism through engagement with classical Marxist texts: "The entire educational system was designed to prevent us from developing a critical mind. Nevertheless, in our third academic year the very process of acquiring knowledge brought us to a stage where we would seriously begin to reflect on all the facts we had learned and assimilated. . . . The first authors who sowed the seeds of doubt about the unquestionable 'ultimate truth' presented to us were Karl Marx, Friedrich Engels, and Vladimir Lenin. . . . In spite of all their (sometimes excessive) polemical sharpness, these works contained a detailed criticism of their opponents' theses, a system of counter-arguments and theoretically sustained conclusions: all of this was in sharp contrast to Stalin's so-called methods of 'debating,' which tended to supplant argument by sheer abuse or, at best, by spelling out unquestionable truths" (1995, 45).

Rebbe didn't make miracles, whether it means that the Baal Shem Tov [the founder of the Hasidic movement] never existed, whether it means that the Rambam [Maimonides, the twelfth-century rabbinic luminary] didn't believe in God, or whether Daniel when he wrote the book of Daniel [a biblical book full of apocalyptic visions], he was actually hallucinating. Okay, what bothered me most was that I felt at the time that I could accept the beliefs, but I want to explore it, because I'm interested in ideas and I'm interested in intellectually understanding it, and I wanted to see the arguments. Of course, you could sit in your house and read books. It's not that kind of community where you can't. But it bothered me that I had to sit in my house, and there was nobody that I could talk to about it, and I'm supposed to hide the fact that I read books.

Similarly, Baruch, a Lubavitcher in his mid-twenties, talked about why he exited and the effect that not receiving answers to his questions had on him:

It gets to a point where I have questions that were never answered, and I don't know if they can be answered—probably not. The realization that a lot of people are doing things based on faith rather than reason. . . . That was a big thing for me. . . . See, there were always questions, but then they would get answered, and I think there are a lot of questions that do have answers. I mean all through my yeshiva years I was always asking and getting answers. It was only after, when I was older, eighteen or nineteen, that less answers started coming through and more people started saying, "Have faith, learn a *maimer* [Hasidic discourse], and you'll feel good; *daven* [pray] and it will work." . . . This happened all the time.

Baruch went on to explain that although he understands that some questions may not have answers, it bothered him that the community was making absolutist claims based on questionable arguments:

There are certain questions that cannot be answered, I think, by definition. I mean, I don't want to put myself out as an intellectual, but you can't know what you can't know. You can't know what's beyond the physical, or whatever; you just can't. Everyone will admit that at some point, and people [*pauses*] they do. You ask people, and at a certain point they say, "Okay, I can't answer that." I think this is an important one. How can you know? How can you be a hundred percent certain? Which is what's demanded. That's important. I mean, then there are others, historical, and so on, but yeah. I mean, that's how it started; then once you're not a hundred percent certain, then you need to weigh everything up.

Similarly, Chesky, a Lubavitcher in his mid-twenties, stated that he thought that life would be much easier if he believed in God, so he tried to force himself into believing:

> I always knew, was conscious of, and still am kind of conscious of the idea that life would be so easy if I would just be able to do that. Just in terms of stress or in terms of everything, life is so easy if you just go along with that crowd. And also the way my brain is wired; if I could just cut the part of my brain that is intellectually above these ideas—there is always a struggle. Would I do that or not because I could do that? There were times when I would sit down and force my brain to believe that there is a God and see how it felt, and I was able to do it, and the relief of believing that was incredible. The relief of, okay everything is settled.

Chesky explained why he thought believing in God would remove a great deal of the anxiety of life, if only he could convince himself of it:

> I think and I've learned that there are two fundamental anxieties in life: (1) of what the reason for something is and (2) of what the end of something is. So religion, I think, is designed to take care of both of those, and when you don't have that religion, it is almost impossible to find those, unless [pauses]. I guess I have to find them somewhere. But yeah, there is constant pressure to, a constant struggle, always. But I think I'm at a point where it would be impossible for me to get [pauses]. I don't think I would be able to ever really believe. . . . It would be too hard for me; I'm way too convinced that I know that it's total BS.

Chesky went on to describe the distinction between his life in the community and his life now as one of intellectual freedom:

> I guess when I think about where I was and where I am, the real big difference is education, if that makes sense. So when I was in a really secluded world, anything outside that world is not okay, and not good. So I was restricted in terms of what I could learn, whereas now not only am I not restricted, but I also have the drive to learn whatever I want and everything. So the big difference is that as a child in Lubavitch I was essentially told what to learn, what to think, what to read, and what is true, whereas now I get to painstakingly try to

figure that out for myself and learn whatever I want and determine for myself whether or not it's true.

Likewise, Yechiel, a Lubavitcher in his early thirties, talked about the impact that college and the scientific method had on his religiosity and the prohibition against asking questions. This describes precisely the different sorts of questioning one encounters inside and outside the ultra-Orthodox world:

> College definitely opened my eyes to think about things that I never really—that I always thought were taboo. All of a sudden, I was not just advised or led to question everything, but it was demanded of me that I question everything . . . the scientific method and things of that nature [*pauses*] to question authority. Whereas my entire upbringing up to that point was never question authority—*kabalas oyl* [accepting the yoke of heaven], et cetera—went against that whole concept, and here not just was I being asked to question authority regularly, but I was graded on my ability to do so. That was definitely a shift. I started asking myself [questions].

Yechiel went on to describe his thoughts about people he knows who are very intelligent and who still are Orthodox:

> Till today I struggle with that. I see very intelligent people, my father included, professors, who are obviously intelligent who pursue that [Orthodox] way of life. To me it does not make sense. . . . Everyone has to make decisions that ultimately make them happy, so if it makes them happy and they understand their way, or they understand that they don't need to fully understand it and it makes them happy, that's okay. For me, certain things that I've conducted my life according to no longer make sense to me, just no longer hold that weight to actually warrant action on my behalf.

I asked Yechiel what kinds of things no longer made sense to him. He responded:

> Well, customs, *chukim* basically [biblical laws that Orthodox Jews consider to have no rational explanation]; *shatnez* [the biblical prohibition against wearing wool and linen in the same garment] is a perfect example. And the fact that you weren't allowed to question it because if you were to question it, you were going against the Torah's edict that you shouldn't be questioning it. It was basically a trap. It was like, "Oh, you got questions? Guess what, you're not allowed to

ask questions!" So that was something, and this ties into the whole scientific method and starting to think about things in terms of questioning authority. It's like, no, I want to ask a question. . . . When I rebelled in my teens, it was more a teenage rebellion; it was more, "You can't be the boss of me!" as opposed to me actually thinking about it and saying, "No, this is not how I want to live my life because it doesn't make sense" . . . because it was too controlling at the time. Whereas later on it became more of something I grew into on my own, and [my religiosity] faded very slowly.

Some interviewees stressed that direct engagement with classical Jewish sources stimulated their doubts about the claims of their community. Mendy, a Lubavitcher in his late twenties, is an example. He describes his training for rabbinic ordination (*smicha*), when he was required to study the *Shulhan Arukh*, the sixteenth-century Jewish law code of Rabbi Yosef Karo, along with the seventeenth-century rival commentaries by authors known as the "Shach" and the "Taz," printed along the sides of the text. Mendy was disturbed by the acrimonious exchanges between the two commentators over their interpretations of Karo's work. This made Mendy doubt the claims he had been taught about their divine inspiration.[13] His doubt began there and then expanded to eventually include all traditional Jewish texts, including the Bible. Mendy explained:

> When I learned *smicha*, we learned eight to ten hours a day *Yoreh De'ah* [a section of Jewish law dealing with many issues, including the laws of not mixing milk and meat]. Learning this material contains the work of Rabbi Yosef Karo, with two commentaries on the side, the Shach and the Taz. It caused me to doubt the entire Oral Torah [rabbinic tradition]. I came to see that on every line of *Shulhan Arukh* these two commentaries battle with each other, and the language that was used was at times vicious and unbecoming of a rabbi. I came to see that their differences of opinions had to do with these rabbis' psyche and that in general it was a human creation and not from Sinai. The language the rabbis used was very unusual to me. I mentioned to several people that learning this was my downfall, and I was told that I didn't learn it right. For me it challenged the notion that *torah min hashamayim* [Torah comes from Heaven], and it reinforced that it was a human creation and did not fall down from heaven.

---

13. Among Lubavitchers, and for the most part Satmars as well, it is believed that "all rabbinic authors until and including the Taz and Shach, composed their works with *ruach hakodesh*, the Divine Spirit" (M. Schneerson [1942] 1973, 17).

Mendy went on to describe how he came to realize the human intelligence of the Shach and Taz and how intellect, not divine inspiration, determined whose arguments won out and became accepted as law. Mendy then explained how this realization had a ripple effect on his belief in other sacred texts:

> The Shach was very young and the Taz was very old when they wrote their commentaries. It was clear to me that the Shach was much smarter. Generally, the Shach won the battles. In general, it appears to me that the rabbinic books that got accepted were the ones that were smarter, not the ones that came from God. I came to doubt the basic Lubavitch belief that the Shach and Taz were written with *ruach hakodesh* [divine inspiration]. The Taz was creative, but the Shach had a much greater command of rabbinic literature, and the Taz couldn't compete. It was clear to me that the Shach's winning had nothing to do with *ruach hakodesh*—it was about human intelligence. He was a lot smarter. Once I doubted *Torah sh'bal peh* [the rabbinic tradition], I came to question *Torah shebiksav* [the Bible]. It started with *halacha* [Jewish law]; then it went to the Mishnah and the Talmud [ancient rabbinic texts], and then it went to the Torah itself. It's ironic that the texts that were meant to make us rabbis caused me to doubt.

A different kind of intellectual narrative was articulated by Yehoshua, a Lubavitcher in his early thirties who argued that he personally had nothing against the belief in God or the Rebbe and exited Lubavitch because of the community's unsustainable financial reliance on a dwindling number of *baal teshuvas* who joined the community as adults after they acquired secular education:

> Lubavitch survived as a pyramid-based scheme where we've been lucky enough to get in enough *baal teshuvas* who have secular education and secular financing to pay for the community to fund yeshivas and other programs. There comes a point where your intake is lower than your outtake, and the pyramid scheme collapses. Lubavitch is not replacing the funding quickly enough. And this shit [a Lubavitch life] does not matter, and it will not give me a better quality of life, and the things that will matter is how much money I can make so I can support my family and my children and their children. This is not a safe place for anybody. . . . All I care about is people able to make a living and support themselves. Let people choose where they find meaning and how they practice, but don't cripple them before they have that opportunity.

Yehoshua made it clear that his objection to staying in the Lubavitch community did not relate to its theology or rituals. It was pragmatic, based on his fears regarding the financial viability of the Lubavitch community moving forward:

> I have no issue with *Hasidus* [Hasidism] or *Gemara* [Talmud] or *halacha* [Jewish law] or Judaism; it is one of many effective ways for people to form communities, to mobilize, to do fantastic things for people. It's a beautiful thing. My issue is when the ideology doesn't make your life better. Everything is good until it makes you worse. . . . It is making people's lives shit. It is ruining lives and families and crippling generations, and that's where for me it stops. Lubavitch now needs a middle class to fund schools, to pay membership dues, to pay for community programs, to pay for the community infrastructure. No longer can they rely on external people funding that community. They need their own people to fund it. There [are] not enough George Rohrs or Lev Levievs [two famous philanthropists who contributed significantly to Lubavitch global activities]. Lubavitch is too big; it's impossible. And instead of breeding a middle class, they are breeding poverty. They're crippling people. It is institutionalized poverty. People come to Lubavitch, and they don't come out better. They come out poor for a lifetime. . . . You do this in a sustainable way, in a financially sustainable way, I'm in.

The specifics of Yehoshua's narrative are highly unusual—it was the only one of its kind I heard—but it is nonetheless an example of an intellectual reason for leaving rather than an emotional one. Sydelle Brooks Levy (1973) analyzes the role the Rebbe played in providing jobs to community members, and she argues that this economic function is pivotal in bolstering the spiritual claims of the Rebbe's charisma. It is possible that as Yehoshua saw the economic foundation of the community in jeopardy, it also weakened his belief in the spiritual aspect of the Rebbe's charisma.

Social-Emotional Narratives

A social-emotional narrative frames the reason for exiting as largely, if not entirely, the result of an emotional disconnect, a feeling of alienation from the community because of how the community deals with a certain issue or set of issues. Of the interviewees who described social-emotional narratives, key issues that came up were prioritization of religion over people's needs, sexual abuse, struggles with homosexuality, and the oversexualization of women's clothing because of a focus on modesty.

A good example of a social-emotional narrative is provided by Yael, a Lubavitcher in her early thirties who described her reasons for exiting. She attributes her exit to the feeling that her school and her parents put religion before her needs:

> I don't believe that people just change their life. I don't believe people change their life because they're so smart—it's always a negative reason. Maybe I'm a very black-and-white person, but I think that people don't just change their entire life. It's not natural; if we're comfortable and happy, why change? A lot of the OTD people have this thing that we are so intellectual, we're so smart! I'm a pretty smart person, but that's not why I left. I think I had negative experiences that kind of taint Orthodoxy in a negative way for me. I don't think Orthodoxy is negative at all. I think I had negative experiences that made me feel that this was not for me. I do feel that if I was happy and comfortable, I would be there today. And a lot of times I wish I was still there. . . . Nothing crazy happened to me—I wasn't abused; I wasn't molested, thank God. But I do think sometimes that religion was taught in a way that it came before the person. And I believe that was the fault of my parents and the fault of my school, but I don't think it was the fault of religion. . . . Negative for me [were] really instances where I felt as a child that religion came before my personal well-being.

Yael continued, explaining that she came to believe that her school placed religion above her well-being:

> As a child, when you find that you almost—even if you're not consciously resisting it—you kind of [*pauses*]. Looking back, I would have to say that it is the reason—I don't hate religion or Orthodoxy, but it is the reason why I didn't feel connected to it. I just didn't feel like it was for me. . . . I don't remember a specific story, but I remember in Bais Rivka [the flagship Crown Heights Lubavitch girls' school] I felt that there were a lot of instances where there was no real concern for the individual. You know, when you're a girl in your teens, it's very important to feel cared for and feel important, and you're just one in hundreds, and you're valued when you're the top *frum* [pious] girl. . . . We had a principal who never talked about our health, either physical or mental, and they just talk about you in terms of your tights [referring to adherence to modesty rules] and how *frum* [pious] you are. And I just don't think that that is something that creates a positive feeling for a girl.

Yael went on to note that her parents also put religion before her needs:

I also think that in my own home my parents also sometimes made me feel that religion comes before me. So I think when you have that at home and you have it at school, it kind of magnifies it. Some people don't have it at home, and [when] they go to school, it washes right over them. It's okay. "My school's crazy; my school's whatever." And a lot of people would agree that it's not the best school. . . . I'll give you an example of my father. I don't want to put my father under the bus, but I remember one time it was dead of winter and one of my little sisters went outside naked. Dead of winter, snowstorm. My father kind of said, "Get inside; you're not *tznius* [modest]!" And I'm like, you're not *tznius*?! The kid's going to get sick! So I feel like that is the epitome of why I have this feeling toward religion—not religion but Orthodoxy.

Another theme that some of the social-emotional narratives discussed is sexual abuse in ultra-Orthodox communities. This problem is compounded by the way that the community responds to it, which is to deny the problem and silence victims and their advocates. As Amy Neustein observed, "It happens that some of the most heartrending accounts of sexual victimization (and of powerful institutionalized denial) come from within the Orthodox sector of Judaism, even though Orthodox Jews make up only 20 percent of U.S. Jewry" (2009, 6). Furthermore, as Joyanna Silberg and Stephanie Dallam, two experts in the field of childhood sexual abuse, have noted, sexual abuse at a young age can have profound effects on victims' religious commitments: "Jewish survivors often associate their inability to disclose or to be protected with aspects of their religious identity. This can lead to spiritual crisis in which survivors reject the religion that they see as having been the fertile ground on which the abuse was fostered" (2009, 84). David H. Rosmarin and colleagues (2018) also found a link between a history of sexual abuse and lower rates of religious involvement across Jewish denominations, including among the ultra-Orthodox.[14]

Five interviewees reported that they were personally sexually abused while inside their community by other members of their community, and their abuse is a prominent part of their exit narrative. Another reported that learning about the sex abuse in her community, including that a close friend was abused, influenced her to exit her community. The actual number of people abused among interviewees may be higher. They were never explicitly

---

14. Rosmarin and colleagues also found that the "formerly Orthodox" were more than four times as likely to report childhood sexual abuse than those in their study who remained Orthodox or who were never Orthodox. Although this finding must be taken seriously, it is possible that it reflects a greater willingness on the part of the formerly Orthodox to candidly discuss the abuse they experienced rather than an actual higher instance of abuse.

asked about sexual abuse or any other kind of abuse; these five chose to disclose this information on their own during the course of their interview.

One example of a social-emotional narrative that focuses on sexual abuse is that of Shoshana, a Lubavitcher in her early thirties. She described a gradual process of exiting the community, but one that she thinks ties directly back to her abuse:

> By the time I was eighteen and a half or nineteen, I was curious and started to try different things, like this or that food, so I started to go in that direction a little bit. But I was still pretty religious. The big switch happened [*pauses*]. I had been through certain stuff as a child that really affected me and kept resounding through the years—you know, abuse, molestation, and stuff, and it happened more than once. And I didn't really have the context for how to handle it, how to deal with it.

Shoshana went on to state that her parents did not properly respond to her sexual abuse and only through a therapist from the outside did she begin to receive support:

> When I would tell my parents, they would shut it out and not deal with it. They'd tell me to shut up. So there were no real tools. . . . So I think that's where a lot of the anger and unfairness [*pauses*] many things came together, like the chaos of the home and going through that [*pauses*]. At the time I had developed a sense of individuality and started working on my own. Once I was on my own, I was like, I want to be well, I want to be a happy person, and I know that I'm not well emotionally now. I'm in a very damaged place, and I need therapy. I actually found a therapist that was willing to take me; she took me on a sliding scale, and she was amazing. She a little bit began to open my world, that there is more than just the community you came from, and she gave me the space to focus on my emotional health.

It is worth highlighting, as Shoshana makes clear, more than the sexual abuse itself, what connected this to her decisions about her religious life was the fact that her community and her parents were unwilling to help her deal with the abuse—they did not provide her with any "tools" to make sense of her abuse and help her move forward.

Nachman, a Satmar man in his late thirties, also focused on sexual abuse, but in his case, he felt an almost immediate impact of his abuse on his religious observance:

I grew up in Borough Park [in Brooklyn] in the Hasidic community, and I was an extremely *frum* [pious] kid. I did everything, all what was asked of me to do. I believed in everything, I learned everything, and when I was twelve years old, I was molested by my teacher in *chader* [religious day school], and that night I pretty much [*pauses*] I went from the Shabbos [Sabbath] before—I would go to the *mikva* [ritual bath] and say *tehilim* [Psalms], and I believed in everything—and the next Shabbos I was turning on lights [which is strictly forbidden on the Sabbath], and nothing made sense to me anymore. . . . As far as my *yiddishkeit* [religious observance] goes, it went downhill very quickly. At the time my bar mitzvah came around, I really didn't believe in anything. I was kind of forced to go to yeshiva because, you know, I was living at home. Being that I didn't believe in anything, I was pretty much kicked out of yeshiva when I was fifteen. . . . I would go from yeshiva to yeshiva because I was kicked out of everywhere. By the time I was seventeen, I was already openly not *frum* [Orthodox] anymore.

Another type of social-emotional narrative centers on sexual orientation. Six people discussed the fact that they were either gay or bisexual and that their community's negative attitude toward their sexual orientation had a major influence on their decision to exit.

Daniel, a Lubavitcher in his early twenties, focused on realizing how poorly he was being treated in his community because of his homosexuality and learning to embrace his own sexual orientation:

I started getting closer to coming out and accepting myself, and I was more and more frustrated by the intolerance I was facing, especially from religion. . . . That's really what started sparking the questions. It was like, "What is this?" This religion that is terrorizing me and my people, practically, because of the way we are. I started to really realize what the gay rights struggle was. It started sparking the questions, and then [*pauses*] I guess it became—I guess I stopped caring and started caring more about myself than what I was supposed to do. . . . And also the fact that gay people weren't addressed in a public or official level in Lubavitch was also pretty disturbing to me, because, like, I didn't understand why, and—well, I did understand why—but to me it just showed a lack of courage, and [*pauses*] I just started going out on Shabbos, taking the train [which is strictly prohibited on the Sabbath], and doing different "very bad things." I started becoming like I was all right with it, and I started giving myself the right to live my life the way I choose, the way I want to, which is the way I'm supposed to because it is the way I want to. It's my decision.

Another example is Ruchy, a Satmar woman in her early twenties who began by describing feeling alienated from the movement of Orthodox queers, even though she greatly appreciated what they were doing:

> Last week I went on a *Shabbaton* [Sabbath retreat] for the weekend for Orthodox Jewish queers, men and women. It was a beautiful experience. It was great—they had the meal, the Shabbat [Sabbath] meal; they had the prayers; and they consider themselves Orthodox, to the point where they have a *machitza* [a traditional barrier between men and women used during prayer] between the men and the women, which to me is ridiculous. Shouldn't we be having the *machitzas* in between? The point is, I feel like how could I identify as an Orthodox Jew when Orthodoxy is so oppressive to people like me: (A) as being a woman and (B) as being a homosexual?

Ruchy explains that her "breaking point" with her community occurred when she felt her community rejected her for being gay, and she came to believe that there was no place for her in that community:

> I don't want to be a part of something that is so sexist, racist, misogynistic; I don't want to be a part of that. I don't want to be a part of any of that! . . . Although I always had religious doubts, the breaking point, the straw that broke the camel's back, was definitely my sexuality. It was like, why do I have to even try to make sense of it all? This religion is taking everything about me, me being a woman, me being a homosexual, me struggling with questions; it's taking everything that I have and telling me that "I don't approve of anything! I don't support you. I oppress you. I restrict you, and I want to put you in a little box and hide you." Why would I want to continue trying to be a part of that anymore? At least till then I was struggling, I was questioning, whatever, but I was always trying, trying to fit in. . . . I got married [within the community]. . . . I had a kid. I was trying; I was trying; I was trying. It came to a certain point, and it was like, hold on a second. Who am I doing this for again? This religion has no place for me. I'm not disowning it; it's disowning me! It is forcing me out the door, and as much as I wake up today and say, I went to an Orthodox queer retreat, and I'm glad that I can show my son that part of Judaism, it's beautiful for me, but I'm still never going to feel a part of it.

Ruchy stated that she felt she was "struggling with questions." But her exit narrative is dominated much more by a sense of alienation than an intellectual problem.

Several female interviewees, almost all Lubavitch, talked about their being disturbed by the dress-code restrictions in their community.[15] They spoke about feeling restricted by the rule against girls or women wearing pants and how they longed for their whole lives to wear pants. Dina, a Lubavitcher in her late twenties, talked about her feeling that the extensive restrictions on girls' clothing and the policing of those restrictions by teachers and parents made her feel oversexualized. Dina began by describing how her father was very controlling over what she wore:

> The attitude the community has about *tznius* [modest dress] and how they try to enforce it had a huge effect on my life and where I ended up. My parents used to be really uptight about my clothing when I was a kid. When I was a teenager, they were really, really cruel, my dad especially. . . . He was a very loving dad; he was a very, very good father. He was very much the main parent in our family, but because of his beliefs he became very cruel to me as I hit adolescence. He was very disrespectful to me about anything I would wear. I was a teenager, and I wanted to wear trendy—I wanted to wear what all the teens [*pauses*] what young people were wearing—and he would make me change all the time. I felt very objectified by how he would make me change and tell me how to dress. He kind of would disrespect me. He became very controlling, and he wouldn't let me use the phone or the internet. . . . He's become much more relaxed. At some point I told him, "Why are you so preoccupied with how we dress? It's the soul that counts; isn't that what you teach us?" But he's very fixated on clothing.

Dina went on to describe how this obsession with girls' clothing also dominated the Lubavitch schools she attended:

> In high school, too, they are very, very fixated on dress. We were young girls, and we just wanted to dress trendy. We wanted to—we cared about how we looked. We were self-conscious, we were vain, you know, and they would just objectify us, and it was very sexual almost. It was very—they would like harass us. We felt like the rabbis were undressing us with their eyes because they were always telling

---

15. This is in line with the findings of Karen E. H. Skinazi (2018) that female ex-Orthodox memoirists focus on female liberation from Jewish legal restrictions.

us that what we were wearing is inappropriate and exactly how it was inappropriate. In retrospect it seems very perverse.

Dina continued, explaining that teachers would scrutinize and lecture her and the other girls in her class, saying that trendy clothing was "slutty" and immodest, which made her feel "sexually harassed."

> There were crazy ladies who would come into our school every week. . . . It was very in style in the nineties for Orthodox girls to wear floor-sweeping skirts, long black skirts that swept the floor, so one lady came in and started screaming, "Long skirts are slutty; they're so slutty!" And the next day they came in and said, "Turtle-necks are slutty!" Whatever was trendy that day was slutty. And there was one rabbi who complained, "You guys are wearing Gap shmap all over your chests!" and I was like, why are you looking at our chests, you pervert? It was just so absurd! They sent me to a camp for troubled Lubavitch kids, and there was a woman who said, "I was looking in a magazine, and I saw that if you wear—next to a leather skirt, it said s-e-x-y. [*Screaming:*] WHY WOULD ANYONE WANT TO BE S-E-X-Y? DO YOU WANT TO GET RAPED?" And like, of course, her voice rose to a shrill. It's like so comical in retrospect, and of course it gave us teens a lot of fodder to joke about, you know; these hysterical, puritanical ladies would just get hysterical over the word "s-e-x-y," so leather must make you get raped. If you wear leather, then you will get raped; that was her logical conclusion, in a shrill hysterical voice, and that was supposed to instill the fear of God in us. So men and women alike sexually harassed us constantly on a regular basis.

The Battle over Narratives: Liminality and the Aristocracy of Discomfort

Both those exiters with intellectual exit narratives and those with social-emotional exit narratives are aware of and vehemently denounce the other type. None of the following interviewees were asked directly either about their own or anyone else's motivations for exiting; they brought these issues up completely independently in the course of the interview.

The most significant charge leveled against the intellectual exit narrative is that of self-deception. This charge is clearly articulated by Elimelech, a Satmar interviewee in his late twenties:

> No matter how much we try to rationalize or explain what made us leave the community, in the end . . . we're so biased and trying to

come up with a nice narrative that we're neglecting a certain emotional part. I see people leaving the community coming [*pauses*]. I come, and I say my story; they say their story [*pauses*], especially the ones that say it's completely an ideological thing—they just decided that they needed to be free. Basically, they take out the emotional, strong, strong emotional upheavals that they need to go through disassociating themselves from such a very close-knit type of clan, and they take it out totally from the equation and explain it as a philosophical decision on their part. This especially points me to the fact that they are deceiving themselves.

Elimelech went on to explain that there was a need for a strong catalyst to stimulate a major lifestyle change, a catalyst that he believed must be based on emotions:

I'm trying to be honest with myself, and I've come up with this theory. In order for people to leave, there has to be a certain catalyst. It could be one little thing, or it could be an accumulation of sorts that made them—so I see it's almost as if a planet is orbiting one nucleus, and in order for it to disassociate itself from that, there needs to be a very strong force, and that power can be a traumatic thing that happened. . . . Lots of people went through sexual abuse that happened to them, or any other kind of [*pauses*]. Sometimes people's parents were divorced. . . . Also another thing, either the people had very low IQs, so they were always outcasts a little bit, they struggled, they had problems in school, [and] they were labeled as "misfits" or "troublemakers." Or the opposite—they have very high IQs, people who never could just conform to this whole thing. These things are the prerequisites, the slight catalysts, but then everyone has their own circumstance and how it went about. Sometimes there is like one thing, the straw that broke the camel's back . . . but there must be an emotional push, or at least partially emotional, to get them to leave the community.

In turn, the most significant charge against the social-emotional exit narrative is that these exiters are not "real" exiters at all. Perhaps their fathers punished them too harshly, or they were sexually abused, or their teachers were cruel; but they do not really have a problem with the teachings or practices of their community. As soon as they "get over" their hostility toward the community, or as soon as they realize just how difficult it is to make it in the outside world, they will come running back, eager to be accepted once more. A related criticism of exiters with social-emotional narratives is that since they have not intellectually grappled with their reason for exiting, they have not developed their own sense of who they are and are instead living only "in opposition to" their upbringing.

This latter charge is clearly expressed by Yechiel, a Lubavitcher in his early thirties who began by describing two types of exiters, which he called the "rebels" and the "academics":

> I don't respect a lot of them who went "off the *derech*" [off the proper path] because [*pauses*] okay, so there's two segments—there is the rebel part, which I went through initially, which is just, "Fuck this; I don't want to do anymore of this," and then there is the academic part, in other words, "Oh, I'm educated, I thought about this a lot, and I decided it's not for me." So those people I could respect more, whereas just the kids who do it—the "rebels" is really what I call them—they are lacking the introspection. [*Pauses.*] So I admire the courage they had to go away from their community, but I don't respect the fact that they are not thinking about it logically.

Yechiel went on to describe what his reservations were about the rebels and why he did not respect them as much as he did the academic type of exiter:

> In other words, they kind of leave it at that, and I feel bad for them because in a sense they will always be trapped by that sense of feeling "off the *derech*" because they've never come to their own understanding of what their *derech* is. They've never figured out what [*pauses*] how they want to live their life, other than that they don't want to live that way. I feel like they're beholden to others' perceptions, because they haven't done the research and the introspection to realize who they want to be. I feel like they will always feel like outlaws as opposed to feeling like new—I don't want to use the term "born again," but come to a new sense of self. . . . Maybe the term "disrespect" is strong, and I take it back, but I don't see them as peers, and I don't like being lumped in together with them. I don't see myself as one of them. It's not that I don't respect them, but I don't respect them as much as people who have gone through that process of introspection.

When I asked Yechiel how he knew that the rebel exiters did not do the introspection he felt was necessary, he responded:

> I guess that's just the way I feel about them. You talk to them; they just seem very ignorant. They seem just like rebel kids as opposed to

developed adults. Maybe it's a lack of education, as well. Maybe it's just the stage they're at; it's just an overall vibe I get from them.

Why do exiters, many of whom in fact seek out comradery with other exiters from ultra-Orthodox communities through formal and informal groups online and in person, denigrate each other's exit narratives? One answer is liminality: The practice of denouncing others' perspectives is a carryover from the ultra-Orthodox practice of denouncing other religious communities (see Chapter 2). To the extent that each group of exiters imagines themselves as *authentic* exiters who had *legitimate* reasons for exiting, they incorporate into their new identity—either "intellectual exit narratives" or "social-emotional exit narratives" (of course, they would not use those terms themselves)—concepts of superiority and practices of boundary maintenance that are familiar to them from their upbringing. To use Michèle Lamont's (1992) framework, exiters are relatively similar in terms of their socioeconomic and cultural status (few have extensive knowledge of high culture), so they seek to distinguish themselves based on their moral status, and one way they do so is through their choice of exit narratives.

An alternative explanation views these denunciations as part of a competition over who suffered the most in the process of exiting their community; the individual or group that suffered the most is the winner and deserves the most glory. Kurt Schneider described the focus of this sort of competition as an "aristocracy of discomfort" (1958, 80). The competition plays out in numerous ways besides the denigration of others' exit narratives. For example, several interviewees were interested in describing why exiting was harder for them than for some others.

Two Satmar exiters claimed that it is easier for Lubavitchers, especially the children of *baal teshuvas*, than it is for Satmars to exit because from their perspective Lubavitch is relatively more lax than Satmar, and they assume that *baal teshuva* parents, who themselves were raised in mainstream society, would be understanding if their children wanted to exit the community.[16]

One female interviewee argued that it is easier for men than it is for women to exit, since in general these communities give the men more leeway

---

16. Although my study includes twenty-three Lubavitchers who had at least one parent who joined the ultra-Orthodox community as an adult, it also includes sixteen Lubavitchers whose parents were members of their community from birth. Thus, I do not think it is accurate to say, as some insiders do, that the exiters are exclusively or even primarily the children of those who joined the community from the outside. Nonetheless, the social-emotional exit narratives of children of *baal teshuvas* have unique features. For example, some exiters express anguish over the fact that their community of origin prevented them from receiving the educational opportunities enjoyed by their parents.

than women. Yechiel implied that the exiters with intellectual narratives think that they have undergone the more taxing exit process because they laboriously and painfully examined the beliefs and practices of their community, carefully evaluating them against the sources and ferreting out logical inconsistencies, while the exiters with social-emotional narratives, from his perspective, have done none of this difficult work. At the same time, the exiters with social-emotional narratives think that they have undergone the more grueling exit process since they had to honestly engage with the traumatic experiences they endured inside the community, while the intellectuals avoid their emotional scars and bruises by focusing on impersonal intellectual reasons for exit.

These two explanations, liminality and the aristocracy of discomfort, are not mutually exclusive. Even if we cast these two explanations as separate from each other, they may both function simultaneously or alternately throughout the lives and experiences of the exiters.

Conclusion

Each type of exit narrative focuses on a different aspect of ultra-Orthodox life: either the intellectual commitments that it demands or the social and emotional community that it provides for its members, each finding fault with that aspect that it focuses on. But even as exiters assert that they left the community because it failed to live up to its promise of true intellectualism or its promise of a supportive social and emotional community, they affirm the value of that promise. Exiters with intellectual narratives seek *better* intellectual commitments; exiters with social-emotional narratives seek *better* social and emotional communities. But they learned to seek these commitments and communities from the worlds they left.

Of course, all the exiters grew up in a community that both demanded certain intellectual commitments and provided its members with a social and emotional community. And exit narratives are not the only means by which exiters bring aspects of their ultra-Orthodox identities with them into their new lives outside the community. So an exiter with an intellectual narrative might affirm the value of social and emotional community, learned in Satmar or Lubavitch, in another aspect of his life, and likewise an exiter with a social-emotional narrative might do so with respect to intellectual commitments. Exit narratives are only part of an exiter's identity and experience as an exiter; they do not define it. This brings us full circle; the beginning of this chapter emphasizes that exit narratives are not to be taken as history. We now see how exactly they might function in the life of the exiter. But since they are not historical, straightforward causal explanations, they cannot be expected to dictate the range of pursuits and interests we find among our interviewees as they pursue their new identities.

The adoption of a personal exit narrative and a perspective on others' exit narratives is a central part of the process of exiting. The dynamic role that exit narratives play in the exit process has not yet received sufficient attention in sociological literature. The contribution of this chapter, beyond its part in the larger thesis about the liminality of religious exiters, is to correct this. Exiting is a matter of not only relinquishing or changing one's practices or beliefs but also constructing a narrative about one's relationship to those practices and beliefs. Exiting thus is not a single act or moment but rather an extended process that is responsive both to the community one has exited and to other exiters who are similarly engaged in reshaping their lives.

Habits of Action and Habits of Thought

The past is never dead. It's not even past.

—**William Faulkner,** *Requiem for a Nun*

Do I contradict myself?
Very well then I contradict myself.
(I am large—I contain multitudes.)

—**Walt Whitman,** *Song of Myself*

A Man with one theory is lost. He needs several of them, four, lots!

—**Bertolt Brecht,** *Diaries*

Men make their own history, but they do not make it as they please; they do not make it under self-selected circumstances, but under circumstances existing already, given and transmitted from the past. The tradition of all dead generations weighs like a nightmare on the brains of the living. And just as they seem to be occupied with revolutionizing themselves and things, creating something that did not exist before, precisely in such epochs of revolutionary crisis they anxiously conjure up the spirits of the past to their service, borrowing from them names, battle slogans, and costumes in order to present this new scene in world history in time-honored disguise and borrowed language.

—**Karl Marx,** *The Eighteenth Brumaire of Louis Bonaparte*

Contrary to prior scholarship, which describes exiting religion and emerging from biographical disruption as a binary transition from one state to another, my research shows that the exit process is prolonged and complex and does not yield binary oppositions between a former self and a new post-exit self. The overarching term I have adopted, "liminality," refers in part to the "role residual," to use Helen Rose Fuchs Ebaugh's (1988a, 173–174) terminology, that remains from interviewees' ultra-Orthodox upbringing once they exit their communities.

Building on the work of Lynn Davidman (2014), who introduced into the study of religious exiting the importance of the body as a locus of transition, this chapter begins with the ways in which the bodies of ultra-Orthodox exiters resist simple classification as either "still" or "no longer" ultra-Orthodox. Through years of socialization, interviewees' bodies have developed certain habits of action that have been internalized and remain part of who they are even after exiting the community. Davidman argues that bodily inscribed habits are the most difficult to relinquish, recurring unexpectedly in the lives of exiters even years later.[1] My interviewees indeed retained many such habits, but this was by no means the only or even most salient aspect of their liminality. Numerous interviewees also exhibited a significant persistence of habits of thought, modes of thinking, that likewise demonstrate continuity with their religious upbringing.

Liminality as envisioned here builds on the idea of habitus in the work of Marcel Mauss ([1934] 1973) that focused on the body and the idea of habitus in the work of Pierre Bourdieu (1977, 1990), which included the body as well as attitudes and beliefs. Mauss associated habitus with "techniques of the body" and described them as a "physio-psycho-sociological assemblages of series of actions" ([1934] 1973, 85). For Bourdieu, habitus is about both the body and the attitudes and beliefs that are internalized through socialization. As Claire Mitchell explains, for Bourdieu, "the habitus is a culturally specific way of thinking and doing. The habitus is assimilated into the unconscious, in embodied and entrenched perceptions and reactions, so that it becomes part of shared group understanding and a basis for social action. As we cognitively order social life into categories, we 'know' which categories we belong to and act accordingly" (2005, 5).

I use the term "habits" to refer to an interviewee's behaviors or attitudes that are at least partially unconscious or not completely conscious. If an interviewee were completely conscious and in control of them, the behavior or attitude would not be a habit but simply something that the individual is deciding to do or think. However, the person may be aware of it to a certain extent but unable to refrain from thinking or doing it. In this context, it is useful to think of Anthony Giddens's distinction between practical and discursive consciousness: "Discursive consciousness connotes those forms of recall which the actor is able to express verbally. Practical consciousness involves recall to which the agent has access in the durée of action without being able to express what he or she thereby 'knows'" (1984, 50). Given that so many of the exiters' behaviors and attitudes developed during their upbringing have been internalized without being discussed openly and thoroughly, it is necessary to raise them to the level of discursive consciousness for individuals to successfully disengage from them—to "put things into

---

1. Davidman's focus on the body is trying to correct the near-exclusive focus on the exit process as it relates to belief and intellectual argumentation found among many scholars, such as Louis Frankenthaler (2004).

words" (46)—and then consciously evaluate and choose whether to keep these behaviors or attitudes.

The remainder of this chapter demonstrates that exiters continue to maintain some of the views and attitudes of their original community. A significant mechanism by which they do so, largely unknowingly, is to give these ideas new justifications that do not rely on religious doctrines. The continuation of habits of action and habits of thought illustrates the complexity of religious exiting; they challenge the binary view that one is either "in" or "out" of the community and instead require us to understand exiting as an ongoing process, a continuous negotiation of past, present, and future that plays out in the desires, instincts, and behavior of exiters' bodies as well as the attitudes, ideas, and opinions in their minds.

Habits of Action

The most obvious way in which interviewees' behavior connects them to their upbringing is through consciously continuing to observe religious rituals. As scholars have noted (e.g., Streib et al. 2009; Zuckerman 2012), it is fairly common for those who exit strict religious communities to continue some form of religious practice. Eight of my interviewees could be characterized as Modern Orthodox,[2] in that they continue to uphold Jewish law as a guiding principle in their lives, though they are open to the outside world and modernity. Five actively embrace some form of liberal Judaism, including participating in liberal Jewish synagogue services and accepting its philosophy of pluralism and religious innovation. Only twelve (16 percent of the total) are committed atheists. The vast majority maintain some kind of relationship to religious rituals and observances, such as occasionally lighting a menorah on Hanukkah.

Unlike many who left new religious movements (NRMs) in the 1960s and 1970s and took on "careers" as spiritual seekers as they joined one group after another (Wright 1987), my interviewees tend not to want to join more religious communities. Instead, they mix and match aspects of their own religious upbringing, adopting some things while rejecting others, in a sort of cultural improvisation. Their religious observance often mirrors idiosyncratic religious amalgams that Robert Bellah and colleagues (1985) famously called "sheilaism," named after one of their respondents, Sheila, who produced her own idiosyncratic religious system.

---

2. Modern Orthodoxy is a formal denomination of Judaism with its own institutions. Characterizing these eight interviewees as Modern Orthodox, however, does not mean that they are formal members of any of those institutions or that they would necessarily classify themselves as Modern Orthodox. Still, their level of religious observance and outlook are generally consistent with that denomination.

A typical expression of this kind of amalgamation comes from Elisheva, a Lubavitcher in her late twenties: "I still love the rituals and the tradition and holidays and community aspect and try to instill it in my life today but without the religious aspect. By religious aspect I mean God or the sense that 'I need to do this!'—the sense of obligation." Another typical expression of positivity toward religious ritual but without a sense of obligation comes from Chesky, a Lubavitcher in his mid-twenties:

> For some weird reason, when it comes to Hanukkah and the menorah, there was one year I was like, "Okay, let's just do this," but this year I didn't light it once. I mean, I wouldn't *not* light it. I've come to the point that I could enjoy those things. But I don't of my own volition do anything religious.

Other interviewees take great pleasure in observing some religious rituals and learning Torah but have similarly let go of the sense of obligation that had previously defined their relationship to ritual. Hershy, a Satmar man in his mid-twenties, stated that he sits down to learn Torah "ven es chapt mir a geshmak" (when I feel inspired to).

Regardless of their particular location on the spectrum of religious observance, the interviewees each had a strong and clear grasp of their relationship to religious ritual and found it easy to describe the ways in which they have retained aspects of their ultra-Orthodox identity in regard to ritual. Other behaviors related to their ultra-Orthodox identities, however— habits of action—were not as clear-cut.

Some habits of action were far less clear or even completely unknown to the interviewees; their self-awareness regarding those behaviors was far less sharp than in the realm of ritual. Other habits were consciously engaged in, but interviewees expressed feeling unable to completely suppress them if they wanted to. Despite the exiters' narratives of discontinuity, in which they claimed that they had reshaped their lives and were now "new" people, these habits of action demonstrate that exiters have internalized their upbringing and incorporated aspects of their former lives into their new lives.

This chapter is not about the inevitable litany of physical differences from their ultra-Orthodox lifestyle to which exiters had to become accustomed. Men in particular described numerous initial challenges: They saw and felt their shaven faces for the first time in years; they had to learn that the bear hugs they shared with their male friends were not how women expected to be hugged; and they had to get used to the absence of ritual fringes hanging from the sides of their clothing. As time passed, they adjusted and their disorientation waned. But other habits of action—instincts, behaviors, aversions—remained long term and may in fact remain part of them forever.

It is these habits, the focus of this section, that demonstrate continuity with their religious upbringing.

I Still Love Chicken Soup

One of the habits of action that stayed with several interviewees despite exiting was an attachment to the Eastern European food that they were raised on. This was particularly true for classic dishes such as chicken soup, *cholent* (a stew of meat and potatoes traditionally eaten on Saturday afternoon), and potato kugel.

Etty, a Satmar woman in her mid-twenties, described this attachment while at the same time asserting that nothing else has remained from her Satmar upbringing:

> This is going to sound weird, but I love *haymishe* [homey] food. The chicken soup—there is nothing better than that. That is always going to stay with me. When I'm bored on Friday afternoon, when I'm just very hungry, I'll cook up a pot of chicken soup. Other than the food, I don't think I have anything left in me from there. I think slowly everything went away. I re-created something completely different.

The Satmar exiters reported much more attachment to traditional Eastern European foods than the Lubavitchers did. Such foods may have deeper roots and play a bigger role in the culture of the Satmar community than the Lubavitch community. Specifically, Lubavitch has many more *baal teshuvas* who joined the community from the outside and do not have as strong a connection to these foods. Lubavitch also has many more North Africans and Middle Eastern Jews of Sephardic heritage for whom these foods are completely foreign.

In regard to eating pork, no less a secular personage and son of the Third Republic than Émile Durkheim felt "great remorse" the first time he ate it (Lukes 1985, 44n2).[3] Similarly, several interviewees recounted their physical revulsion toward pork (a food Jewish law strictly forbids). This revulsion was illuminating because these individuals no longer believed that it was wrong

---

3. Steven Lukes and others who make this claim base it in part on Durkheim's comment arguing for the moral and obligatory nature of religious rules. They see the following quotation as autobiographical: "The Christian who for the first time eats a normal meal on Good Friday, and the Jew who for the first time eats pork, experience a remorse which it is impossible to distinguish from moral remorse" (Durkheim 1975, 35). For a thoughtful analysis of Durkheim's relationship to Judaism, including a discussion of a letter he sent his nephew Marcel Mauss that urged him to break off his romantic relations with a non-Jewish woman because it was causing Mauss's mother great suffering that might result in her death, see Birnbaum (2008).

to eat this food; they simply had what they themselves realized was an irrational response to it, which is significant. Norbert Elias notes that the "apparently trivial phenomena" including "people's attitudes to meat-eating . . . are highly illuminating with regard to the dynamics of human relationships and personality structures" ([1930] 2000, 100).

One Lubavitcher, Elisheva, told of having unknowingly eaten a small amount of pork and was surprised by her own forceful reaction to it:

> One day I went to eat at this diner near my work, and I ordered a bowl of split pea soup. One of my favorites. When it came, I noticed that it had some little pieces floating inside the bowl, but I didn't think anything of it. I started to drink the soup and ate a few of these little pieces. They tasted salty. Suddenly I had this terrifying thought that maybe it was pork. I have no idea why I thought this, but it just popped into my head. I asked the waiter what it was, and she told me it was pork. I freaked out. I went to the bathroom and stuck my fingers down my throat to make myself vomit to get the pork out of my body. Afterward I was surprised that I had responded so forcefully to the pork, since I was already eating nonkosher food, but something about pork made me draw the line. I was just grossed out at the thought of pork.

The insights of Yehuda, a Lubavitcher in his mid-twenties, into his own experience overcoming his trained bodily responses highlight just how ingrained they originally were:

> A lot of superstitions were hard for me to get over. I think a lot of people who come from a *frum* [Orthodox] household, when they stop being *frum*, they start eating nonkosher—you know, they'll have some pizza, maybe a little fish—but obviously [nonkosher] meat, and particularly pork, is a hard one. So I'll say it took up to a year after me not believing in anything to actually be completely free of that [revulsion]. So it can be a physical feeling. It's a psychosomatic thing that goes off in your brain. You've been told all your life, "This stuff is dirty, and they stick horse meat in there!" You know—all the BS you're taught your whole life. [*Pauses.*] So that obviously took a lot of unlearning. So there's a lot of learning. It took a couple of years, probably, to get over everything all together.

It is important to note that it takes varying amounts of time for different people to overcome their trained bodily responses. Yehuda reported that it took him only a year or two to "get over everything," whereas others reported that it took longer, and still others reported that they never "got over it," even years after exiting the community. (Although Yehuda states that he "fully got over" the physical revulsion of nonkosher food, including pork, he still exhibits other ultra-Orthodox habits of action.)

Adam, another Lubavitcher in his late thirties, spoke about feeling physically ill after eating pork twice and deciding not to bother trying to eat it anymore:

> I don't eat pork, but I do eat nonkosher meat and sushi, but pork makes me nauseous. . . . So basically the story is, I was out with this group, and the food came, and I didn't really realize what was what, and I just started eating. And I'm like, "Wow, this is really good!" And this girl just starts laughing her ass off. And I'm like, "What?" She's like, "You don't know what that is, do you?" And it was pork ribs, you know. And as soon as she said it, I felt nauseous. And whether there is actually a physiological thing that my body is not used to it, I don't know. But another time, when I did know what was happening, I was like, what the hell [so I ate it]. I felt sick. The brainwashing might do it; it might be physiological. You know what, I don't need this, one way or the other.

Some claimed that they would not eat pig, but it was not because of any religious conviction but because pigs are "gross" or "disgusting" creatures. Leah, a Lubavitcher in her late teens, felt this way and described the negative messages she received growing up about pigs and how they affected her:

> And then when I was fourteen, I just stopped keeping Shabbos. I mean, I still keep stuff—like I'm not going to go out and eat pig [*pauses*] because it doesn't sound tempting. . . . It's just—I think I was told my whole life, "Pig is pretty disgusting." I mean, not taste-wise—that, personality-wise, a pig is pretty disgusting. I don't know; I just wouldn't go out and eat at a Burger King—it's just something I wouldn't do.

Shoshana, a Lubavitcher in her early thirties, seemed to concur: "I ate pork one time, but it was yucky." Yitty, a Lubavitcher in her early twenties, associated not eating pig with the messages she received growing up in Lubavitch schools:

> I keep kosher. It's not so spiritual, really. I just get grossed out by anything that's not kosher. It just grosses me out. They did a really good job at Bais Rivka [the flagship Lubavitch girls' school in Crown Heights] at making pig totally unappetizing. It's also unhealthy, and, like, I rationalize it in a million ways.

Similarly, Elimelech, a Satmar in his late twenties, spoke about his aversion to pig, acknowledging that it was irrational:

> Not for moral reasons or religious reasons, but [*pauses*] I was afraid of eating nonkosher food at that time. And even till this day, I don't eat pork just because—I don't know—I feel like I'm disgusted by it [*pauses*], even though I know—intellectually speaking—I know that it is no different than any other meat, and I understand that, but on an emotional level I just have this aversion to it.

The fact that many interviewees who state that they are no longer Orthodox and no longer feel obligated by Jewish law still are unwilling to eat pork may result from, as Yehuda and Leah noted, the community's messages about pork being "disgusting," which produces a psychosomatic or visceral abhorrence of the food that no amount of rethinking and reflection can undo. (The association between pigs and "uncleanness" is very old in the Jewish tradition. At least as early as the twelfth century, Moses Maimonides writes that Jews are prohibited from eating pork because it is such a "dirty" animal [1963, 598].[4] Hundreds of years earlier, the Talmud [Berachot 25a] records a rabbinic opinion that "the mouth of a swine is as dirty as dung itself.")

Jews' scrupulous avoidance of consuming pig has firm roots in Jewish history and literature.[5] The most famous example of the theme that Jews would sacrifice their lives rather than consume pig is retold in children's stories of Hanukkah in the ultra-Orthodox community: The villainous Hellenists tried to force Jews to eat a piece of pig, but the Jews refused, sometimes paying with their lives.

A minority of interviewees do seem to have become accustomed to eating pork. One such individual, Perel, a Satmar woman in her early twenties, reported, "So like I'll be in a random diner about to eat some bacon, and I'll say *shehakol* [the traditional blessing over meat] out loud, only if I'm with my *Hasidish* [Hasidic] friends though. If I'm with my non-Jewish friends, never. It's like a shtick." Another pork-eating interviewee fantasized about a *bais medrish*, a study hall, where people could come Thursday night to learn and eat *cholent*, but instead of beef it would have pork. Daniel, a Lubavitcher in

---

4. Maimonides states, "The major reason why the Law abhors it is its being very dirty and its feeding on dirty things. You know to what extent the Law insists upon the need to remove filth from out of sight, even in the field and in the military camp, and all the more within cities. If swine were used for food, market places and even houses would have been dirtier than latrines, as may be seen at present in the country of the Franks" (1963, 598).

5. Ancient Romans considered this practice particularly strange. The first- to second-century Roman poet Juvenal noted, "Judaea is the one place in the world where pigs must be happiest, for they can live to a ripe old age" (quoted in Gruen 2010, 184; also see Rosenblum 2014).

his early twenties, was very proud of the fact that he had worked hard at becoming used to eating pork and then said:

> I really worked hard to learn to enjoy bacon. . . . I made sure on Yom Kippur to get—I don't eat bacon every morning, but on Yom Kippur I made sure to get a bacon, ham, and cheese sandwich. It was important. I didn't write it on Facebook, I didn't tell anyone, but it was for myself. It made me feel good.

All three individuals who reported eating pork or fantasizing about eating it mentioned pork in relation to some subverted Jewish ritual or custom—making a blessing and eating *cholent*—or as a defiant act of eating it on Yom Kippur when Jews traditionally fast. That is, a significant attraction to eating pork for them is its subversive quality. In other words, even for these individuals who were eating pork, the value system of their community still preoccupies them, even as they defy it.

Swaying While Reading in a College Library

Unconscious bodily instincts were also reported by several exiters. Multiple men observed that for years after leaving the community they would catch themselves swaying (*shukling*) when they read secular books, just as they had swayed back and forth in the traditional manner of studying Talmud in yeshiva and praying in the synagogue.

Yechiel, a Lubavitcher in his early thirties, described swaying while reading a secular book and the need to resist the urge to do so while in public:

> I'm sure that there are things that I do that I'm not even cognizant of that others are, that label me as an outsider because other people don't do it. Like, I remember *shukling* at my college library while reading a book for class—that obviously made me stand out. . . . You know, once in a while I still find myself *shukling*, but for the most part, I don't—especially in public. I definitely don't do it in public. . . . It's not so much anymore that I make sure not to do it in public but rather that the times I have the urge to do it I'm usually—I won't do it in public. The majority of the time I don't do it anyway, but when I do it, I make sure it's not in public.

It is intriguing to think what Yechiel meant by "the times I have the urge to." What is the basis of that urge? Is it that he sways when alone trying to comprehend a particularly difficult text, as a yeshiva student might do when trying to grasp the meaning of a dense passage of the Talmud? Is it that he feels the urge to sway when he is alone and becomes nostalgic for the life that he has given up, which is shot through with surges of emotional exuberance? One is left to wonder. I observed while interviewing Yechiel that he regularly stroked his trimmed beard in the same manner that men in the community stroke their long, untrimmed beards.

I Can't Stop Thinking about the Right Way to Cut My Nails

Ultra-Orthodox Jews abide by a slew of bodily customs from a young age. These include (but are by no means limited to) putting on the right shoe before the left shoe and then tying the left shoe first; removing the left shoe before the right shoe; cutting every other fingernail and toenail, starting with the left hand or foot and then going back to cut the remaining nails and discarding the nail cuttings by burning them or flushing them down the toilet (it is believed nail cuttings are dangerous, particularly to pregnant women, and therefore must be appropriately disposed of); making sure any religious books, such as a Bible or a prayer book, are resting right side up without anything placed on top of them; and kissing a religious book that has fallen on the floor.

Several interviewees reflected that they continue to "catch themselves" trying to observe—or violate—these customs, regardless of how much they try to put such thoughts out of their mind. One particularly strong example of this phenomenon is related by Chesky, who still struggles with the urge to follow the guidelines of his community in these matters:

> Every single time I put on my shoes, I'm conscious of right left, left right. I don't do it, but I can never get it out of my head. It's almost impossible for me to put on my shoes without thinking about that superstition. Or cutting my nails. I cannot cut my nails without thinking about it. These are like terrible OCDs [obsessive-compulsive disorders] that come up all the time—tons of stuff. I still have to think about all those things. Let's say I see a *sayfer* [religious book] and there is something on top of it. I'm now forced to make a conscious choice to *not* do anything about it, which sucks because why can't I just not have to think about this stuff? Now I'm like, "Why am I making this a conscious thing? Maybe I should just do it; maybe I shouldn't." I know I don't care, but why am I not doing it? I'm not doing it because it's nothing. But that still affects me.

The case of Chesky may be extreme, and he may indeed suffer from OCD; he also mentioned that when he was a child, he was obsessed with turning all the books in all the synagogues in his neighborhood right side up. His teachers would allow him time off to do this because it would upset him so much if he did not. This is something that all Orthodox Jews would agree is proper but may not necessarily devote significant time each day to do so. Still,

Chesky was not the only person to report that he still struggled with such impulses.

Baruch, a Lubavitcher in his mid-twenties who did not mention a history of OCD tendencies, also spoke about struggling with such impulses as an exiter:

> There are still things, little things that pop up, like I had to blow out a candle the other day [ultra-Orthodox Jews avoid blowing out candles because they believe the candles represent the soul]. . . . Cutting fingernails pops up all the time, especially if you bite your nails, and you have to throw them out. I think about not throwing them out. I think about it every time—I just do. It's hard to change. . . . When it comes to which order to cut my nails, sometimes I don't want to fight with myself, so I just do it the old way. Then I put [the nail cuttings] in my pocket, and sometime later when I'm in the bathroom, I flush them. It's honestly a habit that I sometimes do without thinking. A long time ago I used to burn them, but I don't do that now. That was when I was really into things.

I asked Baruch if there were other similar behaviors that he still maintained. He responded:

> No, I cannot think of anything else. I mean, there are other things, like when you get dressed, the order you get dressed. I would probably notice if I did my right shoelace first. I still tie my left shoelace first. Probably, I think so. I don't have shoelaces on these shoes, but I probably would. And if I didn't, I would be aware of it.

Baruch's experience is informative on several levels. Not only does he sometimes still continue to follow the prescribed religious behavior, but he acknowledges that resisting the impulse to act this way would require him to "fight with myself." Moreover, he explicitly notes that these behaviors are so ingrained that they have become "habits" that he follows even without thinking and that even when he does not follow them, he "would be aware of it." This all illustrates the extent to which these behaviors have become embedded in the body and psyche of interviewees; even when these individuals consciously decide to change their lifestyle, aspects of their community carry over to their new lifestyle.

So My Children Will Understand Me

Some of the exiters discussed the issue of instilling in their children an awareness of their religious background. Several spoke about their desire to raise their children with aspects of their religious upbringing so the children could better understand their exiter parents. One such exiter is Shira, a Lubavitcher in her early thirties, who observed the following:

> I continue to do some things from my Lubavitch upbringing, like I still keep my kitchen kosher even though I no longer believe it is morally necessary. I do these things so that when my son grows up, he will be able to recognize who I am and where I came from. I mean, I can't imagine raising a son that has no idea what it means to live in a home with a kosher kitchen. I was raised by parents who were *shluchim* [emissaries] from the Lubavitcher Rebbe, I spent years of my life learning the Rebbe's *sichas* and *maimorim* [public teachings and discourses], and my own child won't know what a kosher kitchen is? It doesn't matter how I feel about my Lubavitch background; the fact is, it is a part of me, and I need my son to know about it, or else there will be this huge gap between us. He doesn't have to like Lubavitch—and he certainly does not need to go to Lubavitch schools or camps—but he needs to know what it was all about.

While Shira speaks about her son "knowing" all about Lubavitch, the example she gives is a physical, bodily experience that she is committing to impart to him. She does not *tell* him about a kosher kitchen to inform him; she keeps a kosher kitchen in her home so that he will *experience* keeping kosher, just as her knowledge of keeping kosher is not merely intellectual but bodily.

In a similar vein, Hershy voiced a fear that an unbridgeable gap will develop in the relationship he has with his child because of his inability to instill in his child an appreciation and sensitivity for the religious and cultural aspects of his upbringing. Hershy reflected:

> I do wonder sometimes. It hurts me because I do acknowledge to myself the intensity I feel about Jewish texts, of *zmiros* [religious music]. I highly doubt my child will have that, and it saddens me sometimes. . . . But I'm sure they'll have their own things that are beautiful and intense for them. . . . I am afraid about the distance I'll have from my child, that things that are so important for me just won't be—how will I relate to them when there is such a big gap? For me these things are so beautiful, so intense and amazing, and for my child they will be nothing, you know. But maybe it won't. I don't know.

One can forget while reading the quotation that Hershy is an exiter at all; it sounds almost as though he is a religious parent raising a secular son. This epitomizes the extent to which it is possible for a religious sense of self to persist in an exiter.

Habits of Thought

Habits of thought are attitudes and opinions that exiters carry over from their ultra-Orthodox upbringing that one would expect them to have shed. We look at habits of thought related to God, personal religious identification, perspectives on an exiter's community and its spiritual leader, race, gender, and liberal forms of Judaism. As the introduction to this chapter notes, interviewees do not justify these views in the same ways they would have before they became exiters. Rather, they attempt to justify them with reasons that appear to them to be rational or secular rather than religious or theologically based. This strategy concurs with the insights of Peter Berger and Thomas Luckmann (1966), who describe how those undergoing a major transformation reduce the discontinuity in their lives by reinterpreting aspects of their former lives in ways that make sense in their current lives.

Ultra-Orthodox communities have both theological and nontheological justifications for these habits of thought, and the nontheological justifications are sometimes heard inside the community itself, but they are never the primary reason the community maintains its attitudes and opinions. For example, a handout opposing secular education in Oholei Torah, the main Lubavitch yeshiva in Crown Heights, was placed in all the synagogues in Crown Heights in July 2015. The handout was titled "Crazy Success!" and spent two pages on the rational reasons why secular education was unnecessary; it focused on the highly successful Lubavitch emissaries and businessmen who are functionally illiterate. Then in the last paragraph it stated: "Obviously these reasonings [sic] are only secondary to the primary point, that *Chinuch al Taharas Hakodesh* [exclusive religious instruction] is the way of Torah, as taught to us by our *Rebei'im* [spiritual leaders], and we therefore uphold it unquestionably."[6] Thus, exiters abandon the theological justifications but have a harder time abandoning the pragmatic (secular) ones that are sometimes reinforced by mainstream society.

For example, the opinions on some of the topics covered in this chapter, such as race and gender, are not unique to these exiters and their ultra-Orthodox communities of origin; racism and sexism are rampant in Ameri-

---

6. Another example of this phenomenon was recounted by a Lubavitch interviewee regarding maintaining a full beard. He was at a *farbrengen* (a devotional communal gathering) and heard someone claiming that having a full beard makes one look younger and more attractive. Clearly the primary reason Lubavitchers maintain full beards is not aesthetic. If it were merely a matter of aesthetics, it would not be considered a grave sin to choose to cut it off. Rather, this argument was used to bolster the primary theological argument.

can society, and exiters may be exposed to these views through conservative talk shows, pundits, and bloggers. But these views are also consistent with the dominant views of ultra-Orthodox communities. Certainly, the fact that exiters have not shed these views shows that they have not distanced themselves from the thinking of their community to the extent that they or others might expect. Again, this challenges the binary view of the exiting process and highlights the persistence of residual effects of ultra-Orthodox socialization, including on exiters' thinking.

Belief in God

Interviewees expressed a diversity of views on the topic of God. Approximately a quarter were staunch atheists, a quarter were agnostics, a quarter believed in God, and a quarter were not sure if God actually exists but thought it was good for them to believe, so they have "decided" to believe in God.

Among those who believed in God, eight could be characterized as Modern Orthodox, but the remainder have developed their own style of practice that is not centered on Jewish law. An example of this idiosyncratic system of observance is that of Menucha, a Lubavitcher in her late twenties, who noted:

> I still say *Asher Yatzar* [the traditional blessing after going to the bathroom]. I pray a lot; I pray every day. I don't do it from a *siddur* [prayer book]. I pray from my heart in English. I find that even though I don't keep Judaism the way it was brought down to me, I can still keep it in a way that feels comfortable. So Shabbos I go to a Friday night meal, and then I go home and do what I need to do, whatever it is. If it's watch a movie, if it's call a friend—I do understand that Saturday is a special day. It feels good to me to be able to live a life that feels comfortable and not out of fear. "You can't do this, and you can't do that!"

Menucha went on to describe how her views on prayer and God evolved with the help of people she met along the way:

> I have a couple of prayers that I've been taught over the years. I've met some people who have helped me to find this path. I didn't find it on my own. I didn't know it existed. I didn't know you could pray. I thought, if you're not using a *siddur*, what are you doing? For me, I could barely go into *shul* [synagogue] on Rosh Hashanah. It's not the God I grew up with—the judging God. I just don't think that's how he works. I don't think you need to just go one day and atone for your sins. I atone every day. Like, at the end of the day, I atone and I say:

"Thank you for another day." Every single day. So I found something that works, but it's not Orthodoxy.

We now turn to those individuals who have decided to believe in God even though they do not actually believe there really is a God. These exiters exemplify Paul Ricoeur's idea of "second naïveté," in which the individual knows rationally that the belief is a myth but chooses to embrace it symbolically for the benefits it bestows on him or her (1977, 376).[7] This also typifies a pattern that emerges throughout this chapter of exiters accepting beliefs or attitudes from their community while rejecting the community's basis for those beliefs and attitudes and substituting their own.

Within the ultra-Orthodox community, members take literally the existence of God and his (always using male pronouns) creation of the world. Some may even believe that they have seen signs of his existence through divine providence, visible signs of the hand of God taking an active role in the unfolding of human events. For the group of interviewees under discussion, their belief in God is not based on the theological claims of their community.

These individuals have rejected such claims and the concomitant obligations to follow the Torah and Jewish law punctiliously. Instead, these exiters employ utilitarian arguments for their continued belief in God. Gavriel, a Satmar exiter in his early twenties, observed: "I think it's useful to believe in God. It gives you hope, regardless of whether he actually exists." Similarly, Yael, a Lubavitcher in her early thirties, stated that "believing in God helps keep people moral."

The Community and the Rebbe

Earlier I discuss the role of the organization Footsteps in fostering community among exiters. Although many interviewees reported that they found Footsteps to be a vital asset in their exit process, providing them with crucial services and programing in a welcoming and nonjudgmental atmosphere, some felt differently. One aspect of their objection to Footsteps reveals their

---

7. Second naïveté is not limited to religious contexts and can also operate in secular ones. For example, as Ira Glass (2015) described in an episode of *This American Life*, there was a notorious Lonely Hearts Club scam run by Don Lowry in the 1980s. He pretended to have a group of women, whom he called "angels," write letters to thousands of men and also send them pictures of themselves along with poems and other mementos, and the men would send the angels money. Some of the men who were scammed continued for decades to feel connected to these "angels" and treasured the pictures and mementos they received even after the whole scam was uncovered. They felt a certain connection and received a measure of strength and inspiration from these fictitious "relationships" even after they learned the entire thing was a hoax.

sustained feelings of deep loyalty to the ultra-Orthodox community even after they exit it. In fact, most of those opposed to Footsteps think that the organization is all about a "victim mentality" and is full of "angry people" who "hate" the ultra-Orthodox community. These exiters wanted no part of this.[8]

Akiva and Etty exemplify this criticism of Footsteps. Akiva, a Satmar interviewee in his mid-twenties, thought that Footsteps was all about hating the Hasidic community that its members came from and focusing on the negative aspects of that community, such as allegations of sexual abuse. He thought it was important to focus on the positive aspects of the Hasidic community. He believes that he can make it on his own and does not need Footsteps:

> I was never involved with Footsteps. As far as I've viewed it, I always felt that they could help a lot of people, and it's very good that they have a thing [such] as Footsteps, but I do feel that it's triggered by a lot of hate. That's my opinion, and it could be that it's not true. But the way that I look at it, and the way that the people that I know look at it [pauses], I mean, a lot of hate, a lot of hate on Hasidim, on molestation,[9] whatever it is. I'm not about these things. I see good and bad in people, and I usually try to see if there is more good or more bad, and that's how I'll judge it. You can't just take a concept and completely throw it off because it has failures [pauses] like [the] Hasidish [Hasidic] community.

Akiva went on to describe what he saw as the hate that Footsteps and its members felt toward the Hasidic community:

> They seem to be full of hate for the Hasidish community. Maybe Footsteps is focusing a lot on how to take those kids and fix them into right places. But I've seen Footsteps' gatherings on YouTube; I've checked it out. I've seen the way they gave conversation, the way they'd speak; I saw it's basically how to make fun of Hasidim, and I'm not about that. So I've always figured that it's not my thing—for now. If I really need help, I could help myself—put it this way. I could find

---

8. Interestingly, Lucinda SanGiovanni found that among the ex-nuns she interviewed, all knew about "transitional agencies" designed to help former nuns and priests but only a handful ever visited one. They believed that such agencies were there for those having "unusual problems of adjustment" and were "merely an extension of convent life" (1978, 110n2).

9. This seems to be a reference to some members of Footsteps being outspoken advocates for the victims of molestation and sex abuse within the ultra-Orthodox community. Many within the ultra-Orthodox community view such advocacy with skepticism or outright hostility. Akiva seems to share this view.

out about college and programs and stuff. I don't need an organization; I don't have to belong somewhere.

Etty, a Satmar woman in her mid-twenties, also focused on the negative emotions that she felt consumed Footsteps members and on her ability to make it on her own:

> I'm not really involved in Footsteps because most of the people that attend these events are bitter, sad, angry, or hurt. I don't feel like I have many of those. I don't need those kinds of people to make me who I am. I built myself; I built my own friends; I built my own life. I don't need that kind of people. I actually dislike it a lot.

I asked Etty if she had ever gone to any Footsteps events and seen for herself what they were like. She replied, "Once I went because socially a friend told me to go just to hang out. I wouldn't put [in] an effort to go; I have other priorities that I would rather do instead. So apparently, it's not important to me."

It is unclear why Footsteps members have a reputation among some exiters as people full of hate for ultra-Orthodox communities. It may be a result of false rumors about it that are intentionally spread within ultra-Orthodox communities. Several interviewees reported that they were told while in their community that Footsteps is a "missionary organization," intent on making people give up their faith. It is also possible (and reasonable, given the exit narratives that the previous chapter explores) that some Footsteps members occasionally criticize their ultra-Orthodox community, and these remarks are taken as representing the entire organization and all its members. Akiva made a cryptic reference to molestation, presumably criticizing those who speak out against sex abusers inside ultra-Orthodox communities. This is an extreme form of aversion to criticism of the community that can be explained only as a holdover from that insistence within the community. One recalls the quotation in Chapter 3 from an interviewee who stated that her own parents silenced her report of sexual abuse.

In regard to the attitudes toward the spiritual leaders of their respective communities, Lubavitchers and Satmars were significantly different. The Lubavitchers can be divided into two categories: a minority who denounce the Rebbe and a majority who expressed respect for him. The Lubavitchers' positive views on the Rebbe show that they have maintained the positive attachment to the Rebbe that is universally accepted, and fiercely promoted, within the Lubavitch community, although the interviewees changed the basis for that respect. In the Lubavitch community the Rebbe is revered for his supernatural powers and is considered the community members' connection to God (*memutza hamechaber*). Exiters do not necessarily believe that he had supernatural powers but instead stress what they perceive as his positive secular characteristics, such as his kindness to everyone, his expansive moral vision, and his inspirational leadership.

Dovid, a Lubavitcher in his late twenties, in an expression typical of many Lubavitch exiters, praised the Rebbe's humanity and leadership skills: "I think the Rebbe was a great man because he was a kind person . . . who cared about non-Jews, who cared about the world, and who wanted the world to be a kinder, better place—that he wanted to spread kindness around. . . . He definitely had good ideas for world leadership."

Asked whether the Rebbe had supernatural powers, Dovid responded, "I don't know about the supernatural powers. I highly doubt it, but he sure knew how to inspire people." Yechiel was agnostic about the Rebbe's supernatural powers but certain that he respected him:

> I think he was a holy man. I don't think he was a crony, believe it or not. I think he genuinely tried to do what rabbis do; he tried to lead his congregation. He happen[ed] to be part of a Hasidic dynasty, he happened to know a lot about it, he was a very intelligent man, and he did his best. You know, I don't think he has any messianic powers—I don't think he is still alive or anything like that. [*Pauses.*] Would I go ahead and spit in his face or burn his picture? No. Would I talk bad about him? No. There is a certain respect for him. That being said, he is in the past. It is very hard to say what I would feel like if he were still here [*pauses*] because there is an embedded respect for him that I did grow up with.

Yechiel went on to express his uncertainty about the Rebbe's supernatural powers, while entertaining the possibility that some people might have such powers:

> I struggle with whether the Rebbe had supernatural powers; I'm still not sure; I don't have an answer. I've heard evidence to the contrary. [*Pauses.*] I don't know where I stand on that, and it's hard to say because maybe there are people, genuinely spiritual people, who are capable of those things. Maybe the Rebbe was one of them. I don't know. I simply can't give you a definitive answer.

Several Lubavitch interviewees, such as Yehuda, have a more definite and negative view of the Rebbe: "I think that the institution [surrounding the Rebbe] was a sham—he was not a miracle worker, and he was not speaking to God." Shimon, in his mid-thirties, blamed the Rebbe personally for the lack of intellectual and organizational freedom in the community:

I also see the Rebbe as being very much a part of this failure, very very much. He bred a culture of total dependence on him where there was no room for any kind of initiative. . . . Even if he said that he wanted initiative from his followers, he never allowed for that. He was always . . . maintaining this degree of cultish aloofness where he was looked at as almost godlike, [so] no one could ever develop any kind of secondary level of community leader. It was never there. Everyone was always subservient to what he thought or whatever could be deduced from whatever he said. It was never about what was good, or what was right, or what anyone thinks for themselves. . . . He deliberately portrayed himself like an almost godlike figure, and it was just him being that way and people constantly showering him with more and more titles like they couldn't do it enough. It just didn't allow for any other kind of leadership of any kind of independent community institutions to develop.

The majority of Lubavitch interviewees, however, continued to have positive, even reverential, attitudes toward the Rebbe, and he continues to occupy the thoughts and imagination of many of them. In stark contrast, many of the Satmar exiters reported not feeling particularly connected to or preoccupied with the Satmar rebbes. For example, unlike the Lubavitch exiters, who often mentioned the Lubavitcher Rebbe without any prompting by me, no Satmars ever mentioned any Satmar rebbes without my explicitly asking them. Furthermore, when discussing Satmar rebbes with Satmar interviewees, it often became clear that the individuals were speaking only about Reb Yoel Teitelbaum, who passed away in 1979—as if they did not even recognize his nephew and successor, Reb Moshe Teitelbaum, who died in 2006, much less his two children who are now fighting over the title of Satmar Rebbe.

Perel, when asked, spoke at the greatest length about the Satmar rebbes, and her dismissal of them and criticisms are typical of the rest of the Satmars I interviewed. I began by asking Perel if she believed that any of the Satmar rebbes have or had supernatural powers. She responded:

Fuck no. I do not believe that any rebbe has supernatural powers, not Moshe Rabbaini [Moses] and not Moshe Teitelbaum. When I was very little, I read stories, when I was less than ten or twelve years old, about Reb Yoel having *ruach hakoydesh* [spiritual powers], and I believed it. As I got older, I started to think that I didn't like those stories anymore; I stopped reading them. It's just like some people realize that Santa Claus isn't real; I realized what it says about rebbes isn't entirely real.

I asked Perel if she discussed the Satmar rebbes when she was growing up. She said, "No, not so much. Well, yeah, I mean, in school. My parents didn't care so much. My father saw it as politics and not as rabbinical powers. And my father doesn't discuss politics with his kids." When I asked Perel what she thought of Reb Yoel now, she replied:

When reading more about him now, I respect him; I like a lot of his teachings. I know a lot of people don't. I actually, from what I read about him now, I think he was a brilliant guy, and I think he was very kind. I never believed the whole "rebbes have magical powers." I know other people do; I don't see it like that. I don't know. I respect him because I know about his work and I know about what he did. I don't know all of it. I'm reading more about him, and I like a lot of things. I think after the Holocaust the Jewish community needed a leader like him. The problem is when his nephew took over after he died—his nephew's an asshole. Moshe Teitelbaum. Moshe is Yoel's nephew, and Yoel was a nice guy; he was a genuine person. He had interesting political views, but people liked him. He was a kind person. He preached a lot of values regarding *midos* [kindness to others]. Moshe, his nephew, he's more of, like, a *kanoi* [zealot], like a hard-ass. He's more militant, and he isolated Satmar from the rest of Hasidim and the Jewish community. Moshe was very militant. He was very strict.

I asked Perel what she thought about Reb Moshe's sons, Aaron and Zalman, who are currently fighting over the leadership of Satmar. She responded:

I'm neutral toward them because I never had anything [to do] with them. I don't like the fact that Zalman's community—this girl who was in the Weberman trial [a highly publicized Brooklyn trial in 2012 of Nechemya Weberman, a prominent unlicensed Satmar therapist who was found guilty of sexually abusing a young teenager during school-mandated spiritual guidance sessions]—Zalman is the leader of the community who bashed her coming forth with her story. I don't like that he didn't speak out against that. But Aaron at the same time gave a whole speech that she's a whore and things like that, so they're both guilty of that. That's my specific thing to make me dislike them. . . . Nobody has supernatural powers, besides me, and all the people who live in the Harry Potter books.

Satmar interviewees do not continue to have deep attachments toward any Satmar rebbes likely because even for many committed community members, the Satmar rebbes do not play as central a role as the Lubavitcher Rebbe does for his followers. Shifra, a Satmar woman in her mid-twenties, told me, "We never had the kind of personal relationship to the Satmar rebbe that you guys had to the Lubavitcher Rebbe." (Here Shifra is referring to my upbringing in the Lubavitch community.)

Personal Religious Identification

There is a similar process of reinterpretation regarding personal religious identification as Lubavitchers and Satmars. Within ultra-Orthodoxy, people identify as Lubavitch or Satmar because they study and practice the teachings of the rebbes of their community and they conform to the behavioral norms of that community. Among interviewees, the majority no longer identify as members of their community of origin. However, almost all were hesitant at first to claim that they no longer were Lubavitch or Satmar, as if it hurt to admit it openly, even in the privacy of an interview.

Nonetheless, most did eventually state that they "guessed" they no longer are members of their community of origin since they no longer abide by the community's beliefs and practices. However, a sizable minority maintained that they still thought they were Lubavitch or Satmar. While living in these communities it is inconceivable for one to be Lubavitch or Satmar without being Orthodox. These exiters, the vast majority of whom are no longer Orthodox by any stretch of the imagination, explicitly separate the two categories and claim that although they are no longer Orthodox, they are still Lubavitch or Satmar.

Several such Satmars reported that "Satmar is in my DNA," and Zev, in his late twenties, quoted approvingly a dictum of the late Satmar Rebbe Rabbi Yoel Teitelbaum that "Satmar is a *fleck* [stain] that can never be removed." Binyomin, a Lubavitcher in his early thirties, made a similar point: "There is a little Hasid inside of me, and there probably always will be."

What is interesting is that these exiters make no attempt to justify their claim to still be members of their community of origin based on their present conformity to the community's criteria for group membership. Instead, as the following quotation makes clear, the claim of group membership is based on cultural association and nostalgic feeling toward the community, things that would never be considered acceptable by community members. The case of Yechiel, who is no longer Orthodox but still identifies as Lubavitch, is typical:

> At heart I still consider myself Lubavitch. A common upbringing with other Lubavitchers, an understanding of a culture, sure. In practicality, I'm not going to live in Crown Heights, I'm not marrying a Lubavitcher, [and] my children will not go to Lubavitch schools, I don't think [*laughs heartily*]. But there is a nostalgia toward the movement. I understand them. They're where I come from. The bit-

terness has long subsided and made way for a new coexistence. . . . Even in the broader context, if you look at the word "Lubavitch"—I visited the town of Lubavitch in Russia and broke the ice [to perform a ritual immersion in the local frozen lake]—the term "Lubavitch" is the city of love. You know, it's about acceptance. It should be; it's not like that, but it should be. And so yes, I accept my upbringing, where I came from, and there are certain aspects of it that I do like, but I don't consider myself a Lubavitcher in terms of how I conduct my life—because I realize that they would not see me as such if they were fully aware of how I conduct my life.

There are no formal criteria for membership in Lubavitch or Satmar. In the case of Lubavitch, on various occasions the Rebbe mentioned certain traits that are related to being a Hasid—that is, one of his followers. For example, the Rebbe said that a Hasid is someone who is passionate about three things: defending the Israeli territories, embracing a strict definition of who is a Jew (only patrilineal descent makes one a Jew), and anticipating the coming of the Jewish Messiah. Elsewhere the Rebbe said that anyone who improves a little bit each day would be a person he would be proud to call his Hasid. The Rebbe also said that extra-strict performance of religious obligations, such as praying at length on the Sabbath, is a sign of being a Hasid (for references and numerous other such statements about the traits of a Hasid, see Seligson 2011, 338–339).

These statements are a far cry from a formal, all-encompassing definition or set of criteria for determining who is a Lubavitcher in good standing.[10] Nevertheless, there is a tacit consensus among Lubavitchers that in addition to following basic Orthodox belief and practice, a Lubavitcher must believe in the spiritual status of the Rebbe, always strive to be *mekushar* (spiritually connected) to him, and must follow his directives, study his teachings, and participate in the many religious and social practices of the community. A similar informal understanding exists in Satmar regarding group membership. However, the fact that there are no formal definitions of membership could allow some exiters to consider that they are still members even if they do not maintain any of the basic standards of the community.

---

10. The previous Lubavitcher rebbe, Rabbi Yosef Yitzchak Schneerson, did describe three levels of membership in Lubavitch based on commitment to the movement: "[True Lubavitch] Hasidim—those whose minds dominate their hearts [which is the Lubavitch ideal discussed in the movements' foundational text, the *Tanya*]; liturgical Hasidim—those who use the *Arizal* prayer book [as is customary in Lubavitch]; and ancestral Hasidim—those whose ancestors were Lubavitch." The previous Lubavitcher rebbe wrote regarding the last group: "Even though they are not living the Hasidic life, nonetheless, Hasidic blood flows in their veins" (quoted in S. D. Levine 1996, 128n221; my translation).

Attitudes toward Black People

As Chapter 2 discusses, the Lubavitch and Satmar communities believe that non-Jews are fundamentally different and of lower status than Jews. In Lubavitch this view is also expressed in the formal doctrine that Jews have two souls, one divine and one animalistic, whereas non-Jews have only the animalistic soul. This denigration of non-Jews is particularly intense in regard to black people.[11] One gay Lubavitcher, Benzion, in his early thirties, expressed concern about discrimination against blacks and related it to discrimination against gays. But he also maintained that many of the problems black people face are their own fault:

> Where we are today compared to where we were during slavery and before the civil rights movement, I think we are at a good place. I think we are doing the right thing. I mean having a black president is great. Part of it is also being gay and realizing you can't just pick out someone; you can't just treat someone differently by the color of their skin or by their sexuality. That you have to treat all people equally.

When I asked Benzion if he felt that as a society we are treating people of color equally, he replied:

> I think there are still racists out there. I see it all the time at work. My boss says, "They just want our money." "They don't have *seychel* [common sense]." I'm working for a very Jewish couple, and this is what they say. They have a housekeeper who is black, and if she does something silly, they say, "No *seychel*. I'm telling you they just don't have *seychel*." They are old school in their thinking. Listen, they're racist. Physically they're racists; I don't have to mince words here. But where have we come in general as a society? As a society I think we've given them all they really need to grow and be equal, but a lot of [racism] I think has to do with where they are. Where do they, where do black people, want to be?

I asked Benzion where he thought black people "want to be." He responded:

> I don't know. Meaning, I guess here in New York you see it more often, but you see it all the time with [them] walking around with

---

11. There is a long history within the rabbinic tradition of viewing black people as inferior to Jews (see Melamed 2003; and Schorsch 2004).

their pants hanging down. I'm like, that tells me—I don't know if it's a black thing; it started off as a black thing—but pull your pants up. You want to be treated like a normal [person], like anyone else, well you have to look like, act like a *mensch* [respectable person].

The views of Benzion are significant because even though he states that he is concerned that black people not be discriminated against, he believes that they are to blame for the discrimination they still face in America—because their pants are sagging. This is a "secular" and "rational" justification for blacks' predicament. One might expect that as a person distances himself from his community's explicit belief in inequality between Jews and non-Jews and blacks and whites, he would also question related racist assumptions that are commonplace in ultra-Orthodox communities. But this is clearly not always the case.

Tzvi, a Lubavitcher in his late twenties, had a more extreme view, and he more explicitly replaced religious justifications for racism with "secular" ideas. Tzvi began by talking about his community using the term *shvartzes* to describe black people and how this had affected him:

I'm not a major racist. . . . Nevertheless, part of my upbringing was to refer to blacks as *shvartzes*. And that's derogatory; that's one step away from calling them animals. And I find that even though I'm not living in Crown Heights anymore, and I've seen different parts of the black community, nevertheless, there is a carryover. It's not something that's so easily eradicated—if you're brought up referring to blacks as *shvartzes*, not as African Americans, not Negroes, or blacks, but *shvartzes*. It's us against them. I'm just saying, I find that even today, you know, I will on occasion, especially talking to people that grew up with such a term, will revert to use that term again.

Tzvi went on to describe his exposure to pornography featuring black women and how this has affected his view of blacks in general. He states that he feels that black people are closer evolutionarily speaking to animals and that black women are more animalistic in bed than women of other races:[12]

I guess one of the problems that complicates my relationship with blacks for whatever reason has mostly been through black porn. So on a sexual level, I find, I found, I find many black women attractive. I never really had any intellectual connection with black people,

---

12. Tzvi's view that, based on Darwinian thinking, black people are closer to animals and more sexually uninhibited is by no means a new idea. For a historical discussion of this white sexual fantasy, see Asim 2008.

outside of one black kid in grad school that I spoke to once. He was a friend of a friend, and I bumped into him. I'm just trying to say that my relationship with them has always been through these women that I found attractive. So it was a very kind of physical, you know, sensual, physical [attraction], you know. Which puts me, if that is the case, without having a regular relationship with them, like I've had with white people. It kind of skewers my understanding of them. . . . It kind of accentuates a racist type of notion. That they're good in bed because they're closer [*pauses*], they're more animalistic. I think that's what I'm trying to get at. Maybe it's not clear. [*Pauses.*] I see them [*pauses*] from a Darwinian understanding—they're black, and we came from monkeys; it would seem to me that they probably have certain traits closer—at least I see in the sexual realm, they're closer to—they seem to be, at least from my experience—have traits closer to animals. [*Pauses.*] I guess on some level I believe this.

Tzvi went on to describe his attraction to black women in pornographic videos in exactly the terms the Lubavitch community describes non-Jews: animalistic, unlike those with "thought processes" that intervene between instinct and behavior:

So they're much more in tune, I would say, with, you know, just like animals—like having sex—there is no thought process that could interfere. Meaning it's just a natural thing; there is no thought process that could interfere with the sexual act, right? They're animals! Real animals. Whereas for white people there seems to be something that gets in the middle that sort of weakens—they're less in tune with this basic instinct. If this is all correct, and in my experience of watching black and white porn, I've always felt that black women in porn are always much more of a turn-on because they are more animalistic. They have less filters between their instincts and carrying those out.

Tzvi is the only interviewee who mentioned watching pornography, and he expressed the most extreme views about race. But his subtle and explicit references to the teachings of the Lubavitch community make it clear that his views are not (or not only) the result of exposure to racist elements of American culture. He carries with him the specific racism of his community of origin. Tzvi, however, not only was unaware of this but adamantly contested it:

I am not a racist. What I just told you is an explanation of my attraction to blacks. The Lubavitchers in the community may agree with my Darwinian ideas, but they think that blacks are dirty and disgusting. They would never want to sleep with them. I am horrified by their prejudice toward blacks.

In other words, though he does see some points of agreement between his views and the racist views of the community, he does not identify his own attitudes as racist or prejudiced. Habits of thought such as this are not consciously preserved ideas or beliefs; they are, again using Ebaugh's (1988a, 173–174) term, "role residual" that lingers, sometimes knowingly and sometimes unknowingly, in the minds of exiters.

Attitudes toward Women

Strict gender roles exist in both the Satmar and Lubavitch communities and are in fact central to these communities' worldviews. Although they have somewhat different standards of dress and behavior, both communities place a premium on maintaining "traditional" gender roles. Both think that the most important task of women is to be mothers and raise children. Both believe that women are the *akeres habayis*, the foundation of the home, and that it is essential for girls and women to dress modestly to maintain their virtue and prevent the men around them from becoming distracted. Both stress the importance of men and women performing the roles that God assigned to them to ensure a tranquil home and a healthy society. Both believe that men and women are fundamentally different and have fundamentally different purposes in life (see Morris 1998; El-Or 1994, 2002; Fader 2009). This attitude is reflected in the basic differences in the religious obligations of men and women. These ideas about gender roles are not unique to these two communities; they are quite common in other ultra-Orthodox communities and even in parts of mainstream Orthodoxy.

Many interviewees continue to defend rigid separation between male and female domains and capacities. Those who reject the religious basis of the gender separation in the community but maintain that men and women are fundamentally different rely on physical differences between men and women to support such separation, including an emphasis on different levels of physical strength. This section is based on interviewees' responses to the question, "How do you feel about female rabbis?" Female rabbis are common in liberal Jewish denominations but completely unheard of in ultra-Orthodox communities.

A third of interviewees claimed to be supportive of gender equality but had issues with female rabbis; a third reported that they support a woman's right to be a rabbi but admitted that this was a foreign idea for them, and they were not sure if they would go to a female rabbi for spiritual guidance; and a third, mostly women, strongly supported the idea of female rabbis.

This section focuses on those who said that although they personally did not "have a problem" with female rabbis, men and women were just different and men's innate capacities were better suited to the leadership demands of the rabbinate, while women's capacities were better suited to other things, such as child rearing.

Ariel, a Lubavitcher in his mid-thirties, expressed this view:

> I think I still have a bias against female rabbis. I think there is a part of me that doesn't feel—yeah, it's hard to really put my finger on it, but, yeah, I still think there is an inherent bias. Maybe because I haven't really seen a female rabbi. [*Pauses.*] I'm not against it; I just feel that the rabbinical sense of, like, someone who is strong [*pauses*]. Maybe there is a certain masculinity that I associate with being a rabbi. Yeah, I have a bias. There is something about it that I don't feel right about.

Ariel went on to describe his basic view on gender roles:

> I feel that—and obviously I was brought up this way—that women are more sensitive, more emotional, more soft, [generally] speaking, obviously, than men. I think they are better at things than men, in a certain sense; they are better linguists, they express themselves better, [and] they're more loquacious. And I feel that certain things—I think that men and women are different. I honestly do. I don't think that everything—of course you could do anything you want; anyone could do anything they want. I think, for example, a woman—most women relate to being a nursery teacher more than a man does. Call it the nurturing instinct, or whatever it is. Not to say that if a man wants to be a nursery teacher—*gezunter hayt* [go ahead]. But I just feel that there are certain things in society—yes, a woman could be a doctor or a lawyer or whatever. But at the same time, the masculine culture that some of these things entail, such as aggressiveness, the business school . . . when I meet a woman who went to business school and has this "rrrr competitive, rrrrr rrrr," I'm like, wow wow wow.

Ariel then said that he found "aggressive women" unattractive:

> I dated women like that, and I had no interest. I didn't want to date a man! To me the attraction to a woman is being . . . softer than you, you know. There is a certain sense of pleasantness . . . there is a certain sense of . . . like I feel I'm *shtuping* someone with a *shmekl* [penis]. To me an aggressive woman is not attractive. I don't find that attrac-

tive, me personally. Some others, that's their thing. I'm happy that a woman decides that they are a little bit more emotional, even girly. I don't like girly girls, that kind of thing, but a certain softness, a femininity, I appreciate.

Ariel then explained that women were by nature physically weaker than men:

So yes, can men and women do everything the same, yeah? . . . I do feel that men are physically stronger than women. Even though there probably is a woman that says, "Ah there is a woman that can lift . . ." Women by nature are physically weaker than men, so that's why a lot of the jobs that are, you know, with hands, a man does it—traditionally a man does it—and most women are not interested in it.

It is apparent that even though Ariel realizes that these views on gender derive from his upbringing, he does not associate this with the religion from which he has actively distanced himself. An outside observer can readily appreciate not only that this concept of gender is part of Hasidic Judaism but that it is integral to it and one of its central teachings. This concept of gender is contrary to that of many other forms of Judaism and is generally regarded as conservative or even reactionary in contemporary American society. Still, Ariel's socialization regarding gender was so pervasive that he appears unable to view it with the same critical eye that he views other aspects of his religious upbringing, such as the requirements to maintain a beard, observe the Sabbath, and eat only kosher food.

Why does Ariel, and many others like him, view certain aspects of his upbringing, such as the obligation to observe all of the rituals of Judaism or even the idea of denigrating non-Jews or the negative attitude toward homosexuals, as things that should be abandoned, or at least significantly revised, while viewing other aspects of his upbringing, such as the community's attitude toward black people, gender, and liberal Judaism, as things that should be preserved? Regarding gender in particular, this phenomenon exemplifies the way that ideas about gender and gender roles are considered to reflect human nature. Those who maintain their community's attitudes about gender do not see those attitudes as either religious or distinctive to their community. Rather, they believe that those attitudes reflect human nature.

Ariel and several others who were in support of rigid gender roles stressed differences in physical strength between men and women as proof that strict gender roles are natural. They did so even when physical strength was completely unrelated to the topic at hand. The original question was about their attitude toward female rabbis. Even afterward, when they were asked their general view of gender roles, several brought up physical strength.

This was a common maneuver to justify their views on gender that they have carried over from their communities of origin. In Satmar and Lubavitch these views were largely justified by religious doctrines and reference to biblical, rabbinic, and Jewish mystical teachings. My interviewees no longer accept the validity of those religious sources, so they justify their views with assertions about the "natural" world and "pragmatic" arguments.

George Orwell ([1937] 1972) described similar holdovers in beliefs about poor people among members of the English middle class even after they became socialists committed to the abolition of class distinction. Orwell argues that English middle-class prejudice against the poor relied not only on the belief that the lower classes are lazy or stupid but also that they smell bad from a lack of personal hygiene. Orwell goes on to state that because this class prejudice is based on purported "physical" characteristics, it stays with members of the middle class even if they become socialists who are intellectually committed to the plight of the lower classes. Similarly, Satmar and Lubavitch Jews are taught, secondarily to the theological principles about gender, that men are indeed stronger than women, and this notion stays with them and guides their ideas about gender even after they exit the community.

Attitudes toward Liberal Judaism

Approximately one-third of the interviewees were either personally involved, at least marginally, in liberal Judaism or supportive of it as a legitimate form of Judaism, and another third were not at all involved in it but "had no problem with it." However, a third were openly dismissive of liberal forms of Judaism and would never consider joining a liberal synagogue or even exploring the possibility that it might be able to offer them some sense of community or connection to Judaism. They viewed liberal Judaism as "inauthentic" and "fake"—the precise attitude of the ultra-Orthodox community.[13]

Ultra-Orthodox communities express deep opposition to liberal Judaism. The most fundamental criticisms of liberal Judaism is that it violates Jewish law, that it does not take the Bible literally, and that some liberal forms of Judaism do not believe in God. These are all theological and religious issues, and they should theoretically not hold any sway for exiters who reject the theological teachings of their community of origin. But Leah, a Lubavitcher in her late teens, appeals repeatedly to Jewish law in her criticism of liberal Jewish women who reject the strict gender divisions of Orthodoxy:

---

13. William Shaffir and Robert Rockaway (1987) and Marta Topel (2012) note the contradictions among exiters regarding their attitude toward liberal or secular forms of Judaism but do not develop this point.

The women who ask for *tallaysim* [prayer shawls] and ask for Miriam's cup [a feminist innovation to the Passover Seder]—the strange part is, most of these women aren't religious in any way. They don't keep Shabbos; they're wearing jeans and tank tops. They eat wherever they want—they don't keep kosher. They're just trying to be feministic in every part of their life, even a part of their life they don't keep to in any way.

When asked if she thought it was wrong of these women to act in this way, Leah responded:

No. Not wrong. I just find it funny that they—it's ironic. They say [that the traditional Jewish laws excluding women from certain rituals are] sexist, but—first of all, they don't know, like, the *halacha* [Jewish law]. Not like I know much better; I just know that that's definitely not a *halacha*. And they just—they have—they're just trying [*pauses*], I feel like they're just trying to be like feministic in every way.

While Leah rejects the authority of Jewish law in her own life, it still plays a role in her attitude toward liberal Judaism. Others who maintained their community's negative view of liberal Judaism, however, do not criticize it on these theological or religious grounds, both because they have rejected the theology of ultra-Orthodoxy and because they themselves are often guilty, as it were, of the same things. Instead, they focus on what they see as a pragmatic argument: that liberal Judaism is incapable of maintaining its membership numbers and keeping their children and grandchildren Jewish.[14]

This pragmatic critique of liberal Judaism was expressed by Shimshon, a Lubavitcher in his early twenties:

The problem with those forms of Judaism—it's like Diet Coke; you have the sweetness, but you don't have the calories. It's just not—there's no sustenance there. . . . I do want them to marry Jewish. But I look at that more as a bloodline, if you will, than a religious aspect. I just think it's good as a people . . . to sustain the tribe. . . . With those types of

---

14. Yehudis, a Lubavitcher in her late twenties, criticized liberal Judaism for "picking and choosing" and then realized that the ultra-Orthodox would say the same thing about her version of Modern Orthodoxy. So she settled for the criticism that liberal Jews pick only the easy parts, but she also picks things that are difficult to do, such as the "family purity" laws that require her to go to a ritual bath after she menstruates before she resumes relations with her husband. She noted that she does this even when it is freezing outside and when it is a great inconvenience.

Judaisms you find intermarriage rates at more than 50 percent sometimes. The problem with that is [Jews] will eventually go extinct.

Shimshon's problem with liberal Judaism is tribal or nationalistic, not
religious. However, the quotation begins with a description that relates more
to ultra-Orthodoxy's problems with liberal Judaism: "There's no sustenance
there." This is clearly a reference to the lack of rigorous attachment to the
strict laws of Judaism from an Orthodox perspective. But Shimshon makes
clear what "the problem" with that is. It is not a problem in and of itself to
flout Jewish law, just as he himself does. The problem is pragmatic and based
on a concern for the preservation of the Jewish tribe.
    Similarly, Yechiel also couches his views on the inauthenticity of liberal
Judaism, echoing his ultra-Orthodox upbringing, in a pragmatic concern for
Jewish continuity:

I think liberal Judaism is a great concept—in theory it could work. In
practice, though, what ends up happening is a diminution of Judaism.
It's basically watered-down Judaism; you start hacking away at the very
core concepts of Judaism, such as *tznius* [modesty], such as Shabbos,
such as kosher, and before you know it, there is nothing left. So it's great
for people who kind of grew up religious and need a little bit of a modern outlet or don't want to be as observant. But in terms of instilling in
the youth a Judaism that will prevail, it fails again and again. There are
no, or it's extremely rare for there to be, third- or fourth-generation
liberal Jews.[15] They will either assimilate, or at the very least lose touch
and become nonaffiliated, or will become much more Orthodox.

Yechiel went on to describe what he saw as the "farce" of liberal Judaism:

It's not something that's sustainable. It's a farce in a way. [*Pauses.*] It's
like, "Come here, we have beautiful stained-glass windows," but it's
not something that's proven to last. Because people realize that
it's fake. Those who are really interested in spirituality realize that
they are not getting real spirituality in a liberal synagogue, because
they realize that there is so much more out there that these people are
just not doing, and it may seem to some because they are lazy. Or
they're like, fuck this whole religion thing. Let me just not practice at

---

15. To the extent that it is possible to substantiate such a claim (which is limited by the
fact that liberal Judaism has changed shape considerably over the past one hundred years), it
is unsubstantiated by demographic data. One problem, for instance, is that the terms "Orthodox" and "Conservative" (one of the main denominations of liberal Judaism) were inter-
changeable for a long time in America up until the interwar period and, in some instances,
as late as the 1950s (Sarna 2006).

all. Because once you open up the door to be able to hack away at concepts, they're like, "Hey, I can hack away at the whole thing. What's the problem? If you send me to school with Christina, why shouldn't I marry her, and she ate in our house all the time. Like, what's the problem?" So it really does present a problem for just continuing the Jewish nation. So in that sense I don't like it.

Like Shimshon, Yechiel describes liberal Judaism as a diluted form of the "real" (ultra-Orthodox) Judaism in which they were reared. But they *oppose* liberal Judaism because it is unable to keep the young from intermarrying and thus threatens the continuity of the Jewish people. This is not based on research or data they are aware of but on perceptions that were acquired from their youth in ultra-Orthodox communities. These demographic ideas circulate as well in ultra-Orthodox communities, albeit secondarily to the theological and religious opposition to liberal Judaism.

This point is made clear in a quotation from Elimelech, who begins by noting that his views regarding liberal Judaism are a direct result of the community in which he was raised. He then states that liberal Judaism is "self-deception," because liberal Jews are trying to be religious without believing in God. He then shifts to talking about a recent Jewish demographic survey that shows that liberal Judaism is disappearing. In other words, Elimelech is struggling to find a rationale for his negative attitude toward liberal Judaism, and when all else fails, without any better option, he relies on the "fact" that liberal Judaism is ineffective at keeping people Jewish:

> Liberal Jews are entitled to do what they want, but I don't see the point. It's probably because of how I grew up. . . . The *frum*, the ultra-Orthodox, especially Satmar, they have a very totalitarian view of the world, and . . . to me that was the only thing that Judaism was; anything else was considered completely unholy and unkosher and whatnot, and they [non-Orthodox Jews] were considered worse than the goyim [non-Jews], because goyim are goyim, but these are Jews who are reinterpreting Toras Moshe M'Sinai [the Torah God gave Moses at Sinai], they are *apikorsim* [heretics] and whatnot, so even though I don't believe in that anymore, . . . to me it loses the point. What's the point doing these things that I know, that I was brought up to see?

Elimelech then stated that he probably had an emotional response to liberal Judaism and that it was possible, based on his knowledge of the history of liberal Jewish movements, for him to understand their perspective:

> So again it's probably more emotional [*pauses*] because intellectually I could go and say, "Who said we are right; maybe they are right?"

And even though I know the history of the Reform movement and the history of the Conservative movement and that it was at a certain point that they decided to change certain things, so it's not as if they all claim that they have Toras Moshe M'Sinai. The Reform and Conservative movements do acknowledge their histories—that they changed observances; they acknowledge that what they have now is not what Judaism was hundreds of years ago.

Elimelech then pivoted to his "practical" concerns about liberal Judaism, related to what he saw as a continuity problem:

At the same time, for me, for all practical purposes, I don't know what to make of it because it has no meaning to me. To me it almost looks like self-deception. You want to feel Jewish, so you do all of these things, but again, what's the point? If you don't believe in God or you don't believe in [pauses]. What's this changing around of things? Just leave the whole thing. . . . Maybe because I grew up in such a totalitarian and black-and-white, all-or-nothing [community,] . . . that may make me feel that way. . . . I harbor nothing against them. On a practical level I saw the recent survey [on Jewish demographics], and they are assimilating, and most of their kids are not continuing even on their level, so in that regard it is also problematic.

In addition to the pragmatic view these interviewees adopt, they evince inability to transcend the "rigid mind" (Zerubavel 1991) that they developed in their community of origin and to see the possible benefits of a more modern and less demanding form of religion. They still view religion through a black-or-white, all-or-nothing lens. (This topic of the "rigid" versus the "flexible" mind is addressed more fully in Chapter 5.)

What I Got from My Community

Possibly the most striking examples of habits of thought carrying over aspects of one's upbringing occur when interviewees consciously adapt something that they consider a quintessential feature of either Satmar or Lubavitch for a different purpose in their new life. The data for this section comes from interviewees' response to the following question: "What aspects of your upbringing remain with you?"

In addition to a sensitivity and attachment to Hasidic music and *niggunim* (melodies), the most common answer was that interviewees acquired a sense of chutzpah, audacity, from their community. They saw this as the underlying trait that allowed ultra-Orthodox communities to eschew the behaviors and values of American society. They thought that their Hasidic upbringing instilled in them a sense of self-confidence to buck the system of the surrounding society. (Ironically, they used that chutzpah to buck the ultra-Orthodox system.) They discussed various ways in which chutzpah played a role in their lives.

Adam associated his sense of chutzpah with his upbringing:

> I think my attitude is somewhat shaped by that [*pauses*] chutzpah, you know, I can have. Which I think I use for positive, for the most part. Although I've been told that is not always true. . . . I speak up where often other people won't speak up in the workplace, in social situations. I'll just call out the elephant in the room, and sometimes that's awkward. It's just like, okay, *tuchus oyfen tisch* [a Hasidic expression meaning putting your cards on the table]. Are we doing this or not? I don't have patience. How long do you want to dance around this bush?

Adam went on to give an example of how his chutzpah helped in his job as an administrator in a nursing home:

> There was a patient in my nursing home. In order for a patient to be in hospice, they have to have six months or less to live, in the United States. So there's this patient [whose] chart says she has end-stage Alzheimer's. Now end-stage Alzheimer's is pretty far-advanced Alzheimer's. She's not supposed to remember me. She's certainly not supposed to remember a conversation we had three weeks ago. And so people were busy, and they weren't doing what they were supposed to do. And I pointed it out once; I pointed it out twice. Now a lot of people would say, "You did your part; why are you doing that?" I'm like, "Hello, people, this is not Alzheimer's!" I didn't have to do that; I'm like, this is bullshit. What are we doing here? Are we playing a game here? This is people's hopes and our integrity. So that's an example of me speaking my mind at work.

Yekusiel, a Satmar exiter in his mid-thirties, spoke of the emphasis in his community on seeking the truth and the effect this has had on his life choices:

> The Satmar Rebbe [Reb Yoel Teitelbaum] very much taught his Hasidim, his *talmidim* [students], to search the truth. He didn't stand on BS. He didn't like it. People used to tell him stories that didn't make sense; he used to shrug it off: "That's not true." That's something that has had a huge effect on my life. It has in a way given me

the courage to go out and find my own truth for myself, even if it goes against what Satmar says is right.

Yekusiel took something that he associated with the community, a passion for seeking the truth, and used it to explain why he has left the community.

Similarly, Benzion associated what he viewed as a key feature of Lubavitch, accepting others, as an important value he continues to embrace. Moreover, he felt that this value, along with his experience performing Lubavitch outreach work (during which Lubavitchers interact with outsiders and try to persuade them to be more religiously observant) contributed to his ability to come to terms with his own homosexuality:

> I think growing up Lubavitch has given me that insight to be more liberal. [*Pauses.*] I have friends that grew up *misnagdish* [non-Hasidic ultra-Orthodox], and I feel they have a lot [*pauses*] harder time with being different, with being not *frum* [Orthodox], with being gay than I had, than I have. I think part of it is because, for me, Lubavitch—in my family, there was never the finger pointing and "You're going to go to hell!" . . . There was never that. And I don't know if it was just the way my parents raised us or if it was coming from the Lubavitch.

Benzion went on to explain that when doing Lubavitch outreach, it was necessary to be nonjudgmental to be successful:

> Lubavitch is about being open and talking to people and trying to get them to become more *frum* [Orthodox]. And you couldn't do that by telling people, "Look, if you do this, you're going to go to hell!" . . . I think it's helped me be open to other forms . . . to there's not one way. . . . Going on *mivtzoyim* [Lubavitch outreach activities] and going and talking to people that were different than me, coming from different backgrounds, some of them might have been gay, some of them are married to non-Jews, but we didn't care about that. We were welcoming to them, so I think in doing that, I think it kind of helped me be somewhat okay with; it's kind of given me that. . . . Look, here I am trying to get them. . . . I'm not telling them they're bad; I'm just asking them to try a little harder to do this or to become a better whatever, or to keep Shabbos, or to keep kosher. But in that process I think it's helped me kind of learn . . . that it's not really black and white. There is a lot of room for movement in between.

Not all agree that chutzpah and openness are key features of Lubavitch or that truth seeking is a key feature of Satmar. Nonetheless, these three exiters associated these features with their communities, just as others associated different characteristics with their backgrounds. What is significant is that they made these associations and felt that they were carrying on these traits in their new life. Although they may be using these traits in ways that are unimaginable or completely contrary to how they are used in their communities, it was important for them to associate it with their community.

Exiters' Exposure to Others

Although both the Satmar and Lubavitch communities have very negative views of non-Jews and homosexuals, almost all interviewees were positively inclined toward these two groups.[16] Many were eager to stress that they have abandoned their community's views of both these groups. Many described becoming friends with, and a few described dating, non-Jews and getting to know them as individuals. They said that firsthand knowledge helped them transcend the stereotypes they acquired growing up. Similarly, several noted that they had friends who were gay, and one stated explicitly that his lesbian friend helped him become sensitive to the plight of homosexuals. That a significant proportion of exiters still maintain views about race carried over from their community may be the result of their lack of genuine interaction with black people post-exit.

Experience socializing with people of the opposite sex post-exit did not necessarily change some of the interviewees' views on gender. This is partly attributable to the physical associations that the community had already imbued in them (women as weaker, men as stronger), which continue to anchor their beliefs about gender generally. But an important difference between changing one's views on other religions or sexual preferences and changing one's views on gender, specifically gender roles in society, is that the latter comes at a higher cost to the individual changing her or his views. Whatever gender role one was brought up to envision as fit for oneself changes when one's concept of gender changes. Deeply held ideas about oneself, one's role in the world, and one's future are at stake. Men in particular would have to suddenly give up some of their power and control, both in society in general and in their personal relationships. Of course, holding on to that sort of patriarchal power is another habit of action that persists post-exit.

Conservative ideas about gender (and race), which originate for exiters in their ultra-Orthodox upbringing, are commonplace in certain parts of American culture and media. Exposure to these ideas in American society

---

16. Two interviewees stated that they were opposed to homosexuality, and one of them, following the pattern this chapter outlines of finding nontheological arguments for attitudes carried over from their community, explicitly framed his opposition as based on the view that homosexuality goes "against the natural order."

supports their persistence for exiters. In contrast, exiters are not exposed to negativity toward non-Jews, which they can more readily acknowledge as a distinctively ultra-Orthodox perspective.

Conclusion

This chapter shows how habits of action and habits of thought that persist in the lives of exiters complicate a simple, unidirectional narrative of exiting religion. They challenge exiter's claims of discontinuity with their upbringing. These habits manifest both consciously and unconsciously in the lives of exiters, as they exhibit their own unique combination of habits retained and shed from their upbringing.

This phenomenon speaks to two aspects of religious exiting that have been misunderstood in prior scholarship. First is the prolonged nature of the exiting process. Some habits remain long term and perhaps forever in the lives of exiters, but we see that others are gradually relinquished, often through a concerted effort on the part of the exiter (such as Yehuda, who forced himself to get used to eating pork). Exiters do not gather up all of the traits, behaviors, and ideas that were instilled in them from their youth and leave them at the doorstep as they exit. It does not happen in a single day or even a single year. Diverse habits persist for varying lengths of time in various ways.

Second, the Lubavitch and Satmar habits of action and thought described in this chapter illustrate why these exiters cannot be classified merely as "in" or "out" of their communities. The binary that scholarship usually assumes about religious identity does not stand up to scrutiny when a full accounting is taken of a strict religious upbringing. Exiters from Lubavitch and Satmar exhibited a range of indicators of liminality, living in an in-between state and retaining some characteristics of the community while abandoning others.

While one might be inclined to dismiss the applicability of this analysis to less strict religious groups, it remains to be tested. One of the implications of this study, familiar to scholars of religion but greatly underrepresented in scholarship on exiting religion, is that religion is made up of far more than doctrines and practices. The range of habits discussed in this chapter testifies to that.

No individual manifested all of the particular habits of action and thought discussed here. It is useful to think of Jonathan Z. Smith's concept of a "polythetic" classification system, in which no single factor is necessary to be present but a combination of factors indicates inclusion in the category (1982, 4). While no exiter possesses all of the characteristics of liminality, the combination of a critical mass of characteristics, whether in the exit narratives, habits of action, or habits of thought, yields an unmistakable liminality.

Strategies for Managing Liminality

Still, even in Shelley the note of rebellion is sometimes too
strong. The note of the perfect personality is not rebellion,
but peace.

—Oscar Wilde, *The Soul of Man under Socialism*

A s Chapter 1 describes, there are three kinds of exiters: trapped, hybrid, and disconnected. Since the vast majority of interviewees are hybrids, I focus on their experiences, specifically the strategies that they use to manage the complex and contradictory realities of their current lives. These strategies are not necessarily mutually exclusive, and hybrids may adopt one or more strategies at one time and then change and adopt others. Since there is no linear model of religious exiting that captures the experiences of all exiters, the presentation of strategies does not imply that one necessarily follows the other in an inevitable sequence. However, often exiters go through a predicable sequence of strategies, and the order of the strategies presented is based on that.

The strategies that exiters employ include medicating the pain, bonding with other exiters, using social media as an outlet, embracing Israel, pursuing the academic route, abandoning pure categories, and exploring liberal Judaism. One of the most challenging realms to navigate as an exiter is one's relationship with one's family who still remain in the community. As Chapter 2 discusses, contrary to what is assumed among both laypeople and scholars, neither Lubavitch nor Satmar families cut their exiters off. All interviewees, except the one who cut off her own abusive family, continue to have a relationship with their family to some extent. How is this relationship managed? Two other strategies, engaging in a conspiracy of silence and drawing lines in the sand, are crucial to its management.

Medicating the Pain

On initially beginning the exiting process, exiters often suffer a great deal of pain and confusion. They know that they no longer feel completely at home in their community but are unsure of where to go or how to get there. Many reported not having contacts outside their community and feeling completely at a loss. In addition, often their families respond very harshly to the exiters' religious deviance and lifestyle changes. With few solutions in sight, some exiters turn to alcohol and drugs as a means of alleviating the pain they are suffering.[1] Several even spoke of groups of exiters meeting up for wild parties. Perel, a Satmar woman in her early twenties, explained:

> Once I was already not religious but before I integrated into the real world, I was partying a lot. Footsteps is where the stable OTDs [exiters] go; everyone else goes to parties [*laughs*]. No, it's not like that. . . . I went to serious drug parties. Did I mention I experimented with everything? I literally did a drug in every category. I have not tried DMT. I have not tried crack. I have tried heroin but no needles. I didn't like the heroin. It made me nauseous. . . . And I was doing it with other *Hasidish* [Hasidic] people. Like there [are] a whole lot of them. . . . A lot of those people when they first get out are dealing with a lot of emotional stuff, so a lot of people end up doing drugs. . . . There was a large drug situation. . . .We went to raves in the city, in Brooklyn, right near Williamsburg, these warehouse parties. . . . Go to hipster parties, and you'll see *Hasidish* guys there with their *payis* [sidelocks] tucked under their baseball cap. For girls it's very easy to dress up and go out. For guys, if they're still living at home, it's tricky, but you can always find a way. . . . I did so [many] drugs back then that people meet me now and they're like, "I didn't think you would still be alive!"

As in the case of Perel, for many who turned to drugs or alcohol to deal with the pain of exiting, this was only an initial stage, and they eventually turned to healthier and more constructive strategies.

Bonding with Other Exiters

A strategy that is often undertaken with great enthusiasm is the effort to bond with other exiters.[2] A significant example of this desire for connection

---

1. This is similar to what Robert Merton, in his typology of deviance, called "retreatism" (1968, 241), in which people abandon the previous goals and means without having furnished any new ones, leading them to seek escape through alcohol, drugs, and risky sex.

2. This is in line with Helen Rose Fuchs Ebaugh's (1977) findings that for ex-nuns who left extremely conservative orders, there was strong solidarity, and frequent informal and formal meetings were held with other nuns who left similar orders.

with other exiters is the importance of the organization Footsteps in the lives of about a third of the interviewees. They expressed great appreciation for the social interactions with other exiters that Footsteps made possible. The members of Footsteps spoke passionately about how Footsteps provides the means for exiters to connect with each other and celebrate the parts of their past that they cherish without the strictures and emotional burdens of interacting with the community itself.

The experience of Hershy, a Satmar man in his mid-twenties who initially felt reluctant to join Footsteps but eventually came to embrace it and its members, is typical:

> I joined Footsteps, and it's been a very good experience. I've become very active, and I recommend it to those people who I believe could benefit from their services. Initially I was reluctant to join Footsteps because the only people I knew who left my community were those people we called "bums," who were with drugs and girls and running around with beepers and silly cars, and when I left, I was like, "I'm not going to be like them." I didn't smoke, I didn't do anything, and I didn't want to be associated with such people, and I thought that Footsteps would be full of such people. So I was reluctant.

Hershy went on to explain that his need for assistance getting his GED brought him to Footsteps and ultimately to an embrace of its members:

> I needed to get my GED, and I was having a hard time, so somebody told me [to] try Footsteps. I went to their office, but I decided I was not going to get involved in their social events. Then one day the social worker contacted me and said that Footsteps is having a big social function, and I decided to go. Initially I was worried that it was like I had feared, since one guy made a joke: "When is the *minyin* [prayer quorum] for *mincha* [the afternoon prayer]?" I was like, "Seriously! Are we seriously going to have to sit through these kinds of jokes?" I didn't want to be in a place that is stuck in its past, sitting around rehashing how much we've been hurt and how much we've missed out. But I continued to go to their events, and I was completely proven wrong on two fronts. First of all, the people weren't like that—the people were looking for a journey. And second, there is nothing wrong with having a space where you can rehash that and work through it and have a time in your life, a year or two, where you can voice those things, even if you don't leave the community completely. So I think Footsteps is a valuable place. Being involved in that world has enriched my life; it has given me a community. It is an

amazing place, an amazing space, and there is nothing condemnable [about] people who struggle to find their way out—there is something valuable and holy about that to me.

Hershy came to believe that it was desirable to "rehash" and "work through" the past. He described his involvement with Footsteps as "being involved in that world," which indicates that he experiences it as a community. Orthodox Jews commonly use the language of "our world" to describe their communities, but for Hershy, the former community of like-minded religious Jews had been replaced with a community of like-minded exiters.

Not all exiters, however, were involved with Footsteps. Several simply said, "[I] like to do my own thing" and do not want to be part of any groups or organizations now. At least eight others were very hostile to Footsteps and thought that continuing to socialize with other exiters worked only to further isolate them from the broader American society into which they were so eager to integrate. In that sense they were aware that involvement in Footsteps keeps them connected to their former identities. (But in fact, those who were not involved in Footsteps still exhibited other holdovers.) Shifra, a Satmar woman in her mid-twenties, felt this way. She thinks that Footsteps keeps people stuck in thinking only about their community and that they need to just get away from the community to "move on."

Similarly, Elimelech, a Satmar exiter in his late twenties, agreed:

On the one hand, I feel that Footsteps is an important organization for those who need it, and I want it to be there for them. On the other hand, if the members left the *haredi* [ultra-Orthodox] community to join American society, why do they go to an organization full of people who came from the *haredi* community? Let them just join the broader society! I guess the point is that I don't have much intellectually or otherwise in common with many of the people at Footsteps. If I was still *haredi* or if I was never *haredi*, I wouldn't hang out with most of those people.

It is clear that for the eight people who were hostile to Footsteps, it is not merely that they dislike this particular organization but rather that they reject the strategy of bonding with other exiters as a means of coping with their own transition. Nonetheless, for many others, community building among exiters, whether through Footsteps or some other kind of formal or informal organization (of which there are many), is highly significant. These interviewees choose to spend time socializing with other exiters rather than simply seeking out friendships among other nonreligious Jews or non-Jews. They enjoy the possibility of connecting with others who share their background and can appreciate what they have gone through as well as what they are dealing with now as they exit their community.

In fact, among exiters, the identifier "OTD"—explicitly defining exiters in relation to their ultra-Orthodox communities of origin—has gained widespread use, and at least some exiters embrace the term and wear it as a badge of honor, as indicated by the many Facebook groups that incorporate the term in their group's name. Furthermore, "OTD" has become a term associated with a shared experience that transcends the sectarian divisions within ultra-Orthodox communities themselves. As Etty, a Satmar woman in her mid-twenties, observed, "We used to be separated—we were Satmar, Lubavitch, Litvish [non-Hasidic ultra-Orthodox]—now we're all just OTD."

One reason this bonding among exiters is treasured is that some exiters reveal aspects of their former selves when in the company of other exiters that they otherwise make a concerted effort to hide. Ruchy's handling of her thick Yiddish accent is a good example of this phenomenon:

> I love my Yiddish accent. When I'm sitting with my fellow OTD buddies, I love speaking Yiddish with my thick accent. It's just when I'm speaking English to others I don't want my accent, and I've worked hard to get rid of it. Although my non-Jewish girlfriend tells me she loves my accent.

That is, bonding with other exiters can create a space that is freeing and allows exiters to drop their guard and revisit parts of themselves that they may have strong affection for but that they think mainstream society demands they usually keep hidden.

Using Social Media as an Outlet

Hybrids also connect with other exiters through social media, such as Facebook groups devoted to exiters' lives. Currently there are more than thirty ultra-Orthodox exiter-related groups, many of which use the term "OTD" in the title of their group, including OTD Parenting, OTD University, LGBTQ and Off the Derech, Off the Derech, Off-the-Derech Torah Discussion Group, and Off the Derech Singles. Among other things, the anonymity social media offers allow exiters to vent to a sympathetic and "safe" audience about their negative experiences in their community, the moral failings of their community, and the difficulties they are experiencing dealing with their ultra-Orthodox families. It also allows exiters to receive encouragement and practical advice.

Perel enthusiastically engages other exiters online. She described both the general appeal of such social media for exiters and the way that one particular group was helpful for her and her resocialization:

Because of my background I had no understanding of political and
social issues. I had no idea who to vote for, and I knew that the only
people who understand me are other OTDs. . . . I grew up very racist,
and it is hard to wake up one day and just be no longer racist. So I
needed a place to learn and find out about things. On Facebook OTD
groups I'm finding a community. . . . For everyone in a different way,
it's about finding a community or finding resources.

Perel went on to explain that OTD Facebook groups were especially important to her now that she no longer lived in Brooklyn, surrounded by other
exiters:

Now I live away from Brooklyn and away from other OTDs. So Facebook helps me stay in touch with other OTDs. Suddenly I'm connected to so many OTDs. Recently I joined a women's OTD group,
and it's been great. I can ask about anything. Today we were talking
about whether we wear *tznius* [modest] clothes when we come home
and if we feel weird about looking so frumpy. It was a great conversation. . . . Finding people I can relate to, people who are now where I
was a few years ago, and making new friends—I just love it.

In terms of bringing exiters together, social media has certain advantages over meeting in person. For exiters who are in the early stages of their
journey and are cautious about being "outed" to family and friends, the idea
of going to an organization like Footsteps and revealing to strangers that
they are in the process of exiting can be daunting. With the anonymity social
media allows, Facebook and other sites can be a comfortable place to initially
meet like-minded exiters.

In addition, for exiters who are still living with their family or who frequently return to visit, social media can be a convenient means of connecting with other exiters on the Sabbath or Jewish holidays when it is difficult
to get away and meet in person. Thus, exiters are able to connect with other
exiters at times when family and community pressure may be particularly
intense and support urgently needed. In addition, as Perel points out, for
exiters who have moved away from New York City and are no longer able to
meet other exiters in person, social media can provide a means of remaining
connected.

Embracing Israel

A strategy most interviewees employed to cope is embracing Israel. For several it meant volunteering to join the Israeli armed forces for several years or
at least living in the country for a period of time. For most who live in Amer-

ica and may visit Israel only briefly, this means participating in Israel Day parades and generally taking Israel's side in the Israeli-Palestinian conflict. This embrace of Israel and its politics allows exiters to connect with a strong source of Jewish identity devoid of religious strictures or demands. They may also be influenced by the fact that today defending Israel is a key marker of Jewish identity among many secular American Jews and that this position has become so naturalized and taken for granted that for many it is unimaginable to do otherwise (see Seliktar 2002; Ben-Moshe and Segev 2007). This embrace of Israel can be seen as an attempt, whether consciously or not, to feel more at home in the broader American Jewish community, which in general is strongly pro-Israel.

As noted earlier, Satmar is staunchly anti-Israel and Lubavitch is staunchly pro-Israel. Satmars tend to reject their community's anti-Israel position, while most Lubavitchers tend to accept their community's pro-Israel position. Specifically, although four interviewees—three Lubavitchers and one from Satmar—expressed support for Palestinian rights and questioned the moral claims of Israel, the majority of both groups support Israel, at least moderately, and seven strongly support Israel and reject the claims of Palestinians out of hand.

Although most are equally supportive of Israel, in terms of their exiting experience, this does not mean the same thing to all of them. The majority of Satmar interviewees who are now pro-Israel have abandoned completely their community's position on the subject and instead have adopted a new position. For the majority of Lubavitch interviewees who are now pro-Israel, this is a continuation of their community's position.

Nonetheless, the reasoning behind Lubavitchers' support of Israel represents something of a change. Specifically, the Lubavitch community framed its support for Israel, at least in part, on theological grounds—the Lubavitcher Rebbe often spoke of God having given the Land of Israel to the Jewish people as an inheritance, and the Rebbe opposed giving back land for peace in part on the grounds that Jewish law prohibited the selling of land in Israel to non-Jews. However, Lubavitch exiters who oppose negotiating with Palestinians frame their support for Israel in nontheological terms, focusing exclusively on the lack of a desire for peace on the part of Palestinians. They claim that such negotiations are a waste of time, since Palestinians "just want to kill Jews."

Pursuing the Academic Route

Another strategy hybrids use is to try to get into college and make a career for themselves. Of necessity this strategy takes time to employ, since exiters usually have little or no secular education by the time they are exiting their community. First, they must improve their English reading skills and obtain a high school equivalency diploma, after which they can attempt admittance into a college. In addition, the cost of college tuition often presents a problem, since exiters often do not have financial support from family members, who are usually strongly opposed to their attending college.

Although exiters must overcome significant hurdles to gain admittance to college, there are several major advantages for those who do. Beyond providing the possibility of a career with financial security, the college environment allows for the kind of intellectual stimulation and social interaction that many crave. As Chapter 3 presents in the discussion of intellectual narratives, for some interviewees, such as Yechiel, the type of intellectual freedom encountered in college is a unique experience and one that shapes the rest of their lives. It also allows them to make friends with people of different genders and from different racial, ethnic, and religious backgrounds, thus widening their horizons and assisting them with their process of integration into the broader society.

Abandoning Pure Categories

A key strategy necessary for the hybrid's successful coping is the ability to abandon one central habit of thought characteristic of ultra-Orthodox communities: the quest for pure categories. Hybrids, consciously or not, reject the black-and-white thinking of their upbringing and instead embrace ambiguity. To paraphrase Salman Rushdie's own description of his notoriously "heretical" novel, *The Satanic Verses*, hybrids rejoice in "mongrelization" and fear the "absolutism of the pure" (1992, 394).[3]

The hybrid's ability to move beyond pure categories is an example of what Eviatar Zerubavel calls the "flexible mind" (1991, 120). Zerubavel distinguishes among three mind-sets: the "rigid mind" (33), which sees ambiguity as a danger to the existing classificatory system (akin to the work of Mary Douglas, which he discusses); the "fuzzy mind" (81), which is completely unaware of boundaries and adopts an "oceanic" perspective (82) (building on Freud's "oceanic feeling" [(1930) 1961, 11, 21]); and the "flexible mind," which combines rigidity and fluidity by recognizing boundaries but

---

3. Rushdie writes, "Those who oppose the novel most vociferously today are of the opinion that intermingling with a different culture will inevitably weaken and ruin their own. I am of the opposite opinion. *The Satanic Verses* celebrates hybridity, impurity, intermingling, the transformation that comes of new and unexpected combinations of human beings, cultures, ideas, politics, movies, songs. It rejoices in mongrelization and fears the absolutism of the Pure. Melange, hotchpotch, a bit of this and a bit of that is how newness enters the world. It is the great possibility that mass migration gives the world, and I have tried to embrace it. *The Satanic Verses* is for change-by-fusion, change-by-conjoining. It is a love song to our mongrel selves" (1992, 394). For an analysis of this view of multiculturalism, see Joppke and Lukes 1999, 1–26; and Waldron 1992.

not limiting itself to them. Zerubavel connects the ability to adopt a flexible mind to the idea of "mental plasticity" (1991, 121) (akin to neuroplasticity or brain plasticity more generally). Likewise, some psychologists describe a personality trait that seems to characterize trapped and disconnected exiters: "intolerance of ambiguity" (see Budner 1962). But it is difficult to know if a person's level of intolerance of ambiguity or mental plasticity is inborn or is developed under certain social conditions. These traits, therefore, cannot be considered causal factors of an exiter's classification as trapped, hybrid, or disconnected. They do, however, seem to accurately describe these categories.

It is instructive to compare hybrids' relationship with their upbringing to the cultural project undertaken within Yiddish culture after the Holocaust that David Roskies (1999) calls the Jewish search for a "usable past." Roskies argues that Yiddish literature and culture have served as a bridge connecting the past to the present and future by allowing Jews to find a "usable past," aspects of the old shtetl life that they can reinvent in a way that seems relevant to the new circumstances Jews found themselves in after the devastation of Eastern European Jewish society.

Roskies explains that what made the past usable was, in large measure, the fact that there was such a dramatic rupture caused by the Holocaust between the past and the present. Post-Holocaust Jews experienced their pre-Holocaust past, even when it was not actually very long ago, as profoundly distant. Likewise, it is perhaps only when exiters separate themselves from their own past long enough to review and evaluate it that they are able to access the usable past of their own upbringing and incorporate it into their new lives.

Exploring Liberal Judaism

One example of where embracing ambiguity is crucial is interviewees' contemplating engagement with liberal Judaism's institutions and culture. Although as Chapter 4 discusses, a third of interviewees were dismissive of liberal Judaism—not unlike the attitude of ultra-Orthodox communities themselves—a third were at least somewhat involved in liberal Judaism, such as attending liberal religious services. They needed to move beyond the black-and-white thinking characteristic of their upbringing that viewed the Torah as either completely true in every word and requiring total submission or completely false and of no value at all.

These exiters have come to realize, for example, that although the Torah may be a human creation, it can still contain great wisdom and provide guidance and emotional sustenance. Exploring liberal Judaism is a strategy that allows these exiters a great amount of personal freedom while also allowing them to stay connected to some form of Jewish heritage.

Chavi, a Lubavitcher in her early thirties, embraces liberal Judaism and relishes the fact that it allows women to perform religious functions prohibited to her in her Lubavitch upbringing:

> I'm really into alternative rituals and creating my own version of what *Yiddishkheit* [Judaism] is supposed to look like. We had a tree-planting ritual for both our kids in the neighborhood park, and it was very meaningful. . . . I feel so buoyed by the community of friends I've pieced together. The friends are from the two liberal synagogues I'm involved in. I'm part of a chanting group in one of the synagogues. Once a month we meet for a potluck and do Hebrew chanting. I regularly go to the two synagogues. I *layn* [read the Torah for the congregation] at one of the synagogues. I like that. I get a lot out of that.

Engaging in a Conspiracy of Silence

A key strategy that hybrids use to maintain the peace with their family is to keep secret who they really are. It is a form of a conspiracy of silence. Zerubavel explains that a conspiracy of silence is not simply the absence of speech but an active social relation, an agreement by the parties involved to avoid certain topics. In effect, it is a form of denial. "Furthermore, it usually involves refusing to acknowledge the presence of things that actually beg for attention, thereby reminding us that conspiracies of silence revolve not around those largely unnoticed matters we simply overlook but, on the contrary, around those highly conspicuous matters we deliberately try to avoid" (Zerubavel 2006, 9).

Exiters maintain a conspiracy of silence with their families regarding the fact that they have exited ultra-Orthodoxy.[4] The goal is to deny as much as possible the basic fact that the exiter has fundamentally changed his or her lifestyle and is now no longer ultra-Orthodox. This conspiracy operates both within the exiter's family and between the family and the rest of the community, from whom the family tries to hide the "shameful" truth. The primary mechanisms that allow this conspiracy of silence to function are the exiter's conformist behavior and speech while in the presence of family members.

A salient example, since it is immediately noticeable, is exiters' adherence to the communal dress code while in the presence of ultra-Orthodox family members. This may include head coverings for both men and married women (yarmulkes and either fur hats or fedoras for men; wigs or kerchiefs

---

4. Ephraim Tabory and Shlomit Hazan-Stern (2013) found a similar dynamic of self-censorship, which they call "bonds of silence," among Modern Orthodox exiters when interacting with their parents.

for married or formerly married women), long skirts and blouses that cover the collarbone and elbows for women, and slacks rather than jeans for men. There are different degrees to which exiters are willing to accommodate their families in this regard, but the vast majority extend themselves at least somewhat in this direction. Many described their adherence to these norms as a form of showing "respect" to their family and as a means of sparing their family greater pain.[5] Part of what the exiters are "respecting" is their parents' interest in preventing younger children and other ultra-Orthodox relatives from being negatively influenced by the actions of the exiter.

Most interviewees never had a formal discussion with their parents about how they would act in their presence. Instead, they have an unspoken agreement. As Naftuli, a Satmar exiter in his late twenties, explained,

> There's never been a discussion about how I would act or dress when I'm home for a visit. There was sort of an understanding. But I've always been very respectful of them, for the most part. At home I would always wear a yarmulke. I could wear whatever kind of crazy T-shirt I want. I have an earring, and I would take it off when I was home. If they were sitting down to a meal and everyone was making a *hamoytzi* [the blessing over the bread], I would mumble a *hamoytzi*. My father still insists when I go there that I lead *bentching* [the blessing] after the meal. He says I should have the honor because I'm a guest. . . . My father would include me in a *minyan* or part of a *mizuman* [two types of prayer quorums]; he'd rather not think about [whether I'm religious and can technically take part in these rituals]. I don't think it's a conscious decision on his part to think about whether I can or can't take part.

In other words, Naftuli's father would prefer not to think about whether his son is religious or not, so he pretends that his son is religious, and the son does what he can to support this illusion.

Some go out of their way to never mention anything about their beliefs or practice that could possibly make their parents think that they are no longer Orthodox. Yechiel takes this approach:

> My parents are still in denial, which is why I still continue to perpetuate the myth that perhaps I still am religious. I remember

---

5. However, Daniel, a Lubavitcher, explicitly rejected the entire discourse of "respect" as a justification for pretending to be Orthodox while in the presence of the ultra-Orthodox community: "I know a lot of people use the 'respect' argument against me just doing my thing while in the community. But it's not respecting me pretending to keep Shabbos around you; that's not respect. That's you disrespecting me by demanding I do that! If you take offense by me walking around not keeping Shabbos, that's your problem, not mine!"

initially when my father found out that I wasn't putting on *tefillin* [phylacteries for prayer] when I was seventeen. He was shocked. Ever since then I kind of made a point not to put it in their faces, because back then I just did it to hurt them. When I was seventeen, I was like, "You could take these home; I really don't need [phylacteries]." But later on, you know, I would never do it in front of my parents. . . . If they try to put the pieces of the puzzle together and think about the things I've done and the places I've been to, they would probably figure out that I'm not Orthodox. But I've never done anything in front of them that was against the Torah.

Yechiel went on to describe how his strategy of "respect" left his parents free to think whatever they wanted:

So they probably think that I'm still *frum*, but if they dig deep down, they probably know that I'm not, but they're in denial about it. We never had a discussion about me not being *frum* anymore. So the status quo is that I'm still *frum*. And I have been careful not to do anything in public that would jeopardize that status quo, to an extent they must believe that I am still *frum*, but we never really discussed it. My main concern is not to cause them unnecessary grief.

Similarly, Hershy spoke about pretending to be Orthodox while around his parents to prevent causing them further pain:

I've never openly acknowledged to my parents that I'm not religious anymore. They still think so, and they still ask me, "Where are you eating for Shabbos?" and "Where are you eating for *Paisech* [Passover]?" It's a little bit difficult. . . . I used to think that it was important that everyone know the full truth about me, but now it's okay. If that's the world that it's easiest for them to live in, then I'm okay helping them live in that world. So I pretend to be religious when I'm around their house, and I do what I need to do.

I asked Hershy how he "pretends to be religious," and he replied:

I don't go out of my way. I don't leave for *shacharis* [morning prayers], but I wear a yarmulke, I make a *bracha* [blessing], I wash my hands before bread, I *bentch* [recite blessings after meals]. I try, you know; I don't eat nonkosher there. If my parents came to visit me at college, I would put on a yarmulke to help them keep their worldview of me.

The conspiracy of silence often encompasses the extended family and prevents any relatives from even mentioning "deviant" or nonconformist behavior. Yehudis, a Lubavitcher in her late twenties, reported an extreme case of this silence. She was never told that her cousin got married, because her cousin married a non-Jew. Her family thought that it was wrong to tell young children about the non-Orthodox behavior of relatives because it might influence others to do likewise:

> As a teenager I was close with one of my Lubavitch cousins. She did not tell me—I found out after I got married that she had been married for years, because she was married to someone who wasn't Jewish. So out of respect for my parents, she hadn't told me. That's what I'm saying. There's like a respect thing. It's like we're not going to go ahead and say, because we decided something, we're going to help someone else decide their thing by giving them something else to think about. We're going to respect what you're trying to teach your child, and then once they've made a decision about your religious life, then it's like [an] all-cards-on-the-table kind of thing.

The conspiracy of silence also extends to the children of exiters who must be taught the difference between how they should act when in their own home and how they should act when visiting their ultra-Orthodox grandparents. For example, Ruchy explained that she coaches her son to be respectful of the rules when visiting his Satmar grandparents on the Sabbath. A key rule he needs to know is that his grandparents believe it is prohibited to turn the lights on or off on the Sabbath:

> I'm extremely open with my son. When I go to my parents' for a meal on Shabbos and my father is going to yell at him because he put the light on, I'm going to take him aside and be like, "Sweetheart, for some people on Shabbat they don't like turning lights on. That's part of their rules. That's not part of Mommy's rules. In Mommy's house you don't have to do that, and it's even okay if you do it in Bubby's house, but they don't like when you do it in front of them. So we're not going to do it in front of them, because we're going to be respectful of their rules." And I feel like, yes, some people are going to be like, "He's only three years old; he doesn't understand what you're saying." He understands exactly what I'm saying.

Similarly, Chavi described the stress of trying to cajole her children to abide by unaccustomed rules to prevent the kids from "blowing our cover" when visiting grandparents:

We went to my Lubavitch in-laws for Passover in Chicago. A month before we got there, I told my husband that we need to talk about it. We need to talk about how this is going to go down. Yenkel [my son] is going to blow our cover. He's going to be five, and he's not going to want to wear a *kippa* [skullcap] the whole time. My husband is like, "We don't need to talk about it. We're just going to go, and it's just going to be fine. I'm just going to bribe Yenkel to behave." Whatever. I'm like, "That's really great!" For a month I was promoting the idea of going to Chicago to my kids. I was like, "Yay! We're going to Chicago! You're going to eat pizza and ice cream, and you're going to wear a *kippa* and *tzitzit* [fringes] because that's what they do at Bubby [grandma] and Zaidy's [grandpa's] house. It's going to be awesome!" I just sort of [*starts to cry*]. We survived, but it was a huge emotional ordeal. We were doing this ridiculous emotional tiptoe pretending to be something that we are not. Family dynamics are stressful enough as it is, and add the fact that you are lying trying to pretend, like seriously. It was so crazy!

Although the conspiracy of silence helps maintain a basic peace, a major consequence is that many exiters believe that they are hiding a great deal of who they really are from their parents and loved ones. They are never able to discuss issues that they care deeply about, and they cannot present themselves physically in the clothing that reflects their true identity. This leads, unsurprisingly, to their feeling that they "have nothing to talk about" with their family and that their relationship with their family is "very superficial."

For example, Ruchy talked about feeling that her identity is completely suppressed when visiting her family. Still, she is willing to go along with this charade to be with her family and avoid causing them more pain:

We don't talk about my religious or sexual preferences with my extended family. My real life doesn't exist. If I go visit my extended family, I don't put a wig on because I'm not doing that shit anymore, but I wear a dress. I look very *frum*, an *eydel meydel* [a modest young girl]. And I'm willing to do that because I don't go every day and I'm not here to cause shame or embarrassment for my family. Although I'm sure there are a lot of pictures going around the community of me ["immodestly" dressed], but at least my grandparents and parents don't have to have that kind of pain. Because a lot of the pain inflicted on my parents is what the outside world, the "neighbors," will think and not about what they themselves think. The neighbors—I don't give a shit, get over it! But when it comes to my grandparents, I don't want to cause them that pain, and I'm understanding of that. Whether it's right or wrong, and you can argue both ways [*pauses*]. It isn't fair, but life isn't fair. This is the best I can get, and I'm very appreciative of it.

An essential part of any conspiracy of silence is to determine what is to be seen and talked about and what is not. When the exiters return to visit their family, they reported that it is important that they "look" Hasidic. Thus, several noted that their parents, particularly their mothers, were more concerned with the outer appearances of their religious conformity than with their inner religious convictions. As Yehoshua somewhat exaggeratedly put it, "I could tell my mom that I ate pork on Yom Kippur, and she would still say, 'But why aren't you wearing your black fedora?'" She says this because outward demonstrations of nonconformity violate the conspiracy of silence. They challenge the fiction that the conspiracy of silence is intended to maintain—that everything is okay and no one is deviating from the religious path.

Although as a rule parents are extremely resistant to openly engaging with exiters about the religious, philosophical, or other disagreements they have with their upbringing, there are exceptions to this rule. Mordy, a Lubavitcher in his mid-twenties, is one such exception. His parents sought to openly discuss their differences:

> With my parents we established that it was more important to be open to each other than to have pleasant conversations. There are no secrets; I just avoid talking about some things. My mother is just very sad when she hears [that] I'm not religious. My father is not as emotionally affected; I think he takes the intellectual stuff more seriously. He really thinks that intellectually I'm wrong. So the last time I was home, we had a nice little debate about evolution and atheism, and it was totally open. It was great. Everyone knew that when I argue the atheist side, I'm not playing devil's advocate. . . . It's open; that's how I would describe it.

I asked Mordy how he and his parents came to the decision that it was more important to be open than to be pleasant. He responded:

> This was something that my mother said very explicitly while she was crying and begging me to "at least keep kosher! What's the big deal? At least say *kriyas shema* [a prayer before going to bed]!" While she was doing all that, in one of those intense conversations about me shaving my beard, it came up that she wanted to have an honest relationship with me. I was talking to her about a friend who was keeping all these secrets from his parents, and he was saying that his parents were so crazy and abusive, and my mother said, "That's not how we do

things." She told me basically, "Don't hide things from me." Telling her things definitely makes her unhappy, so on my own I would maybe think of hiding things. . . . It was really great to be able to tell things to my parents. It made it easier to tell things to relatives and friends.

Mordy's experience is highly unusual and is not at all representative. In fact, he is the only interviewee who described such an open and honest relationship with his parents, in which the substance of their disagreements was openly discussed. Although it is impossible to know exactly why his parents wanted or allowed such a relationship, several factors seem relevant. Both his parents are involved in the outside world, and his father is extremely learned in Jewish matters as well. They were also both born into the Lubavitch community rather than joined it from the outside. All this may give them a sense of security in their own religious convictions and allow them the latitude to hear "heretical" ideas and discuss "heretical" behaviors without feeling threatened. Whatever the reasons, this openness is extremely rare; most families maintain the conspiracy of silence.

Gender also plays a role in the conspiracy of silence. Specifically, it is possible for female exiters to dress up in all the clothes of the community, including wearing a wig, to blend in when visiting family. However, for male exiters, all of whom have trimmed or shaved off their beards completely, regardless of how much of the community's clothing they don, given that they no longer have a full beard, they will always stick out and reveal that they are not actually fully in the community anymore. This seriously undermines the conspiracy of silence. At the same time, it highlights that what is key for the conspiracy of silence is not the attempt to actually fool family or neighbors into thinking the exiter is fully in the community but rather to not say or do anything while in the community that could offend.

This tendency of exiters to remain silent and not offend their family also extends to remaining silent and not offending or challenging the community as a whole. Albert O. Hirschman (1970) described three types of responses to institutional failure: exit, which means simply leaving the institution; voice, which means remaining within the institution and agitating for reform; and loyalty, which means quietly remaining in the institution and supporting its continuation.

To use Hirschman's terminology, interviewees adopted the "exit" strategy for the most part, but as I describe at length, they remain liminal. One feature of this liminality, which Chapter 4 discusses as a habit of thought, is that in general they do not publicly voice their opposition to the community.[6] Another way of thinking about this practice is as part of the conspiracy of

---

6. One significant caveat to this rule is that some exiters use social media and the anonymity it allows to strongly criticize the community and its customs.

silence, a tacit agreement not to publicize one's objections to ultra-Orthodoxy. Hirschman also observed that an organization from which it is impossible to ever fully exit may cause exiters to be concerned about its future and the public's perception of it even after they leave, since in some respects they are still attached to it.

Two organizations are exceptions to this practice of avoiding public criticism of the community: YAFFED, which advocates for improved secular education within the community's private schools; and Jewish Community Watch, which advocates and raises awareness about child sex abuse inside the ultra-Orthodox community. But both of these organizations frame their efforts in Orthodox religious terms. For example, YAFFED designed billboards promoting both the religious and secular legal obligations for parents to teach their children secular studies so they will be able to earn a living. The billboards contained the following quotation from the Talmud: "A person is obligated to teach their son a trade" (Kiddushin 29a) and the words "It's Your *Mitzvah* [Jewish legal obligation]. It's the Law."

Similarly, Jewish Community Watch urges ultra-Orthodox rabbis to speak on the topic at their functions by stressing the Jewish legal obligation to protect children from abuse. In other words, although both organizations challenge a certain aspect of the norms and institutions of their community, they frame this challenge as a critique from within rather than as an attack from without. In contrast, exiters who voice their objections to their communities of origin would not be doing so "from within."[7]

Drawing Lines in the Sand

Although the parameters of the conspiracy of silence usually go unstated and are maintained through tacit consent, occasionally there are explicit negotiations. These discussions tend to center on two themes: clothing and intermarriage. It seems that these two topics have the greatest potential to dispel the myth that the exiter is still Orthodox. There may be concern over marrying a non-Jew because this is considered a grave sin and is seen as a point of no return for the exiter. As long as the exiter is single or marries a Jew, he or she can always come back to the community, or at least the couple's Jewish children might "return" to the community. Once an exiter marries a non-Jew, whether or not the children are considered Jewish according to Orthodox Jewish law,[8] the specter of a non-Jewish upbringing is, from the

---

7. For an analysis of a Roman Catholic equivalent of a movement criticizing the church from within that uses the discourse of the church to substantiate its moral claims, see Dillon 1990.

8. Orthodox Jews consider children of a Jewish woman to be Jewish, but Jewishness is not passed on through patrilineal descent.

perspective of the exiter's family, a grave indicator of a permanent break with the community.

Simcha, a Lubavitcher in his mid-twenties who has a relatively open relationship with his parents, spoke about the lines in the sand that his parents set out:

> My parents are okay with me walking around the house without a yarmulke, but they tell me that they want me to wear it at meals and in front of the grandchildren. . . . The only line that I cannot cross is marrying a non-Jew. My mother told me once if I marry a non-Jew, she would still speak to me, but she wouldn't let me come home to visit.

Simcha described his parents as laid-back *baal teshuvahs*. This may explain their unusually permissive expectations regarding his head covering. But the line drawn in the sand about intermarriage is typical.

Similarly, Sheindy, a Satmar woman in her late twenties, discussed explicit negotiations with her mother over what she should wear when she comes home to visit:

> My mother would call to tell me how to dress because it bothered my father. My mother would ask me to dress a certain way. I try to be respectful. I used to take off my nail polish before coming over. If my father didn't like what I was wearing, he would come out with a housecoat and ask me to put it on. I would put it on.

Efraim, a Satmar interviewee in his early twenties, spoke about his parents asking him to dress a certain way, especially on the Sabbath, to "blend in" with the rest of the family and not draw attention to his personal religious status:

> My parents ask me, "When you go out from the house, you should be dressed . . . with a white shirt and black or blue pants." They'll ask me to do that kind of stuff. But that's about it. They tell me, "At home, respect where you are. Try to blend in more." Look more Yiddish [ultra-Orthodox]; you know what I mean. And the point is, I respect it. It's not like if I won't do it, they'd kick me out. I know for sure that even if I tell them that I'm going to wear whatever I want and look however I want, they'll still keep me there. I kind of respect them and do it as much as possible. . . . If I walk out of my parents' house on Shabbos, they want me to wear at least a *bekeshe* [a long silk coat traditionally worn by Satmar men on the Sabbath] and look like a Jew that is dressed for Shabbos. You know what I mean.

Similarly, Hershy described a conversation with his grandmother in which she bluntly stated her condition for accepting him in the family. The one line she would not allow him to cross was marrying a non-Jew:

> My grandmother actually found out that I wasn't religious, and I had a long conversation with her. We had a conversation. She's a very smart and intelligent woman, and she said, "Hey, I can't argue with you. It bothers me you're not religious, but whatever. The only thing is, if you marry out, then I can't accept you in the family. Otherwise, it bothers me that you are not religious, but marrying out is the only line I wouldn't let you cross."

External Factor: Worldly Success

A key factor in determining how exiters reflect on their past and how they feel about their community is whether they have achieved what their communities would call "worldly success" post-exit. Worldly success does not necessarily mean becoming very wealthy but simply achieving professional goals, such as sustaining a career or even securing stable, long-term employment. Those who have achieved this sort of success are also more philosophical about their upbringing than those who are professionally frustrated, and they express some affection for their community. They do not see their upbringing as a hindrance to achieving success outside their community. From their perspective there is a causal relationship: Their upbringing did not hinder them professionally, so they have less reason to bear animosity toward it. Hershy, a quintessential hybrid, expressed this point clearly:

> I interact with my Jewish history. I feel very rich by having had the education of knowing it. People ask me, "If you could do it over again, would you go to a high school [where secular studies were taught]?" And I say, "No." My yeshiva education made me who I am today, and I like who I am today. It was painful and difficult, but I like who I am today, and that education made me. There were some gaps and stuff, and there was some stuff I wish they gave me, but they gave me other things, and I'm happy with that.

Similarly, Yael, a Lubavitcher in her early thirties who is a highly successful professional, reported having "no use for sad, depressed people full of anger toward the community."

In contrast, Mendy, who was very successful in the Lubavitch community growing up but is still struggling to find his place professionally in the broader society, harbors a great deal of resentment toward Lubavitch as a result. This informs his resistance to embracing what he might find positive in Judaism while rejecting other aspects of it; his resentment about his professional frustration colors nearly his entire perspective on the community. He is the quintessential trapped exiter.

It is of course impossible to determine whether hybridity leads to (or includes) worldly success or whether worldly success paves the road to hybridity. Not only chronological factors but also psychological factors (beyond the scope of this research) and other social factors would have to be taken into account in each case to determine that sort of causal relationship. But the correlation between hybridity and professional success emerged clearly from numerous interviews.

Conclusion

This chapter describes the strategies that hybrids employ to cope with the contradictions in their lives. These strategies include medicating the pain, bonding with other exiters, using social media as an outlet, embracing Israel, pursuing the academic route, abandoning pure categories, exploring liberal Judaism, engaging in a conspiracy of silence, and drawing lines in the sand. Finally, this chapter addresses one external factor strongly correlated with hybridity: worldly success.

These strategies are not necessarily mutually exclusive. Rather, exiters adopt various strategies at various points in the exit process. Although there is no one model that fits all exiters, as a rule certain strategies tend to be used at predicable times in the exiting process. Specifically, the strategy of medicating the pain is often employed early in the exit process while individuals are still struggling to create a new social support network and redefine who they are. The strategy of remaining close to their family—which involves engaging in a conspiracy of silence and drawing lines in the sand—is often adopted later in the exiting process, since it usually takes the family some time to recover from the shock of their loved one exiting the community before they can engage constructively with the exiter.

There are several significant relationships between the exit narratives that exiters choose (described in Chapter 3) and the kinds of coping strategies they use. These are not perfect correlations but patterns that are often observed. Those who chose intellectual narratives often used the strategy of pursuing the academic route. This makes sense both because those who are intellectually inclined are more likely to be interested in and better prepared to attend college and because, having attended college and absorbed its intellectual norms, they are more likely to describe their journey in intellectual terms. In addition, those who chose intellectual narratives were less likely to identify with the term "OTD" and less likely to choose a strategy of bonding with other exiters. They tended not to privilege their exiter experience and just wanted to "get on with their lives" and connect with people who were unrelated to ultra-Orthodox communities and their exiters.

However, those who chose emotional-social narratives were more likely to choose a strategy of engagement with liberal Judaism. This makes sense since they did not approach religion primarily from the perspective of doctrine and logic but experientially and pragmatically. These individuals were also more likely to identify with the term "OTD" and more likely to seek out avenues for engagement with other exiters, whether in person or online. They tended to feel that it was important and emotionally healthy to engage with their exiter experience and with other exiters to better understand themselves and to heal. Both those who chose intellectual narratives and those who chose social-emotional narratives tended to follow a strategy of remaining connected to their families and engaging in the two strategies related to that aim.

Conclusion

This book presents an in-depth analysis, based on seventy-four qualitative interviews, of the process of religious exiting from the
Lubavitch and Satmar ultra-Orthodox Hasidic Jewish communities.
The interview data are supplemented with historical and textual research on
these communities, including data from their print and online publications
and statements, as well as their classical texts. This is contextualized most
generally in terms of sociological literature on religious exiters and life transformations, and other areas of scholarship are integrated into each chapter
as they arose.

My research first shows that conceiving of religious exiting as a process
through which one transitions from "in" a religion to "out" of that religion
is simplistic. Religious identity is not binary. To the extent that exiters themselves erroneously conceive it to be binary, they struggle post-exit (as disconnected or trapped exiters). By establishing that exit is a process and that
features of a totalizing religious worldview affect exiters throughout the process, this study is able to interrogate the role that the old identity plays in the
new and thus suggests certain variables and constants at work in certain
identity transitions, such as habits of thought and action and coping mechanisms.

Second, my research also pushes beyond the question of why exiters
leave their communities of origin and, significantly, demonstrates alternative ways of understanding exit narratives—as serving as continuing acts of
exit. This development might be viewed as compatible with larger shifts in
the study of narrative across the social sciences wherein narrative is studied
not only as evidence of change but as an analyzable aspect of change itself.

Additionally, the points of emphasis uncovered as a result of this study might be employed productively to study other populations of exiters, specifically in its threefold focus on the community of origin itself, the meaning and functions of exit narratives, and the lives of exiters after exiting their communities. This concluding chapter summarizes the data and findings presented with particular attention to these contributions.

Chapter 1 introduces the theoretical background on religious exiting in scholarly literature until now and demonstrates how the present study takes advantage of opportunities to build in new directions. Two primary directions are identified. First, people who exit their communities of origin offer important differences from exiters of communities of choice; most of the literature focuses on people who exit NRMs ("cults") that they joined in the first place as adults. The findings from those studies cannot be applied directly to the kinds of exiters this book addresses, and in fact my interviewees offer numerous new conclusions. Second, at *least* regarding exiting from one's community of origin, exiters retain considerable elements of their former religious identities in greater need of understanding, and their connections to their former religious communities offer fertile ground for new inquiry. Research shows that exiting is a long process that does not necessarily have a demarcated end. This realization necessitates greater engagement with exiters who remain somewhere in between, redefining, stretching, and repeatedly traversing various sorts of boundaries, which this book aims to provide.

The period of this "liminality," to borrow Victor Turner's term (1967, 93), is not a brief, temporary state; rather, it comes to define the exiter indefinitely. Therefore, I avoid whenever possible referring to exiters as having *exited* in the past tense; rather, they are continually in the process of *exiting*. This does not mean that they are stymied or unsuccessful. On the contrary, the acceptance of this aspect of their identity and life journey corresponds with an exiter's professional success and social and emotional well-being.

If such an engagement is to be insightful, it naturally requires informed attention to the exiter's life before exiting. The nature of the community of origin, and especially the boundaries it constructs and maintains for itself, relates directly to the exiting process and outcome. Therefore, both in Chapter 1 and more extensively in Chapter 2, I provide a great deal of background on the Lubavitch and Satmar communities. This is the only way to fully understand the data collected from exiters. Chapter 2 addresses various concentric circles of boundaries that Lubavitch and Satmar use to insulate themselves and to prevent insiders from exiting. The data reveal that these boundaries are indeed formidable and in some cases elaborate, but they are also, in some measure, permeable. This permeability is multidirectional. Community members regularly cross boundaries to interact with outsiders for various practical and personal reasons. But more strikingly, an empirical finding that contradicts both scholarly and public assumptions is that nearly all exiters, including from Satmar, maintain some form of relationship with their families. The assumption that Satmar cuts off or even sits shiva as a sign of mourning for exiters is unfounded.

It is impossible to draw causal connections between all of the background and data on the life of an exiter. But correlations are important to find because patterns can then be sought and tested in other, similar communities. There is a strong correlation between exiters maintaining a relationship with their former communities, whether through conversations, visits, or deep emotional and social bonds, and the liminality of the exiters.

Multiple factors inform liminality, and it is unreasonable to assume that any given factor is either necessary or sufficient to lead to liminality. But following Jonathan Z. Smith (1982), assembling the factors present in a polythetic assessment of liminality among exiters leads to a robust understanding of the phenomenon and, moreover, to an understanding of related phenomena. That is to say, if we know that a range of features correlates with liminality, when we find one of them in another population, we will know to look for the other factors we know of and for liminality (which we may or may not find). We can then determine how related various populations of exiters or various kinds of life transitions are to one another.

Thus, for instance, we can begin to understand whether the transformations undergone by transgender individuals, people returning from military to civilian life, or immigrants are of a piece with those of religious exiters. Do they too experience liminality? Helen Rose Fuchs Ebaugh (1988a), for example, deals with a range of transitions—including getting a divorce, retiring from a medical practice, and even graduating from a school—along with religious exiting. But a deeper analysis of the shared and distinct features of the communal structures around which these transitions take place would yield a much richer analysis of them. It may also, with enough different populations examined, allow for an understanding of causal relationships among certain factors and outcomes.

Built into the communal boundaries of Lubavitch and Satmar, as Chapter 2 also shows, are exit narratives that these communities ascribe to their exiters. It is broadly understood among sociologists and historians alike that conflict, rupture, and deviance affect not only the protagonist but also the community in which he or she operates or from which he or she exits. But this has not yet been translated into an interest in the exit narratives of either the exiter or the community suffering the deviance, though Kai T. Erikson (1966) pointed us in that direction decades ago. In turn, the community's narrative about the exiter affects the exiter, his or her own narrative, and the process of exiting itself. Most significantly, analyzing the community's narrative about exiters as a form of exit narrative helps bring into relief the subjective and utilitarian nature of exit narratives generally, which can then be applied to the exit narratives of the exiters themselves.

Chapter 3 analyzes those exit narratives of the exiters. While such narratives have formed the basis of other studies of exiters (most recently, Davidman 2014), the most significant lacuna in such studies has been attention to the function of those narratives in the exit process itself. Instead, scholars have searched those narratives for *why* exiters left (for example, Zuckerman 2012) and how their exiting affected the way they view their lives in retrospect (Davidman 2014). My analysis shows that the exit narrative itself serves to distance exiters from particular aspects of their upbringing from which they sought to disconnect and to cement other aspects of their upbringing as central elements in their new identities, albeit in altered forms. In the case of my Satmar and Lubavitch interviewees, the adoption of an intellectual exit narrative or a social-emotional exit narrative reflected the commitment to one or the other as the true aim or meaning in their community of origin. They sought better versions of those outside Satmar and Lubavitch, but they also remained attached to those aspects of their upbringing by focusing their attention on one or the other of those two broad spheres.

The fact that a battle over narratives emerged from the interviews with no prompting from me shows that exiters are aware that the adoption of one or the other type of narrative is highly significant, as indeed it is. (Naturally, the significance they ascribe to it is different from what emerges in the context of this book's fuller analysis.) Again, one of the main contributions this book makes to the study of exiters and personal transformations is the contention that exit narratives are not to be taken merely as *evidence* of the process but as an integral part of the process itself.

Chapter 4 presents and analyzes the most central evidence of liminality among ultra-Orthodox exiters: the persistence of habits of action and habits of thought from their upbringing into their new lives. The first significant finding is that these habits are not based on decisions the exiters make to retain this or that aspect of their former lives, for instance, one's decision to continue lighting the Sabbath candles every Friday night. Rather, in many cases interviewees were not even conscious of these habits, and it was only through my own analysis of the data in the context of background knowledge of the community that I discerned them. Often my interviewees' level of consciousness of these habits could be described as "tacit knowledge" ("knowing without knowing"; Polanyi [1966] 2009, 237). In other cases, interviewees were aware of them but had no control over these habits (particularly habits of action). These habits, therefore, are not evidence merely of the "new" identities (in the sense of being divorced entirely from the old) that exiters construct, simply using the building blocks of the past. Rather, these habits are concrete evidence of the persistence of the "old" life in the new. More accurately, they show that exiting does not yield a separate, new life at all. It generates a state of liminality, of being in between, in which boundaries are redrawn and continually traversed and identities are poorly defined.

Chapter 5 turns to the various kinds of strategies the vast majority of exiters who are hybrids used to cope with the contradictions liminality created in their lives. These interviewees replaced some aspects and maintain others of their community's goals and means. These strategies include medicating the pain, bonding with other exiters, using social media as an outlet, embracing Israel, pursuing the academic route, abandoning pure categories, and exploring liberal Judaism. They also often made an effort to maintain a relationship with their family that involved two other strategies: engaging in a conspiracy of silence and drawing lines in the sand. Through using these various strategies and managing their liminality, hybrids demonstrate that rather than serve as a hindrance to exiting or a thorn in the side of exiters, liminality should be understood as a healthy phenomenon. Of course, since liminality is not a personal characteristic that one chooses—again, habits of action and thought were unconscious and/or out of the control of exiters—this is not a prescriptive determination, which would in any case be beyond the interests of this book. Rather, the primary significance of this finding from the perspective of this book's contribution to scholarship is that liminality should be explored in other cases of life transformations. It should not be assumed that healthy transitions do not yield liminality.

Again, if more populations are studied with attention to this phenomenon such that it becomes possible to assemble a meaningful polythetical assessment of its features and correlations to other factors, causal connections might finally begin to be drawn.

The methodological contributions of this study are threefold. Understanding the relevant communities of origin, particularly their systems of boundary construction and maintenance and the narratives they construct about their own exiters, informs the entire study. The exiter's experience is not examined in a vacuum. Second, exit narratives are understood to be part and parcel of the exit process itself, subjective and functional in the lives of exiters. While this is widely accepted within qualitative sociology, scholarship on religious exiting and life transformations has not sufficiently incorporated that concept into its analysis of data collected from exiters.

Third, and most significantly, the outcome of exiting the ultra-Orthodox Hasidic Jewish community, this book shows, is not to be simply "out" of that community and to adopt a "new" life. The assumed binary of religious identity—religious or not, part of the community or separate from it—is overturned by the overwhelming evidence of long-term liminality among interviewees. In conclusion, it is my humble hope that these three parts of my study can be replicated in studies of other populations and that dynamic boundaries, exit narratives, and liminality are further plumbed among exiters and other examples of biographical disruptions.

Every study has its limitations, and this one is no different. There are many aspects of the ultra-Orthodox exiter experience that require further attention. It would be most helpful for future research to pay special attention to the family environment of exiters pre-exit. Did exiters generally get along with their family and feel loved and supported by them, or did they suffer chronic abuse, neglect, or dysfunction? This could inform our understanding of the motivations of exiters as well as the kinds of relationships they maintain with their family post-exit.

It would also be beneficial to explore more fully the similarities and differences between exiters whose parents joined the community from the outside (*baal teshuvahs*) and those who were born into it (*frum* from birth). My book already shows that the assumption that parents who joined the community from the outside will necessarily be understanding and sympathetic to their children who want to join the broader society is false. Still, there may be significant ways that the experiences of these two groups of interviewees differ.

It would also be useful to investigate the romantic life of exiters and see what kinds of relationship choices they make and the effects those have on their liminality. Do they tend to date and marry Jews or non-Jews? How do their families respond to these choices? What kinds of decisions do exiters make regarding having children and how many to have? What role do these decisions play in their relationships to family and to organized religion?

And most important, longitudinal studies of exiters need to be conducted. Does time heal the rupture caused by the exit, or does it cause a hardening of differences? Does the passage of time cause exiters to miss some form of engagement with religious life, or does it lead them to feel that they have no need for religion? Only longitudinal studies can address these and similar questions.

Exiting Other Total Institutions

The persistent habits of action and habits of thought that this book describes should make it clear that those who exit religious total institutions grapple for years with the residual effects of the institution they exited. The question remains: To what extent would individuals who exit from other forms of total institutions likewise manifest similar residual effects? This conclusion only begins to address this question, but it can hopefully open doors for further study, both of specific total institutions and of comparisons between them. There are aspects of personal transformation that are shared by all who undergo a transformation, as captured by Ebaugh's (1988a) model of becoming an ex, and there are aspects that are distinct to each particular type of transformation. Here we look at some of the distinct aspects: those who exit the total institution of marriage and get divorced, those who exit prison, and those who immigrate. Again, this discussion is of necessity preliminary and intended only to show the potential usefulness of adopting this framework to the analysis of other types of exit.

Before discussing these individual cases, it is worth mentioning the issue of stigma and its relationship to the exiting process. Not all total institutions are equal. Some may have little or no stigma attached to them in the public mind, while others may have a great deal. The extent to which society attaches stigma to the former identity or to a particular type of transition will perforce influence an exiter's decision regarding how candid to be about his or her exit. This in turn could impact the exiter's ability to move beyond the exiting process and comfortably settle into his or her new identity.

Thus, for those exiting religious total institutions such as ultra-Orthodox Judaism, since there tends to be little or no stigma attached to this transition—on the contrary, such exiters are often viewed by the general public as heroic and idealized—religious exiters are free to openly discuss their former identity and their exit process. Although Nora Rubel (2010) may be correct that non-Orthodox Jews feel anxiety and a sense of inferiority regarding the ultra-Orthodox, it is also true that these feelings are often mixed with admiration and even envy. Certainly, there is tremendous admiration for those who exit from ultra-Orthodoxy. I personally have experienced this on countless social occasions. Given the extremely high rate of divorce, similar conditions of nonstigma pertain to those who get divorced.

In stark contrast, there is tremendous stigma, and potential social and economic repercussions, attached to being formerly incarcerated. As Devah Pager (2007) amply demonstrates, those with criminal records had a much harder time becoming employed than those without one. Thus, those who exit prison have strong incentives to hide their history of incarceration. The case of immigrants may fall somewhere in between such cases in terms of the stigma attached to that identity, depending of course on where the immigrant comes from and the circumstances of the migration.

Divorce

Possibly the most common form of exit from a total institution occurs when a person exits a marriage, since almost half of all American marriages end in divorce. As Stuart Wright (1991) points out, there are many parallels between religious exit and divorce in terms of reluctance to separate, postinvolvement effects such as depression and loneliness, and disassociated states and obsessive review of the events that led to the exit.

Nonetheless, the experience post-exit, specifically the adjustment and rebuilding of one's life after exiting, is quite different. In the case of divorce, the person needs to rebuild and find a new mode of being in the world—but the person getting divorced was once a single adult before getting married and therefore possesses some "materials" to use to build a new identity. Those exiting from a religious total institution in which they were born and lived their entire life have never known another identity outside the community. They do not need to reconnect with a former way of life but to build an entirely new identity. Thus, there is intense pressure to incorporate aspects of their old identity into their new one.

Furthermore, as Diane Vaughan points out regarding those who get divorced, "For some, uncoupling can never be complete. One or both of the partners may not be able to develop a new life that becomes self-validating" (1990, 178). But this is a minority. Most who divorce eventually succeed in finding a way to move forward.

However, there may be aspects of a marriage that persist postmarriage. As Vaughan notes, "Even though people separate, move away, or divorce, visible indications of the bond between partners often remain" (1990, 179). This is seen in continued interaction patterns and similar habits and lifestyles. If the couple had children, that certainly connects the partners after divorce. But even if not, there are points of connection that remain.

Significantly, however, certain things predate their marriage. As Vaughan states regarding how people handle divorce, "Others increase their investment in resources *that have given structure to their lives in the past*" (1990, 161; emphasis added), meaning their past prior to the marriage that ended. Religious exiters born into a community have no such past to go back to. They must build their future from scratch both in the sense of material and social resources and in the sense of understanding the world beyond their current identity. Religious exiters have nothing that predates their exiting and almost nothing (if anything at all) that is unrelated to their religious upbringing.

What conceptual tools developed in this book might be applied to the study of divorce? Scholars of divorce may seek to understand how the habits of thought and action from marriage persist even years after divorce. Do people who are divorced continue to think of themselves as married and have to continuously remind themselves that they are in fact no longer with their original spouse? Do they persist in cooking certain dishes or doing other house chores that their ex-partners preferred? Do they persist in attending certain cultural events that they began at the encouragement of their partners? Do they avoid new sexual encounters out of a sense of loyalty to their former partners? Are certain sorts of marriage more lingering in their effects than others, just as certain religious communities affect exit differently? Assuming any of these patterns exist, what is the level of awareness or tacit awareness of these habits by those who are divorced? What steps do they take to manage these habits? Do they create narratives for their friends and families that incorporate these habits? Do they claim that these habits were always part of "who they were," or do they acknowledge that they are residue of their marriage that they have either willingly embraced or that they now seek to jettison?

Exit from Prison

With several notable exceptions, including Shadd Maruna (2001) and Bruce Western (2018), scholars who research those who were formerly incarcerated tend to focus more on the policy side of reducing recidivism and formal discriminations and increasing access to various types of social services and less on questions of identity, attitudes, and personal narratives. The field of criminology could benefit from research that delves into the personal life of the formerly incarcerated and explores the residual effects of their incarceration.

Thinking about the relationship between religious exit and exit from prison, one important difference is the issue of the time of exit and control over the time of exit. There is a definite departure date for when the incarcerated person exits prison that is based on a set of criteria whose control rests primarily with the controlling institution rather than the incarcerated person.

In stark contrast, religious exit is usually a much more fluid process that can take years to effectuate. Furthermore, depending on the nature of the religious group one is exiting, exiters often have much, and sometime total, control over when they exit (see Wright 1998). In addition, because of the constraints of prison life, although the people incarcerated may think about rebuilding their lives before leaving prison, they may be prevented from taking concrete steps in that direction. In contrast, religious exiters, similar to those initiating divorce (see Vaughn 1990), often prepare for their life post-exit years in advance of exiting.

What tools from this book might be most effectively applied to prisoner reentry? For those who were formerly incarcerated, does integrating aspects of their prison life into their post-prison life put them in a better position to make a healthy transition than those who try to start from scratch? In what ways does the intense stigmatization of the formerly incarcerated make it that much more difficult for them to disassociate themselves from the label "felon"? Given that it is often a stipulation of probation that the formerly incarcerated not associate with known felons and those engaged in criminal activity, to what extent do the formerly incarcerated maintain connections with people they knew before prison or whom they met in prison, and do such connections help or hinder their reentry into society? Do the formerly incarcerated struggle with habits of action they learned while in prison, such as hypervigilance regarding their personal space and the perception of threat to them? Michelle Alexander (2010) notes that there is often silence within the African American community regarding family or community members who are incarcerated. What effects does this silence have on the prospects for reentry for the formerly incarcerated?

Immigration

The best analogy to religious exit may be the experience of immigrants in their new environments. They leave the environment they have known their whole life, possibly with few resources to start anew, and retain various things from their former life, such as their accents, mannerisms, food preferences, and cultural sensibilities. Like immigrants, religious exiters may be forced to deal with internal barriers and constraints, overcoming years of religious socialization, as we observe with many of the interviewees in this book who struggled with embracing gender equality and religious pluralism.

One difference between immigrants and religious exiters, however, is a set of external constraints that may await immigrants. Immigrants to America—especially since 1965 when the demographics of the immigrants changed, with the majority now coming from the Caribbean, Latin America, and Asia instead of Europe—may be forced to deal with widespread prejudice and even violence (see Sobczak 2010).

This widespread prejudice thrives on a racist myth that the current wave of immigrants is inferior to the massive wave of European immigrants who arrived at Ellis Island in the early twentieth century. However, as Nancy Foner (2000) notes, many immigrant children today do better in school than those of the earlier immigration wave, and the current immigrants are as prepared, and sometimes even more prepared, for the job market as the previous immigrants were. This prejudice against immigrants can make it difficult for them to find a job or access housing.

Another difference between immigrants and religious exiters is that many immigrants today maintain close connections to their family and country of origin, sending back money, visiting, and remaining in touch with its culture. Scholars often use the term "transnationalism" to refer to families (and whole diasporas) that straddle multiple countries and cultures (see Schiller, Basch, and Blanc-Szanton 1992), and Foner (2000) argues that although the phenomenon of transnational families has intensified in recent decades, the basic arrangement flourished even among immigrants to America a hundred years ago. In fact, according to Ewa Morawska (2007), it is possible that transnationalism may actually assist certain immigrant communities with assimilation into broader American society by giving them an initial cultural, social, and economic base in America on which to build. In stark contrast, religious exiters may be prevented from visiting their families or may face hostile receptions when they do.

Scholars of immigration can investigate how immigrants view the trade-off between integration into their new country and maintenance of needed social structures and ties from their country of origin. How do immigrants determine which habits of action and thought to maintain and which to discard? What narratives do they develop to justify these decisions? How does their country of origin shape the degree to which their first identity is mutable in the transition? How do immigrants compare their journeys with those of others going through the same process? Do they think they are doing a better job, and if so, why?

Directions

When people choose to distance themselves from the religious community of their birth, they cross a boundary, often physical, always emotional and social, and sometimes deeply psychological. While it has often been understood among sociologists that this boundary crossing can be fraught and complex, an assumption persists that people who make the decision to cross the boundary can and will ultimately do so in a complete, clearly identifiable way. That is, communal affiliation has usually been assumed to be binary: One is either an insider or an outsider.

This book focuses on individuals who chose to distance themselves from the religious community of their birth and demonstrates how despite many successful efforts to separate themselves from that community, their boundary crossing was never complete. The persistence of their religious identity, trained bodily responses to communal taboos, denigration of outsiders to the community, attitudes toward the community's leader and protectiveness of the community's public image, and even some spiritual beliefs and practices of the community all defy a binary characterization of their relationship to the community.

For my interviewees, distancing themselves from their community to become members of general society involved a complex form of identity transformation and boundary crossing and revealed strategies of gradual distancing from their community while simultaneously remaining connected to it. These insights highlight the profound effect socialization has on each of us and the extent to which the cultural norms and behavioral patterns we internalize throughout our upbringing stubbornly persist throughout life, even when conscious efforts are undertaken to push beyond them.

As Americans and cultural descendants of the Enlightenment, with its focus on the power of reason to shape human behavior, we would like to believe that if we put our minds to something and decide to change our lives, we can do so. Our culture tells us that everything is a choice in our own hands, and mind can be exerted over matter. This book's findings should temper our estimation of the freedom we have to change ourselves.

Appendix A

Three Structural Factors That Enable Exiting

How do people exit the community in which they were raised? According to Helen Rose Fuchs Ebaugh (1988a), there are four basic stages to all exiting processes, including exiting a religion: first doubts, seeking alternatives, the turning point, and creating the ex-role.[1] Lynn Davidman (2014), who essentially follows Ebaugh's model and applies it to individuals exiting ultra-Orthodox Judaism, describes the four stages thus: tears in the sacred canopy, first transgressions, passing, and stepping out. The details of the stages of the exit process itself were not the focus of this study since they had been explored in previous scholarship (e.g., Wright 1987; Ebaugh 1988a; Jacobs 1989; Davidman 2014).

This study focuses instead largely on the lives of exiters post-exit. Nonetheless, to provide the reader with a more complete picture of the exiting phenomenon, I briefly describe three structural factors that enable exiters to exit, which are in line with the literature on the subject: physical separation from the community, access to outside information, and support from the outside.

---

1. Although generally the experiences of ultra-Orthodox exiters are similar to those of other types of exiters described by Ebaugh, there is a significant difference during the stage of seeking alternatives. Ebaugh emphasizes that in this stage exiters consciously evaluate their current role by comparing it to specific other potential roles they may adopt instead. Although ultra-Orthodox exiters certainly go through a stage (potentially very long and exhaustive) of evaluating their current role, given their lack of information about the outside world, it is less a comparative analysis between their current role and other roles and more an internal comparison between the positive and negative aspects of their current role. Ebaugh assumes that all agents have access to information about other potential roles and does not entertain the possibility that one of the features of the institution from which actors may seek to exit is precisely that it prevents them from accessing such information.

PHYSICAL SEPARATION FROM THE COMMUNITY

Although this was not the case for all, many interviewees reported that a period of time when they were physically separated from their community was crucial to their exiting process. For some Lubavitchers, their traveling for Lubavitch outreach activities provided them this opportunity. For Satmars, and for some Lubavitchers, spending time in Israel at a yeshiva or seminary for a year or two provided them this opportunity. Still others took advantage of tourist trips they managed to arrange.

The physical separation from their community has two possible functions. For some this allows them to travel and become exposed to people from various backgrounds to learn about the world. This could lead people to question their own upbringing and its assumptions. Mordy was powerfully affected by people he encountered during outreach activities:

> I was sent by Lubavitch headquarters to Wyoming for a summer to do outreach work. While there, I met this woman who was . . . being sort of pantheistic and being a little incredulous that God would talk to Moses and dictate a book. This was very difficult for me because I was trying to give her all the right answers, but what she was saying was so appealing to me. It was so appealing to my heretical side, but my religious side was scrambling so hard to come up with answers. And when we left, she thanked us and said it was so enlightening and such a wonderful conversation. We really made her think and opened up her mind. And I was saying, "Yes, same here!"

As the experience of Mordy illustrates, for some Lubavitchers, the people they meet while they are doing outreach work can have a huge effect on their own religious outlook and thinking. Others are affected by their travels to Israel. Zev, a Satmar interviewee in his late twenties, was powerfully affected by his travels in Israel and the people he met there:

> I used to go to a certain person's house in Jerusalem very often. This guy had an open house, and anyone could come for Shabbos, Jews and non-Jews. Everyone was welcome to come and experience what a Shabbos was. He had the idea of being nonjudgmental. I have no idea how I got into this guy. I do not remember that. He, his house, had a major impact on me. I had long discussions with people from all around the world. There were regulars who would come week after week, so I would talk to them and get to know them. There were a lot of scholars who came by for Shabbos. It was a very very open house.

I asked Zev how long he visited this open house, and he responded:

> I don't remember if it was a year, but I used to go a lot—months for sure. Whenever I was in Jerusalem, I would go for the meal Friday night or the meal Shabbos day, or I used to go over Friday night after the meal just to schmooze. Everyone had a chance to stand up and give their *drusha*, their speech. Once someone got up and started speaking about Jesus, and people started booing. So the host said, "Let him finish. Two minutes." Then the host got up and ex-

plained that what the person said was his opinion and that it was okay for everyone to share their opinions in a respectful way. In other words, the host was showing how everyone should respect and accept other's views. . . . There were all kinds of activists coming by. . . . The walks of life, the experiences I had there, I think you rarely find a place like that. . . . When you're looking for an answer about Africa, here's the guy from Africa—ask him! What more do you need? So going to this house was a really amazing experience.

Other interviewees already had ideas about how they wanted to change their lives or their appearance and simply needed time away from the community to feel safe to go ahead with their plans. An extreme example of this was the case of Ariel, who used the time on the plane away from Brooklyn to do a personal makeover:

I never had a big beard; I never let it grow big. I used to "pick" it out by hand since I learned that there was a rabbi that said that this was permitted [rather than shaving with a shaver]. But I had a beard, and I kept it the whole time I lived in Crown Heights. I took a trip for a summer to Greece. That was like my official, "I'm going to a place where nobody knows who I am," to do my own thing. I was in my early twenties. I took a plane from JFK to London and from London to Athens. On the plane to London, I went into the bathroom and just shaved off my whole beard. Yep.

I asked Ariel why he did not shave his beard before he left. He replied, "Because I was still living in Crown Heights, and I didn't want to be—I was still, whatever. . . . I didn't want to be the guy [pauses], but I knew that when I come back, this was going to be it; I'm done. When I came back, I think I went home and then I moved right away to Manhattan."

It is clear that Ariel felt uncomfortable shaving his beard as long as he lived in Crown Heights surrounded by Lubavitchers who knew him and his family. However, knowing that he would be in Greece for the summer removed from other Lubavitchers with time to prepare mentally for coming back home without a beard, he felt safe to go ahead and shave it off. Similarly, physical separation from their community allowed others the necessary space to experiment with altering their appearance to match where they considered themselves to be both religiously and emotionally.

ACCESS TO OUTSIDE INFORMATION

Given that most of the religious schools that interviewees attended provided them with little or no secular studies and that many of their parents prevented them from reading such materials at home, a key place to access this information was public libraries. These libraries provide the curious exiter with books on many different subjects—such as evolution, atheism, and sex, as well as critical academic studies of Judaism—which were strictly forbidden inside his or her community.

Thus, for many exiters libraries became places of refuge where they could explore these unknown worlds. In addition, libraries had computers with internet access, and for some interviewees whose communities outlawed the use of the internet, these computers were the only means of connecting with other exiters online. The books and the internet that libraries provide often had a huge impact on exiters' lives, causing them to question many of the assumptions and principles of their community.

Mendy was deeply affected by visiting libraries:

> When I was in high school, I started to go to the Brooklyn Public Library intensively. I started to take out books generally about Jewish things. One of the reasons I went to the library was to look at anatomy books to teach myself about sex ed. I didn't have any sex ed from school, so I was trying to teach myself about sex. I was trying to figure out how things worked. I never took out any of these books. . . . The library that probably had the biggest effect on me was the Jewish Theological Seminary library in Manhattan. It opened up a whole world of Jewish scholarship to me. I had access to two hundred thousand books at my fingertips.

Mendy went on to explain that the books he read at these libraries helped him contextualize the theological beliefs of his community:

> Reading some of these books put Lubavitch, the world that I was growing up in, into context. It helped me understand how Lubavitch came about. You come to realize, not only was Lubavitch not always around, but Hasidim in general were not always around. I came to realize that a lot of the historical criticisms of the Hasidic movement were still warranted. . . . Eventually I read books about Jewish false messiahs that helped me understand that the messiah craze that was sweeping Lubavitch at that time may be part of a larger trend within Judaism. It helped me start to question basic assumptions within Lubavitch at that time. . . . Later on, wherever I would travel around the world when attending various Lubavitch yeshivas, I would always have access to public and private Jewish libraries to further my personal exploration.

To take advantage of public libraries, it is necessary for exiters to learn how to read English. Most, if not all, Lubavitch interviewees know English by the time they start exiting the community. Some of the males learned English from sisters who learned it inside the community. Others learned it in after-school classes in the community or from private tutors. And others learned it from a secular relative or some other outsider who was willing to assist them. Many Satmar interviewees, using one of the methods just described, master at least the rudiments of English by the time they start exiting. For some, beginning to exit the community also corresponds to the time they begin to learn to read English, thus significantly compounding the challenges all exiters face on exit.

SUPPORT FROM THE OUTSIDE

A key factor that enables exiters to begin to exit their community is having support from someone on the outside. This person could provide emotional, financial, or educational support or may provide some kind of support with finding housing. This outside supporter could be a relative, especially in the case of Lubavitch exiters whose parents joined the community as adults and thus have many non-Lubavitch or even nonreligious relatives on the outside. This support could also be friends or organizations such as Footsteps who are willing to help.

Mendy, whose parents joined Lubavitch as adults, had many relatives on the outside and received several kinds of support from some of them:

> I had a great-aunt who was not religious at all, and she was always encouraging me to do what I want. She would always say that I should go out of the community and get a secular education. She was probably the most important relative in the early stages of my leaving. It wasn't so much financial, but she also did support me financially, allowing me to go to college. It wasn't a lot of money, but at that time I didn't have much money, and it was crucial. Another relative who had a big effect was my grandmother. She was always bitter that my father joined the Lubavitch community as an adult, so my grandmother looked at me as a "correction" because I was coming back "home"; I was rejecting Lubavitch and becoming more secular. She took a lot of pride in what I was doing.

Mendy went on to describe how his grandmother in particular had a huge effect on him:

> When I would visit her when I was in elementary school, she would teach me math. This was the only secular education I was getting at that time. So in a sense she planted the seeds of my interest in secular education. Later on, when I was in my early twenties, she allowed me to come live with her and let me stay with her rent-free. This allowed me to focus on my college education without the need to hold down a job at that time. She was also a very knowledgeable person, and I was able to discuss with her whatever books I was reading, whatever lectures I was attending, and whatever classical films I was watching. She became a sort of mentor to me. She had a huge effect on my thinking.

Although the particular psychological dynamics of each family may differ, having a relative on the outside who can act as a role model, a source of financial and emotional support, and a font of secular knowledge and practical advice is crucial in enabling individuals to exit. For those who do not have such relatives, friends or organizations such as Footsteps can serve a similar function. Although several exiters may have taken the initial stages alone, for the most part they tended to have some kind of support from the outside.

Appendix B

Demographics and Method of Study

DEMOGRAPHICS

The basic inclusion criterion for both my Lubavitch and Satmar interviewees was that the individuals were born and raised in one of these two communities but no longer live an ultra-Orthodox lifestyle. In practice, no longer living an ultra-Orthodox lifestyle requires more than privately doubting the principles of the faith or secretly diminishing levels of religious observance. It requires some visible act of rejecting the norms of the community.

To use Erving Goffman's language, this study focuses on "discredited" rather than "discreditable" individuals (1963, 41–42). For the men, this could include cutting their religiously mandated beards or refusing to wear the mandated head covering (the yarmulke); for the women, this could include wearing pants (rather than skirts) and low-cut tops. For the women who were already married prior to exiting, this could also include refusing to wear the community-mandated *sheitel*.

According to the evidence from the General Social Survey, the largest demographic study of American attitudes and public opinion, the process of leaving a religion typically takes place before age thirty (Streib et al. 2009). Therefore, I chose to interview exiters between the ages of eighteen and forty who were not too far removed from their previous lives and identities to recall their experiences and to recount the process of exiting.[1]

I interviewed thirty-nine Lubavitchers, twenty-four Satmars, and eleven members from other Hungarian Hasidic communities that share very similar dress, religious intensity, and, most important for this study, communal response to religious deviance

---

1. To shed some light on historical changes regarding the Satmar community's response to exiters, I also interviewed three Satmars who were older than forty. These three were ages forty-four, fifty-five, and sixty-five. I also interviewed the parents of a Satmar exiter who were in their sixties.

with the Satmar community (which also has Hungarian roots). All the "Satmar-like" interviewees come from sects that are historically linked to Satmar, such as Kasho, and they live among the Satmar community. These exiters self-identified at first explicitly as Satmar (which is how they were admitted into the study in the first place). They all share the basic characteristics of Satmar today. Therefore, they are grouped in the same category as Satmar for the purposes of this study.

I interviewed twenty-two Lubavitch men and seventeen Lubavitch women; seventeen Satmar men and seven Satmar women; and five Satmar-like men and six Satmar-like women. The total gender breakdown, in other words, is forty-four men and thirty women, or 60 percent male. Since there are no large quantitative academic studies available on Hasidic exiters, it is extremely difficult to determine if there is a gender differential among exiters.[2] My sample is slightly skewed toward men because I had many more male than female contacts in the Lubavitch community. In addition, it is likely that for both communities men were probably more comfortable than women with being interviewed by a male interviewer.

There is, however, a perception among the exiters that there were many more male exiters than female ones. This was expressed by one Satmar female, who ended the interview by saying, "Good luck finding another girl who left Satmar!" She was convinced that there were many Satmar male exiters but that she was the only female. I managed to find thirteen. Interestingly, the Footsteps membership data also show more males than females. Specifically, of the 134 new Footsteps members in 2018, 55 percent were male, 43 percent were female, and 2 percent were gender nonconforming/questioning (Footsteps 2018). However, this again is likely due more to the reticence of some female exiters to join a group they know little about than an actual gender differential among exiters.

According to Mark Trencher's (2016) study of more than six hundred ultra-Orthodox OTDs, within the category "Chasidic" (excluding Chabad), he found that 60 percent were male, 38 percent female, and 2 percent trans or other; and within the category "Chabad," 47 percent were male, 51 percent female, and 2 percent trans or other. These numbers certainly do not support the claim that most of the OTDs are men. Despite the slightly larger number of men than women in my study, this was a fairly balanced sample in terms of gender.

In terms of exiters' sexual orientation, two identified as gay, three as lesbian, two as queer, and one as bisexual. The remaining sixty-six identified as straight. Forty-eight were single, seven were married, and nineteen were divorced. Seventeen had children, most of them born within the ultra-Orthodox community.

Twenty-three interviewees, all Lubavitchers, had at least one parent who joined the ultra-Orthodox community as adults. However, even among the thirty-eight Lubavitch interviewees, a significant proportion had parents who were members of their community from birth. All of the parents of Satmar interviewees, with the exception of one case, were members of their community from birth.

A small portion of interviewees, mostly Lubavitchers, continue to reside in the same Hasidic community in which they were raised. The rest live mostly in neighboring communities that consist of other less Orthodox Jews or non-Jews. Several also live in large metropolitan cities far away from where they were raised.

---

2. Hella Winston (2006) also had significantly more men in her study than women but was not convinced that this indicated that there were more male exiters in general.

METHOD OF STUDY

The interview questions were structured to provide comparable information about each individual while being flexible enough to incorporate new questions as the project progressed and allow for the interviewee's idiosyncratic perspectives and experiences. The interview consisted of questions that tap each respondent's level of religious observance, belief, and identification while inside the community as well as the individual's current attitudes and opinions and current relationship to family and community. The interview employed questions designed to uncover both change and continuity among all respondents, which in turn made it possible to locate the structural and cultural forces that both bind people to the community and loosen those ties.

Beyond collecting basic demographic data on each interviewee, the questions are designed to address embeddedness, exiting, and current location. To what extent were the individuals embedded in their religious community of birth? To what extent did their formal education, family life, and personal behavior conform to religious rules? What is the nature of their exiting from their religious upbringing? What form did the exiting take, and when did it begin? What was occurring during this period in their family and community? How do they make sense of their transformation? What is their current location religiously, socially, philosophically, behaviorally, and politically, and where do they see themselves headed? What is their current relationship to their family and community of birth?

The first twenty individuals were interviewed using one interview protocol that consisted of seventy-three detailed questions. The remaining fifty-four were interviewed with a somewhat different format, inspired by Irving Seidman (1998). This format was much more open-ended and included only six broad questions with prompts for the interviewer to ensure that certain basic topics were covered (see Appendix C for the text of both protocols). Although the second protocols included an emphasis on the punitive response of the community to exiters and a section on the exiters' views on several topics such as race, gender, and current events, for the most part both protocols covered the same material, just in different ways.

The initial plan was to ask interviewees detailed questions about exiting and what was going on in their life during that time to match their exiting trajectory with other life developments. Yet interviewees tended to have a difficult time remembering with any certainty when they reached particular milestones in their exiting trajectory: "I can't remember exactly when I stopped eating kosher." So I developed the more open-ended questions that allowed individuals to recount their exit experience in a way that made sense to them.

Since Lubavitch communities dot North America, it was beneficial to interview members from various Lubavitch locations to determine if there are regional differences that affect the exiting process. Even though I conducted face-to-face interviews in the New York metropolitan area, it was still possible to include Lubavitchers from various communities, since many visit New York to see extended family members and attend Lubavitch social and religious functions. My location in the New York metropolitan area proved ideal for interviewing Satmars, given that it put me in close proximity to the two largest groups of Satmar members, those in Williamsburg in Brooklyn and those in Kiryas Joel (Monroe) in Orange County, New York. Furthermore, although I am studying Lubavitch and Satmar exiters, many of them still live near where they were raised, either in those communities themselves or in neighboring communities that are now becoming gentrified.

I also conducted eighteen of the interviews using Skype. This allowed numerous people who live in the New York City area but who were too busy to meet in person to participate in the study. It also allowed several people who live in other cities or other states to participate, which contributed geographical diversity to the study. All the interviews, including those on Skype, were recorded with the interviewees' permission. The face-to-face interviews were usually conducted in my office, at the interviewee's home, or another location of the interviewee's choosing, such as a local café. The interviews lasted between two and four and a half hours, depending on the time constraints of the interviewee. Most interviews lasted approximately two and a half hours.

My recruitment technique for the Lubavitch and Satmar sample began with personal contacts in these communities to find individuals to interview. I then used a snowball technique to enlarge my sample. I also contacted Footsteps to ask the organization to send out a flyer publicizing my study. Twenty-four individuals contacted me as a result of the Footsteps flyer and then joined the study. In the end, many of the Lubavitch interviewees and almost all of the Satmar ones were people I had not known prior to beginning the study.

The interviews explored how community institutions function and the interviewees' diverse and potentially unexpected responses to these institutions. By learning how individuals experienced their own yeshivas' and seminaries' responses to religious divergences, for example, and comparing this information to that gathered from other interviewees, I created a composite picture of how Lubavitch and Satmar institutions respond to individuality and nonconformity. Furthermore, in an effort to present the "lived religion" (Hall 1997) of the Hasidic community rather than merely the official perspective of the community leaders, in addition to official texts and statements of the leadership and the data derived from the interviews, I include comments from internet forums and other popular cultural sources to give a sense of the culture of the communities being explored.

Since it is helpful to know how interviewees' parents and family respond to their decision to exit, aside from the one set of parents of a Satmar exiter who agreed to be interviewed, I gathered this kind of information by asking interviewees about their parents' and families' responses to their exiting. This is a means of including the reaction of exiters' families without interviewing them directly, a process that most families would not consent to.

The interview process strove to put interviewees at ease and encouraged them to use whatever words or phrases from Hebrew, Aramaic (the language of the Talmud), and Yiddish that felt comfortable to them. I wanted them to speak freely and not translate their thoughts for me. Foreign-language words and phrases were transliterated based on the speaker's usage, and contextual explanations are provided.

Because of the open-ended nature of the interview questions, readers cannot read too much into the fact that only a few individuals mentioned a particular theme or piece of information. It is entirely possible that had they been asked directly about that issue, they would have agreed that it applies to them as well. I refrained from such direct questions to prevent interviewees from simply agreeing with me out of a sense that that was the "correct" answer I was looking for. The upshot is that sometimes only a few interviewees mentioned a particular idea that I believe is in fact quite prevalent.

I have therefore not given the exact number of interviewees who stated a particular idea. Instead, I have used more general language to indicate how common that particular response was. Thus, I am not arguing that all interviewees have the same response to their community and that they all raised the same issues in the interviews. Rather, various individuals raised various issues that when taken together form a pattern of response. It is useful to think of Jonathan Z. Smith's (1982) concept of a polythetic classification system where no one factor is necessary to be present but where a combination of factors indicates inclusion in the category.

Although interviewees show visible signs of deviance from the norms of their original communities, this does not mean that their community is completely aware of their precise religious status. For example, men who shave their beard but wear a yarmulke while in public in their community are often believed to be "Modern Orthodox," a loose category that means something to the effect that although they are no longer strictly ultra-Orthodox, they are still bound by traditional Jewish law.

Many interviewees are not particularly eager to disabuse this false impression within their community for fear of the possible consequences. For those with strong familial or communal connections inside their communities, the penalty for their secret being exposed can be severe. Those who still work inside their communities fear that their employment may be summarily discontinued. The majority who operate largely outside the community may still fear that exposure will suddenly cost them old friendships and that they will now be treated differently by their erstwhile friends and community members. They may also fear that this exposure will prove painful for their family or that it may hurt the marriage prospects for the rest of their family members who remain in their communities.

For these reasons, those in this predicament tend to be very cautious about sharing information regarding their personal religious views and practices. This caution can have a profound effect on individuals' willingness to participate in a research project on this topic and their willingness to divulge personal information once in such a study. Although this caution did cause several individuals to refuse to participate, the primary way that it manifested was that potential interviewees needed to be continuously assured during the initial phone conversation of the anonymous nature of the study and that their identity would be assiduously protected. Once they were assured of this, most of those who called were willing to participate. The fact that I had grown up in an ultra-Orthodox community myself and am no longer Orthodox comforted them, because it meant that I was fully aware of the risks involved in their participation and that I would do all that was possible to keep their identity confidential.

As Seidman argues, "The extent to which the interviewer needs to resort to disguise is in direct relation to how vulnerable the person might be if identified" (1998, 105). Thus, given the possible dangers to my interviewees should their identity be exposed, and given the extremely close-knit nature of Hasidic communities where even minor biographical details can be used to discover who the interviewees are, it was necessary to take extreme caution to protect them. In addition to changing their names, I altered all personal identifiers from the record. However, such changes in no way alter the basic meaning of the individuals' statements. I have also occasionally altered the grammar and style of the transcripts from the interviews to clarify the interviewees' statements. This is in accordance with Seidman (1998), who permits such alterations as long as the main goal is to preserve the dignity of the interviewees and make it easier to understand their statements.

A word is in order about the veracity of the accounts of religious exiters. As Daniel Carson Johnson notes, "Apostasy accounts are essentially autobiographies, and autobiographies are never perfect works of non-fiction" (1998, 118). Indeed, this concern exists in all research based on self-reporting. However, the purpose of this study is not to determine the objective facts of the participants' lives but their subjective narrative and the ways they view their lives and their relationships to their communities.

My technique for analyzing the data used a grounded theory approach and looked at what was said by the various interviewees, trying to find similarities and differences, especially between the Satmar and Lubavitch exiters. I spent countless hours looking for patterns as I listened to the audio recordings of the interviews and read the transcripts of the interviews. Many of the insights were simply things that jumped out at me and were not at all expected. This is especially the case regarding the issue of how Satmar families respond to their children's deviance, which contradicted the assumptions of the literature.

Appendix C

Interview Protocols

FIRST-INTERVIEW PROTOCOLS

Demographic Information

    0. Gender of interviewee

    1. Where were you raised?

    2. How old are you now?

    3. What is your marital status?

    4. Are your parents still married to each other?

    5. What do your parents do for a living?

    6. How many siblings do you have?

    7. Where are you in the birth order?

    8. How would you describe your religious background growing up?

    9. Were your parents raised in the same religious community as you?

    10. If not, how were they raised?

    11. Which elementary school, high school, and yeshiva/seminary/college did you attend?

    12. Are you employed now, and how did you get this job?

Before continuing with further detailed interview questions, please briefly describe all the stages of your religious life that were significant to your development in terms of your relationship to your community of birth.

The Community

    13. Thinking as far back as you can remember, how would you describe your community?

    14. Thinking as far back as you can remember, how did you feel about attending religious schools?

    15. How did you feel toward the rituals and customs in your community?

16. Was there a general agreement between your parents, teachers, and the community leadership in terms of your expected level of religious observance?
17. (*for female interviewees*) In thinking about your intellectual curiosity and development, would you say that it was encouraged or discouraged by Orthodox culture and its authorities?
18. Do you think that your community placed religious restrictions on your activities or behaviors (such as prohibiting TV viewing, the reading of "secular" books or newspapers, the prohibition on eating only kosher food)?
19. If yes, how did you feel about this?

The Outside World

20. How did your teachers, parents, and friends describe secular American culture?
21. Did you feel that there was an attempt on the part of the leadership of your community to insulate you from the "outside" secular world?
22. If yes, how did your community try to do this?
23. Do you feel that such efforts were successful?
24. If yes, how so, and if no, why not?
25. While in the community, did you access knowledge of the outside world (e.g., books, movies, and internet)?
26. When did you learn to read English?
27. How old were you when you went to a public library for the first time?
28. When did you watch your first popular American film, and do you remember what it was?
29. How old were you when you started to date?

Doubts

30. Growing up in the community, did you ever feel that there were aspects of your community that you disagreed with or that you hoped were different?
31. If yes, what were they?
32. How old were you when you first had this feeling?
33. At the time, how did you respond to those feelings (e.g., did you feel that it was permissible to have such thoughts or that it was sinful even to think such things privately)?
34. Did you feel that you were alone in thinking such thoughts, or did you know others who had similar thoughts?
35. What effect, if any, did these feelings have on your general attitude toward the community?
36. Did you ever feel that you no longer "belonged" in the community?
37. Did you ever feel like you wanted to distance yourself from the community?
38. If yes, when did you start to think about this?
39. At the time, what did you feel was wrong with the community (was it cultural, theological, philosophical, psychological, political, familial, sexual)?
40. At that time, what did it mean to you to "separate yourself" from the community (e.g., to simply move away geographically, to stop dressing according to community guidelines, to stop following Jewish law)?

41. When considering whether to distance yourself from the community, were there any particular factors that caused you to hesitate (e.g., the loss of your family, friends, or community)?
42. Were there any particular individuals who influenced your religious life, either to stay in the community or to leave it?
43. What was going on in your life while you were thinking about distancing yourself from the community?
44. Was there a time when you "passed" between both the religious and secular worlds?
45. If yes, how long did that last, and how did it make you feel?

Self-Transformation

46. How would you describe your current religious status?
47. Would you say that you have left the religious community in which you were raised (e.g., would you still consider yourself a Hasidic Jew)?
48. If no, what does it mean to you to still be a part of the community?
49. If yes, what is different about your life now that you have left (e.g., do you no longer keep certain parts of or all of Jewish law)?
50. Would you marry a non-Jewish person?
51. Would you marry a non-Orthodox person?
52. Has your self-transformation changed your relationship with your family?
53. Has it changed your relationship with your friends (e.g., do you now have a new group of friends)?
54. Has this transformation affected your general outlook on life (e.g., your political or philosophical perspectives)?
55. How do you view your act of self-transformation (e.g., are you proud or ashamed of what you have done)?

Adaptation to the "Outside" World

56. Are there any aspects of Orthodox culture that you felt you needed to unlearn or new things you felt you needed to learn to integrate yourself in the broader American culture?
57. Do you find nonobservant life easier or more comfortable to you than your former life?
58. Have you ever struggled with "too much freedom" since leaving the community?
59. Do you feel like people in the outside world could relate to your experiences?
60. What was your biggest surprise in the process of transformation?

Current Relationship to the Community

61. How do you feel toward the community of your birth (e.g., do you feel anger, hate, love, pity, indifference)?
62. How do you feel toward the religious leaders (or leader) of the community?
63. Do you ever find yourself "defending" the community to outsiders even though you strongly disagree with the community?
64. If yes, why do you think this is the case?

65. Do you ever go back to visit?

66. How likely do you think it is that you would one day return to the community and reaccept the strictures and practices of the community?

Reflections

67. Why do you think that you decided to transform your life?

68. Were there other members of your family or close friends who were making similar decisions?

69. Do you have any regrets with regard to your self-transformation or wish you had made a different decision?

70. Do you think that those ultra-Orthodox individuals who transformed themselves were less embedded in the community in the first place?

71. How embedded in the community do you think you were?

72. Do you think that the likelihood of people transforming themselves is directly related to the mental and emotional connection they have with their parents?

73. Is there anything I have not covered that you would like to tell me before we conclude the interview?

SECOND-INTERVIEW PROTOCOLS

State gender, age, marital status, and former religious affiliation.

What does it mean to you to be OTD (off the *derech*, off the path)?

What did it look like for you to be on the *derech* (path), and how is it different from being off it? (How integrated into the ultra-Orthodox community were you? Were your parents raised in the community you were raised in? Did you finish the educational system of your community?)

What was the journey that led you to this point? (When did you start to feel discontent in your community? How did you make the transition? Were there inside/outside influences of note? During the transition process, did you know other OTDs? Are there aspects of the broader American society that you found [or still find] difficult to deal with? Was there anything that caused you to hesitate to transition away from ultra-Orthodoxy?)

How did the community you were raised in respond to your lifestyle changes? (What punitive measures, if any, were taken against you or your family? Did your religious transformation affect your access to your children?)

Now that you are "OTD," what does your life look like today? (What is your current religious, political, and philosophical situation? Where do you live? What relationship do you have to your family, former friends, and old community? What do you want your children's relationship to be to Judaism and to the community in which you were raised? Did you need to unlearn things from your past or learn new things to integrate yourself into broader American society? Have you changed your name, or do you sometimes use a different name from the one you used inside the community? Do you still consider yourself a member of your original community? What aspects of your upbringing remain with you?)

What is the response of your new environment to you? (How integrated are you into mainstream society? What do you think about affirmative action, Israeli/Palestinian conflict, the BDS movement, the LGBTQ community, Liberal Judaism, female rabbis, and gender roles? Was there anything that surprised you about your transition process?)

Is there anything I have not covered that you would like to tell me before we conclude the interview?

Glossary

Amalek: The nation in the Bible that tried to destroy the ancient Israelites and that is believed to be the source and model of all future anti-Semites.

Ashkenazi: Jews of Central and Eastern European descent.

baal teshuva: A non-Orthodox Jew who joins an Orthodox or ultra-Orthodox community.

bocher (singular; plural, *bocherim*): A yeshiva student.

Chabad: A transliteration of the Hebrew acronym for *chochmah, binah, da'at*, meaning "wisdom, understanding, and knowledge," describing core values of the Lubavitch community and often used as a synonym for Lubavitch.

cholent: A meat, potato, and bean stew traditionally eaten on Saturday afternoon among Eastern European Jews.

Crown Heights: A neighborhood in Brooklyn, New York, that has served as the headquarters of the Lubavitch Hasidic community since 1940.

farbrengen: A common Lubavitch term to describe a devotional communal gathering.

frai: A Yiddish word with negative connotations derived from German, meaning "free," often used by the ultra-Orthodox to describe people who leave the ultra-Orthodox community.

frum: A Yiddish word meaning "religious," "pious," "Orthodox," or "ultra-Orthodox," depending on the context.

goy (singular; plural, goyim): Literally, someone of a different nation, a non-Jew; often used as a derogatory term in the Hasidic community.

Hanukkah: A Jewish festival, a key feature of which is lighting of menorahs, commemorating the rededication of the second Temple in Jerusalem in 165 B.C.E.

haredi: A Hebrew word that literally means "those who tremble" (referring to Isaiah 66:5, "those who tremble before God"); commonly used as a synonym for the ultra-Orthodox.

Hashem: A Hebrew appellation for God (literally, "the Name").

Hasidic: A way of life that combines strict observance of Orthodox Jewish law (*halacha*) while also maintaining distinct beliefs and rituals, especially the reverence for a leader called a "rebbe" who is believed to possess great spiritual powers.

Haskalah: The Jewish Enlightenment, a movement begun in late seventeenth-century Europe, that sought to modernize and rationalize Judaism while preserving its distinct characteristics.

haymishe: Homey, describing a warm and comfortable environment.

Kiryas Joel (or Yoel): A village in Monroe, New York, that has served as a center for Satmar Hasidim since 1974.

kosher (noun, *kashrut* or *kashrus*): Referring to the laws and practices pertaining to Jewish dietary restrictions.

kugel: A baked pudding often made with noodles or potatoes and traditionally eaten by Eastern European Jews on the Sabbath and Jewish holidays.

Lubavitch: A Hasidic sect founded in the late eighteenth century by Rabbi Schneur Zalman of Liadi, which for over a century was based in the town of Lyubavichi, Russia. The headquarters of the movement has been based in Crown Heights, Brooklyn, since 1940. Lubavitch now has thousands of emissaries throughout the world endeavoring to strengthen world Jewry.

l'vish: A term popular among Satmar and other Hasidic communities to refer to traditional Hasidic garb.

menorah: A nine-branch candelabrum traditionally lit on the holiday of Hanukkah.

misnagdim: Historical opponents of Hasidism; nowadays referred to as the Litvish or Lithuanian tradition; also called *yeshivish.* "Snag" is a derogatory term for this group and is used ubiquitously in Lubavitch.

mitzvos: Jewish commandments.

Modern Orthodox: A stream of Judaism that adheres to traditional Jewish law but does not isolate itself socially and culturally from secular society as ultra-Orthodoxy does (for example, it tolerates television, accepts social dating, and encourages college education).

Oral Torah: Refers to the rabbinic tradition, which from an ultra-Orthodox perspective was also given by God to Moses and from him to the Jewish people but was not written down in the Bible (the "written Torah").

Orthodox: A branch of Judaism that adheres strictly to Jewish law.

OTD: Off the *derech* (off the path), a popular phrase within the American Orthodox community to describe the action of someone who has left the community.

paiyyes: Long side curls worn by many Hasidic boys and men.

Purim: A Jewish holiday with a carnivalesque atmosphere, including revelers dressed in costumes, that is rooted in the biblical story of Esther that describes how the ancient Persian Jews were saved from the plot of Haman, who wanted to destroy them.

rebbe: A spiritual leader of a Hasidic community, believed by his followers to possess supernatural powers. In the context of Lubavitch, "the Rebbe" refers to the seventh Lubavitcher Rebbe, Rabbi Menachem Mendel Schneerson, who died in 1994.

Satmar: A Hasidic group founded by Rabbi Joel Teitelbaum in the early twentieth century in the city of Szatmárnémeti, Hungary (now Satu Mare, Romania). The group currently has members in South America, Europe, and Israel but is primarily based in Williamsburg (Brooklyn) and Kiryas Joel (Monroe, New York).

Sephardic: Referring to Jews of Spanish descent; often used as well to refer to Jews of Middle Eastern or North African descent.

Shabbos (or Shabbat): The Sabbath.

shaygets: A word that derives from the Hebrew *sheketz,* meaning "abomination," and is used colloquially to mean rascal or scoundrel and a non-Jewish male.

sheitel: A wig worn by Hasidic married women as a sign of modesty.

shiksa: A derogatory term for a non-Jewish female.

shiva: The traditional Jewish seven-day period of mourning.

shul: A Yiddish word meaning "synagogue."

Shulhan Arukh: The sixteenth-century Jewish law code of Rabbi Yosef Karo.

shvartzes: A derogatory Yiddish term for black people, commonly used in Hasidic communities.

smicha: Rabbinic ordination.

Torah: Can refer to the collection of biblical scriptures as well as more generally to Jewish religious texts.

tzitzis: Ritual fringes attached to a garment worn by Hasidic boys and men.

ultra-Orthodox: A strict form of Judaism that follows all of Jewish law as well as additional customs and conservative theological beliefs.

Williamsburg: A neighborhood in Brooklyn, New York, that has served as a headquarters for the Satmar Hasidic community since 1947.

yarmulke: Skullcap.

yeshiva: Rabbinical school for boys or men.

Yiddish: A language originally spoken by Jews in Central and Eastern Europe before the Holocaust that began as a dialect of German and incorporated words from Hebrew and other modern European languages. It is still spoken by most Hasidim as well small groups of secular Jews.

Yom Kippur: The Jewish Day of Atonement, when Jews traditionally fast.

References

Albarelli, G. 2000. *Teacha! Stories from a Yeshiva*. Thetford, VT: Glad Day Books.

Albrecht, L. S., M. Cornwall, and P. H. Cunningham. 1988. "Religious Leave-Taking: Disengagement and Disaffiliation among Mormons." In *Falling from the Faith: Causes and Consequences of Religious Apostasy*, edited by David G. Bromley, 62–80. Newbury Park, CA: Sage.

Alexander, M. 2010. *The New Jim Crow: Mass Incarceration in the Age of Colorblindness*. New York: New Press.

Anonymous. 2015. "Education????" Comment on "NY to Probe 39 Brooklyn Yeshivas." *COLlive*, July 30. Available at http://collive.com/show_news.rtx?id=36501&alias=ny -to-probe-39-brooklyn-yeshivas.

Aron, R. 2015. "We Are Hearing Their Cry." *COLlive*, August 4. Available at http://www .collive.com/show_news.rtx?id=36574&alias=we-are-hearing-their-cry.

Asim, J. 2008. *The N Word: Who Can Say It, Who Shouldn't, and Why*. Boston: Houghton Mifflin.

Ballis, P. H. 1999. *Leaving the Adventist Ministry: A Study of the Process of Exiting*. Westport, CT: Praeger.

Barker, E. 1998. "Standing at the Cross-roads: The Politics of Marginality in 'Subversive Organizations.'" In *The Politics of Religious Apostasy: The Role of Apostates in the Transformation of Religious Movements*, edited by D. G. Bromley, 75–94. Westport, CT: Praeger.

Belcove-Shalin, J. S., S. C. Heilman, W. Shaffir, L. D. Loeb, E. Koskoff, L. Davidman, J. Tocks, D. R. Kaufman, B. Morris, G. Kranzler, S. Epstein, and S. Poll. 1995. *New World Hasidism: Ethnographic Studies of Hasidic Jews in America*. Albany: State University of New York Press.

Bellah, R. N., R. Madsen, W. M. Sullivan, A. Swidler, and S. M. Tipton. 1985. *Habits of the Heart: Individualism and Commitment in American Life*. New York: Harper and Row.

Bengtson, V. L., N. M. Putney, and S. C. Harris. 2013. *Families and Faith: How Religion Is Passed Down across Generations.* Oxford: Oxford University Press.

Ben-Moshe, D., and Z. Segev, eds. 2007. *Israel, the Diaspora and Jewish Identity.* Eastbourne, UK: Sussex Academic Press.

Berger, D. 2001. *The Rebbe, the Messiah, and the Scandal of Orthodox Indifference.* Portland, OR: Littman Library Jewish Civilization.

Berger, P., and T. Luckmann. 1966. *The Social Construction of Reality: A Treatise in the Sociology of Knowledge.* New York: Doubleday.

Biale, D. 2010. *Not in the Heavens: The Tradition of Jewish Secular Thought.* Princeton, NJ: Princeton University Press.

Birnbaum, P. 2008. *Geography of Hope: Exile, the Enlightenment, Disassimilation.* Stanford, CA: Stanford University Press.

Botticini, M., and Z. Eckstein. 2014. *The Chosen Few: How Education Shaped Jewish History, 70–1492.* Princeton, NJ: Princeton University Press.

Bourdieu, P. 1977. *Outline of a Theory of Practice.* Translated by R. Nice. Cambridge: Cambridge University Press.

———. 1990. *In Other Words: Essays towards a Reflexive Sociology.* Translated by M. Adamson. Stanford, CA: Stanford University Press.

Bromley, D., ed. 1988. *Falling from the Faith: Causes and Consequences of Religious Apostasy.* Newbury Park, CA: Sage.

———, ed. 1998. *The Politics of Religious Apostasy: The Role of Apostates in the Transformation of Religious Movements.* Westport, CT: Praeger.

Budner, S. 1962. "Intolerance of Ambiguity as a Personality Variable." *Journal of Personality* 30 (1): 29–50.

Caplovitz, D., and F. Sherrow. 1977. *Religious Drop Outs: Apostasy among College Graduates.* Thousand Oaks, CA: Sage.

Chabad.org. n.d. "The Chassidic Masters on Food and Eating." Available at https://www.chabad.org/library/article_cdo/aid/73827/jewish/The-Chassidic-Masters-on-Food.htm (accessed September 7, 2019).

Chomsky, N. 1969. *American Power and the New Mandarins.* New York: Pantheon Books.

Cohen, S. M. 2014. Correspondence with the author.

Coser, L. A. 1956. *The Social Functions of Conflict: An Examination of the Concept of Social Conflict and Its Use in Empirical Sociological Research.* New York: Free Press.

———. 1974. *Greedy Institutions: Patterns of Undivided Commitment.* London: Collier Macmillan.

Dalfin, C. 2002. *Attack on Lubavitch: A Response.* New York: Jewish Enrichment Press.

Davidman, L. 2014. *Becoming Unorthodox.* New Brunswick, NJ: Rutgers University Press.

Davidman, L., and A. L. Greil. 2007. "Characters in Search of a Script: The Exit Narratives of Formerly Ultra-Orthodox Jews." *Journal for the Scientific Study of Religion* 46 (2): 201–216.

Dein, S. 2012. *Lubavitcher Messianism: What Really Happens When Prophecy Fails?* London: Bloomsbury.

Deutscher, I. 1968. *The Non-Jewish Jew and Other Essays.* London: Oxford University Press.

Dillon, M. 1990. *Catholic Identity: Balancing Reason, Faith, and Power.* Cambridge: Cambridge University Press.

Douglas, M. (1996) 2002. *Purity and Danger: An Analysis of Concepts of Pollution and Taboo*. Reprint, London: Rutledge.

Dresner, S. 1987. *Zaddik: The Doctrine of the Zaddik according to the Writings of Rabbi Yaakov Yosef of Polnoy*. New York: Schocken Books.

Dubnow, S. 1916. *History of the Jews in Russia and Poland: From the Earliest Times until the Present Day*. Translated by I. Friedlaender. Philadelphia: Jewish Publication Society of America.

Dubov, N. D. 1999. *To Love a Fellow Jew: The Mitzvah of Ahavas Yisrael in Chassidic Thought*. Brooklyn, NY: Sichos in English.

Durkheim, É. 1960. *The Division of Labor in Society*. Translated by G. Simpson. Glencoe, IL: Free Press.

———. 1975. "Review: 'Guyau—L'Irréligion de l'avenir.'" In *Durkheim on Religion: A Selection of Readings with Biographies and Introductory Remarks*, edited by W.S.F. Pickering, 24–38. London: Routledge and K. Paul.

Ebaugh, H.R.F. 1977. *Out of the Cloister: A Study of Organizational Dilemmas*. Austin: University of Texas Press.

———. 1988a. *Becoming an Ex*. Chicago: University of Chicago Press.

———. 1988b. "Leaving Catholic Convents." In *Falling from the Faith: Causes and Consequences of Religious Apostasy*, edited by D. G. Bromley, 100–121. Newbury Park, CA: Sage.

Ehrlich, M. A. 2005. *The Messiah of Brooklyn: Understanding Lubavitch Hasidism Past and Present*. Jersey City, NJ: Ktav.

Elias, N. (1939) 2000. *The Civilizing Process: Sociogenetic and Psychogenetic Investigations*. Reprint, Malden, MA: Blackwell.

———. 1987. "The Retreat of Sociologists into the Present." *Theory, Culture, and Society* 4:223–247.

Elior, R. 1998. "The Lubavitch Messianic Resurgence: The Historical and Mystical Background, 1939–1996." In *Toward the Millennium: Messianic Expectations from the Bible to Waco*, edited by P. Schafer and M. R. Cohen, 383–408. Leiden, Netherlands: Brill.

El-Or, T. 1994. *Educated and Ignorant: Ultraorthodox Jewish Women and Their World*. Boulder, CO: Rienner.

———. 2002. *Next Year I Will Know More: Literacy and Identity among Young Orthodox Women in Israel*. Detroit, MI: Wayne State University Press.

Endelman, T. M. 2015. *Leaving the Jewish Fold: Conversion and Radical Assimilation in Modern Jewish History*. Princeton, NJ: Princeton University Press.

Erikson, K. T. 1966. *Wayward Puritans: A Study in the Sociology of Deviance*. New York: Wiley.

Fader, A. 2009. *Mitzvah Girls: Bringing Up the Next Generation of Hasidic Jews in Brooklyn*. Princeton, NJ: Princeton University Press.

Feldman, J. 2003. *Lubavitchers as Citizens: A Paradox of Liberal Democracy*. Ithaca, NY: Cornell University Press.

Fine, G. A., and I. Khawaja. 2005. "Celebrating Arabs and Grateful Terrorists: Rumor and the Politics of Plausibility." In *Rumor Mills: The Social Impact of Rumor and Legend*, edited by G. A. Fine, V. Campion-Vincent, and C. Heath, 189–205. New Brunswick, NJ: Transaction.

Fishkoff, S. 2003. *The Rebbe's Army: Inside the World of Chabad-Lubavitch*. New York: Schocken Books.

Foner, N. 2000. *From Ellis Island to JFK: New York's Two Great Waves of Immigration*. New Haven, CT: Yale University Press.

Footsteps. 2013. "State of Footsteps, 2013." Unpublished report in the author's possession.

———. 2018. "New Member Trends, FY18." Unpublished report in the author's possession.

———. 2019. "Membership Growth, FY17–19." Unpublished report in the author's possession.

Frankenthaler, L. 2004. "Leaving Ultra-Orthodox Judaism: Defection as Deconversion." Master's thesis, Hebrew University of Jerusalem.

Freud, S. (1905) 1962. *Three Essays on the Theory of Sexuality*. Translated by J. Strachey. New York: Basic Books.

———. (1930) 1961. *Civilization and Its Discontents*. Translated by J. Strachey. New York: W. W. Norton.

Fuchs, I. 2014. *Jewish Women's Torah Study: Orthodox Religious Education and Modernity*. New York: Routledge.

Gans, H. J. 1979. "Symbolic Ethnicity: The Future of Ethnic Groups and Culture in America." In *On the Making of Americans: Essays in Honor of David Riesman*, edited by H. J. Gans, N. Glazer, J. R. Gusfield, and C. Jencks, 193–220. Philadelphia: University of Pennsylvania Press.

———. 1994. "Symbolic Ethnicity and Symbolic Religiosity: Towards a Comparison of Ethnic and Religious Acculturation." *Ethnic and Racial Studies* 17:577–592.

Giddens, A. 1984. *The Constitution of Society: Outline of the Theory of Structuration*. Cambridge, UK: Polity Press.

———. 1991. *Modernity and Self-Identity: Self and Society in the Late Modern Age*. Stanford, CA: Stanford University Press.

Gitelman, Z. 1972. *Jewish Nationality and Soviet Politics: The Jewish Sections of the CPSU, 1917–1930*. Princeton, NJ: Princeton University Press.

Glass, I. 2015. "The Heart Wants What It Wants." *This American Life*, October 30. Available at http://www.thisamericanlife.org/radio-archives/episode/571/transcript.

Gluckman, M. 1963. "Gossip and Scandal." *Current Anthropology* 4 (3): 307–316.

Goffman, E. 1961. *Asylums*. Chicago: Aldine.

———. 1963. *Stigma: Notes on the Management of Spoiled Identity*. New York: Simon and Schuster.

Goldberg, H. 1989. *Between Berlin and Slobodka: Jewish Transition Figures from Eastern Europe*. Hoboken, NJ: Ktav.

Goldberger, F. 2013. "Blurring Out Satmar History." *Forward*, August 2. Available at http://forward.com/opinion/181566/blurring-out-satmar-history.

Goldschmidt, H. 2006. *Race and Religion among the Chosen People of Crown Heights*. New Brunswick, NJ: Rutgers University Press.

Gorbachev, M. 1995. *Memoirs*. New York: Doubleday.

Grant, E. 1996. *The Foundations of Modern Science in the Middle Ages: Their Religious, Institutional and Intellectual Contexts*. Cambridge: Cambridge University Press.

———. 2001. *God and Reason in the Middle Ages*. Cambridge: Cambridge University Press.

Green, A. 1977. "The *Zaddiq* as *Axis Mundi* in Later Judaism." *Journal of the American Academy of Religion* 45 (3): 327–347.

Greenwald, G. 2014. *No Place to Hide: Edward Snowden, the NSA, and the U.S. Surveillance State*. New York: Metropolitan Books.

Gruen, E. S. 2010. *Rethinking the Other in Antiquity*. Princeton, NJ: Princeton University Press.

Hall, D. D. 1997. *Lived Religion in America: Toward a History of Practice*. Princeton, NJ: Princeton University Press.

Heilman, S. 1994. "Quiescent and Active Fundamentalisms." In *Accounting for Fundamentalisms*, edited by Martin E. Marty and R. Scott Appleby, 173–196. Chicago: University of Chicago Press.

———. 2000. *Defenders of the Faith: Inside Ultra-Orthodox Jewry*. Berkeley: University of California Press.

Heilman, S., and M. Friedman. 2010. *The Rebbe: The Life and Afterlife of Menachem Mendel Schneerson*. Princeton, NJ: Princeton University Press.

Heilman, U. 2014. "Where Chabad's Lost Boys Go to Find Themselves." *Jewish Telegraphic Agency*, June 9. Available at http://www.jta.org/2014/06/09/news-opinion/united-states/where-chabads-lost-boys-go-to-find-themselves.

Helfgot, N. 2013. "Modern Orthodoxy's Welcome Alternative." *Jewish Press*, June 20. Available at http://www.jewishpress.com/indepth/opinions/haredi-dropouts-should-try-modern-orthodoxy-first/2013/06/20.

Helmreich, W. B. 1986. *The World of the Yeshiva: An Intimate Portrait of Orthodox Jewry*. New Haven, CT: Yale University Press.

Hirschman, A. O. 1970. *Exit, Voice, and Loyalty: Responses to Decline in Firms, Organizations, and States*. Cambridge, MA: Harvard University Press.

———. 1991. *The Rhetoric of Reaction: Perversity, Futility, Jeopardy*. Cambridge, MA: Belknap Press.

Hofstadter, R. 1963. *Anti-intellectualism in American Life*. New York: Vintage Books.

———. 1964. *The Paranoid Style in American Politics and Other Essays*. Chicago: University of Chicago Press.

Hoge, D. R., K. McGuire, and B. F. Stratman. 1981. *Converts, Dropouts, Returnees: A Study of Religious Change among Catholics*. New York: Pilgrim Press.

Holden, A. 2002. *Jehovah's Witnesses: Portrait of a Contemporary Religious Movement*. London: Routledge.

Hostetler, J. A. 1993. *Amish Society*. Baltimore: Johns Hopkins University Press.

Jackman, M. R. 1994. *The Velvet Glove: Paternalism and Conflict in Gender, Class, and Race Relations*. Berkeley: University of California Press.

Jacobs, J. L. 1987. "Deconversion from Religious Movements: An Analysis of Charismatic Bonding and Spiritual Commitment." *Journal for the Scientific Study of Religion* 26 (3): 294–308.

———. 1989. *Divine Disenchantment: Deconverting from New Religions*. Bloomington: Indiana University Press.

Jacobs, L. 1990. *Holy Living: Saints and Saintliness in Judaism*. Northvale, NJ: Jason Aronson.

Johnson, D. C. 1998. "Apostates Who Never Were: The Social Construction of *Absque Facto* Apostate Narratives." In *The Politics of Religious Apostasy: The Role of Apostates in the Transformation of Religious Movements*, edited by D. Bromley, 115–138. Westport, CT: Praeger.

Joppke, C., and S. Lukes, eds. 1999. *Multicultural Questions*. Oxford: Oxford University Press.

Kanter, R. M. 1972. *Commitment and Community: Communes and Utopias in Sociological Perspective*. Cambridge, MA: Harvard University Press.

Kanya, K. 2018. *Ve-Tinok Le-Lamdo Sefer.* New York: Der Veker.

Kaplan, Y. 2015. "The Truth about Camps." *CrownHeights.info,* April 27. Available at http://crownheights.info/op-ed/481482/op-ed-the-truth-about-camps.

Katz, M. B. 2010. *The Visual Culture of Chabad.* Cambridge: Cambridge University Press.

Keren-Kratz, M. 2015. "Maramaros, Hungary—the Cradle of Extreme Orthodoxy." *Modern Judaism* 35 (2): 147–174.

Kirschenbaum, M. 2009. "The Soul of a Gentile." Avner Institute, December 23. Available at http://portraitofaleader.blogspot.com/2009/12/soul-of-gentile.html.

Kravel-Tovi, M., and Y. Bilu. 2008. "The Work of the Present: Constructing Messianic Temporality in the Wake of Failed Prophecy among Chabad Hasidim." *American Ethnologist* 35 (1): 64–80.

Kuhn, T. S. 1962. *The Structure of Scientific Revolutions.* Chicago: University of Chicago Press.

Labendz, J. 2010. *Socratic Torah: Non-Jews in Rabbinic Intellectual Culture.* New York: Oxford University Press.

Lakatos, I. 1970. "Falsification and Methodology of Scientific Research Programmes." In *Criticism and the Growth of Knowledge,* edited by I. Lakatos and A. Musgrave, 91–196. Cambridge: Cambridge University Press.

Lalich, J. 2001. "Pitfalls in the Sociological Study of Cults." In *Misunderstanding Cults: Searching for Objectivity in a Controversial Field,* edited by B. Zablocki and T. Robbins, 123–155. Toronto: University of Toronto Press.

Lamm, N. 1999. *The Religious Thought of Hasidism: Text and Commentary.* Hoboken, NJ: Ktav.

Lamont, M. 1992. *Money, Morals, and Manners: The Culture of the French and American Upper-Middle Class.* Chicago: University of Chicago Press.

Landau, D. 1992. *Piety and Power: The World of Jewish Fundamentalism.* New York: Hill and Wang.

Levine, S. 2003. *Mystics, Mavericks, and Merrymakers: An Intimate Journey among Hasidic Girls.* New York: New York University Press.

Levine, S. D. 1996. *Zikoron L'Beis Yisrael.* Brooklyn, NY: Kehot Publication Society.

Levy, S. B. 1973. "Ethnic Boundaries and the Institutionalization of Charisma: A Study of the Lubavitcher Chassidim." Ph.D. diss., City University of New York.

Loewenthal, N. 1990. *Communicating the Infinite: The Emergence of the Habad School.* Chicago: University of Chicago Press.

Lofland, J. 1969. *Deviance and Identity.* Englewood Cliffs, NJ: Prentice Hall.

Lukes, S. 1985. *Émile Durkheim, His Life and Work: A Historical and Critical Study.* Stanford, CA: Stanford University Press.

Maimonides, M. 1963. *The Guide of the Perplexed.* Vol. 2, translated by S. Pines. Chicago: University of Chicago Press.

Margolese, F. 2005. *Off the Derech: How to Respond to the Challenge.* Jerusalem, Israel: Devora.

Maruna, S. 2001. *Making Good: How Ex-convicts Reform and Rebuild Their Lives.* Washington, DC: American Psychological Association.

Mather, C. 1820. *Magnalia Christi Americana; Or, The Ecclesiastical History of New-England.* Vol. 1. Hartford, CT: Roberts and Burr.

Mauss, A. 1969. "Dimensions of Religious Defection." *Review of Religious Research* 10 (3): 128–135.

Mauss, M. (1934) 1973. "Techniques of the Body." *Economy and Society* 2 (1): 70–88.

Mayse, A. E. 2017. "The Sacred Writ of Hasidism: Tanya and the Spiritual Vision of Rabbi Shneur Zalman of Liadi." In *Books of the People: Revisiting Classic Works of Jewish Thought*, edited by S. W. Halpern, 109–156. New Milford, CT: Maggid.

Mead, G. H. 1918. "The Psychology of Punitive Justice." *American Journal of Sociology* 23:577–602.

Meisels, D. 2011. *The Rebbe: The Extraordinary Life and Worldview of Rabbeinu Yoel Teitelbaum, the Satmar Rebbe*. Lakewood, NJ: Israel Book Shop.

Melamed, A. 2003. *The Image of the Black in Jewish Culture: A History of the Other*. New York: Routledge.

Mendelsohn, E. 1970. *Class Struggle in the Pale: The Formative Years of the Jewish Worker's Movement in Tsarist Russia*. Cambridge: Cambridge University Press.

———. 1983. *The Jews of East Central Europe between the World Wars*. Bloomington: Indiana University Press.

Merton, R. K. 1968. *Social Theory and Social Structure*. New York: Free Press.

Miller, C. 2014. *Turning Judaism Outwards: A Biography of the Rebbe, Menachem Mendel Schneerson*. Brooklyn, NY: Kol Menachem.

Mintz, J. 1994. *Hasidic People: A Place in the New World*. Cambridge, MA: Harvard University Press.

Mitchell, C. 2005. "Behind the Ethnic Marker: Religion and Social Identification in Northern Ireland." *Sociology of Religion* 66 (1): 3–21.

Morawska, E. 2007. "Transnationalism." In *Harvard Encyclopedia of the New Americans*, edited by M. C. Waters, R. Ueda, and H. B. Marrow, 149–163. Cambridge, MA: Harvard University Press.

Morris, B. J. 1998. *Lubavitcher Women in America: Identity and Activism in the Postwar Era*. Albany: State University of New York Press.

Myers, J. 2011. "Kabbalah for the Gentiles: Diverse Souls and Universalism in Contemporary Kabbalah." In *Kabbalah and Spiritual Revival: Historical, Sociological, and Cultural Perspectives*, edited by B. Huss, 182–211. Be'er Sheva, Israel: Ben-Gurion University Press.

Nahshoni, K. 2013a. "Satmar: IDF Draft Worse than Annihilation." *Ynet News*, April 12. Available at http://www.ynetnews.com/articles/0,7340,L-4365946,00.html.

———. 2013b. "Satmar: No Greater Offense than Voting." *Ynet News*, January 22. Available at http://www.ynetnews.com/articles/0,7340,L-4335420,00.html.

Neustein, A., ed. 2009. *Tempest in the Temple: Jewish Communities and Child Sex Scandals*. Lebanon, NH: Brandeis University Press.

Orwell, G. (1937) 1972. *The Road to Wigan Pier*. Reprint, New York: Houghton Mifflin Harcourt.

Pager, D. 2007. *Marked: Race, Crime, and Finding Work in an Era of Mass Incarceration*. Chicago: University of Chicago Press.

Park, R. 1928. "Human Migration and the Marginal Man." *American Journal of Sociology* 33 (6): 881–893.

Partlan, A., D. S. Davis, S. Heilman, M. Zanger-Tishler, and M. Hamilton. 2017. "Nonequivalent: The State of Education in New York City's Hasidic Yeshivas." Available at https://d3n8a8pro7vhmx.cloudfront.net/yaffed/pages/116/attachments/original/1523680597/Yaffed_Report_online_version.pdf?1523680597.

Pew Research Center. 2013. *A Portrait of Jewish Americans*. Available at https://www.pewforum.org/2013/10/01/jewish-american-beliefs-attitudes-culture-survey.

Polanyi, M. (1966) 2009. *The Tacit Dimension*. Reprint, Chicago: University of Chicago Press.

Poll, S. 1969. *The Hasidic Community of Williamsburg: A Study in the Sociology of Religion*. New York: Schocken Books.

Putnam, R. D., and D. E. Campbell. 2012. *American Grace: How Religion Divides and Unites Us*. New York: Simon and Schuster.

"Rabbis Urge to Marry Young." 2012. *COLlive*, February 10. Available at https://collive.com/rabbis-urge-to-marry-young.

Rabinowicz, T. 2000. *Hasidim in Israel: A History of the Hasidic Movement and Its Masters in the Holy Land*. Northvale, NJ: Jason Aronson.

"Radio Clash: Chabad vs. Reform." 2011. *Shmais*, May 14. Available at http://www.shmais.com/chabad-news/latest/item/radio-clash-chabad-vs-reform.

Ragen, N. 2013. *The Sisters Weiss*. Farmington Hills, MI: Thorndike Press.

Rapoport-Albert, A. 2013. "From Woman as Hasid to Woman as 'Tsadik' in the Teachings of the Last Two Lubavitcher Rebbes." *Jewish History* 27:435–473.

Rapoport, C. 2002. *The Messiah Problem: Berger, the Angel, and the Scandal of Reckless Indiscrimination*. Essex, UK: Ilford Synagogue.

———. 2011. *The Afterlife of Scholarship: A Critical Review of 'The Rebbe' by Samuel Heilman and Menachem Friedman*. N.p.: Oporto Press.

Ravitzky, A. 1994. "The Contemporary Lubavitch Hasidic Movement." In *Accounting for Fundamentalism*, edited by M. E. Marty and R. S. Appleby, 303–327. Chicago: University of Chicago Press.

———. 1996. *Messianism, Zionism, and Jewish Religious Radicalism*. Translated by M. Swirsky and J. Chipman. Chicago: University of Chicago Press.

Richardson, J. T. 2009. "Foreword." In *Deconversion: Qualitative and Quantitative Results from Cross-cultural Research in Germany and the United States of America*, edited by H. Streib, R. W. Hood, B. Keller, R. M. Csöff, and C. F. Silver, 9–12. Göttingen, Germany: Vandenhoeck and Ruprecht.

Ricoeur, P. 1977. *The Rule of Metaphor: Multi-disciplinary Studies of the Creation of Meaning in Language*. Toronto: University of Toronto Press.

Roberts, S. 2011. "A Village with the Numbers, Not the Image, of the Poorest Place." *New York Times*, April 20. Available at http://www.nytimes.com/2011/04/21/nyregion/kiryas-joel-a-village-with-the-numbers-not-the-image-of-the-poorest-place.html.

Rosenberg, S. 2011. "Hasidic Paper Removes Hillary Clinton from Osama Picture." *Failed Messiah*, May 5. Available at http://failedmessiah.typepad.com/failed_messiahcom/2011/05/hasidic-paper-removes-hillary-clinton-from-osama-picture-567.html.

———. 2012a. "Letter from Satmar Va'ad HaTznius." *Failed Messiah*, December 4. Available at https://failedmessiah.typepad.com/failed_messiahcom/2012/12/letter-from-satmar-vaad-hatznius-345.html.

———. 2012b. "Satmar Internet Rules." *Failed Messiah*, June 3. Available at http://failedmessiah.typepad.com/failed_messiahcom/2012/06/satmar-internet-rules-123.html.

———. 2013a. "Audio: What Rabbi Manis Friedman Really Said about Child Sex Abuse." *Failed Messiah*, January 30. Available at https://failedmessiah.typepad.com/failed_messiahcom/2013/01/audio-what-rabbi-manis-friedman-really-said-about-child-sex-abuse-456.html.

———. 2013b. "Satmar-Hasid-Owned Newspapers Cut Slain Woman out of Her Own Wedding Picture for 'Modesty' Reasons." *Failed Messiah*, March 7. Available at http://failedmessiah.typepad.com/failed_messiahcom/2013/03/satmar-hasid

-owned-papers-cut-slain-woman-out-of-her-own-wedding-picture-for-modesty
-reasons-567.html.

———. 2013c. "Satmar Rebbe: 'All Goyim Are Dirty.'" *Failed Messiah*, September 18.
Available at http://failedmessiah.typepad.com/failed_messiahcom/2013/09/satmar
-rebbe-all-goyyim-are-dirty-456.html.

———. 2014. "Satmar Aharon Faction Officially Bans Girls Who Wear Makeup." *Failed
Messiah*, February 17. Available at http://failedmessiah.typepad.com/failed
_messiahcom/2014/02/satmar-aharon-faction-officially-bans-girls-who-wear
-makeup-234.html.

Rosenblum, J. D. 2014. *Food and Identity in Early Rabbinic Judaism*. New York: Cambridge University Press.

Roskies, D. 1999. *The Jewish Search for a Usable Past*. Bloomington: Indiana University
Press.

Rosmarin, D. H., S. Pirutinsky, M. Appel, T. Kaplan, and D. Pelcovitz. 2018. "Childhood
Sexual Abuse, Mental Health, and Religion across the Jewish Community." *Child
Abuse and Neglect* 81:21–28.

Rosnow, R. L., and G. A. Fine. 1976. *Rumor and Gossip: The Social Psychology of Hearsay*.
New York: Elsevier.

Rothbaum, S. 1988. "Between Two Worlds: Issues of Separation and Identity after Leaving a Religious Community." In *Falling from the Faith: Causes and Consequences of
Religious Apostasy*, edited by D. G. Bromley, 205–228. Newbury Park, CA: Sage.

Rubel, N. L. 2010. *Doubting the Devout: The Ultra-Orthodox in the Jewish American
Imagination*. New York: Columbia University Press.

Rubin, I. 1997. *Satmar: Two Generations of an Urban Island*. New York: Peter Lang.

Rushdie, S. 1992. *Imaginary Homelands: Essays and Criticism, 1981–1991*. London:
Granta Books.

Sacks, J. 2013. "The Far Horizon." Chabad.org, December 31. Available at http://www
.chabad.org/parshah/article_cdo/aid/2430669/jewish/The-Far-Horizon.htm.

SanGiovanni, L. 1978. *Ex-nuns: A Study of Emergent Role Passage*. Norwood, NJ: Ablex.

Sarna, J. 2006. "The Break between Conservative and Orthodox in America." Paper
presented at the Modern Orthodoxy 1940–1970 conference, University of Scranton,
June 13–15.

Schiller, N. G., L. Basch, and C. Blanc-Szanton. 1992. "Transnationalism: A New Ana-
lytic Framework for Understanding Migration." *Annals of the New York Academy
of Sciences* 645 (1): 1–24.

Schneerson, F. 1922. *Chaim Gravitzer*. Berlin: Judischer Literarischer Verlag.

Schneerson, M. M. (1942) 1973. *Hayom Yom*. Reprint, Brooklyn, NY: Kehot Publication
Society.

———. (1950) 1991. *Likkutei Sichos* [Collected discourses]. Vol. 2. Reprint, Brooklyn,
NY: Kehot Publication Society.

———. (1982) 2006. *Likkutei Sichos* [Collected discourses]. Vol. 18. Reprint, Brooklyn,
NY: Kehot Publication Society.

———. 1983. *Torat Menachem: Hisvaduyos 5743* [The Torah of Menachem: Gatherings
5743]. Vol. 4. Brooklyn, NY: Vaad Hanochos BLahak.

———. 1986. "14 Adar I 5746, Sicha 1." Chabad.org, February 23. Available at http://www
.chabad.org/therebbe/article_cdo/aid/554266/jewish/14-Adar-I-5746-Sicha-1.htm.

———. 2001. *Eyes upon the Land: The Territorial Integrity of Israel; A Life-Threatening
Concern*. Edited by U. Kaploun. Translated by E. Touger. Brooklyn, NY: Sichos in
English.

———. 2004. "The Rebbe's Letter on the Rescue of Ethiopian Jews." *Failed Messiah*, September 23. Available at http://failedmessiah.typepad.com/failed_messiahcom/2004/09/the_rebbes_lett.html.

———. 2018. *Security for the Land of Israel*. Edited and translated by B. Schlanger. Jerusalem: Israel Stand Strong.

Schneider, K. 1958. *Psychopathic Personalities*. Translated by M. W. Hamilton. London: Cassell.

Schochet, J. I. 2001. "The Professor, Messiah, and Scandal of Calumnies." *Shmais*. Available at https://archive.li/UMd4h.

Schorsch, J. 2004. *Jews and Blacks in the Early Modern World*. Cambridge: Cambridge University Press.

Seidman, I. 1998. *Interviewing as Qualitative Research: A Guide for Researchers in Education and the Social Sciences*. New York: Teachers College Press.

Seligson, M. 2011. *Sefer Hamaftechos l'Sichos Kodesh* [An index of the sacred discourses]. Brooklyn, NY: Kehot Publication Society.

Seliktar, O. 2002. *Divided We Stand: American Jews, Israel, and the Peace Process*. Santa Barbara, CA: Praeger.

Shaffir, W. 1974. *Life in a Religious Community: The Lubavitcher Chassidim in Montreal*. Toronto: Holt, Rinehart and Winston of Canada.

———. 1993. "Jewish Messianism Lubavitch Style: An Interim Report." *Jewish Journal of Sociology* 35 (2): 115–128.

———. 1998. "Disaffiliation: The Experiences of Haredi Jews." In *Leaving Religion and Religious Life: Patterns and Dynamics*, edited by M. Bar-Lev, W. Shaffir, and D. G. Bromley, 205–228. Greenwich, CT: JAI Press.

Shaffir, W., and R. Rockaway. 1987. "Leaving the Ultra-Orthodox Fold: Haredi Jews Who Defected." *Jewish Journal of Sociology* 29 (2): 97–114.

Shapiro, M. 2015. *Changing the Immutable: How Orthodox Judaism Rewrites Its History*. Oxford: Littman Library of Jewish Civilization.

Shragi. 2014. "10 Prerequisites for Going OTD." *Frum Satire*, September 8. Available at http://www.frumsatire.net/2014/09/08/10-prerequisites-going-otd.

Shteinman, A. L. 2017. "Rav Aryeh Leib Shteinman and Accepting Boys into Yeshivah— Every Jew Should Watch This!" *YouTube*, July 31. Available at https://www.youtube.com/watch?v=YP2QIl9Qthc.

Silberg, J., and S. Dallam. 2009. "Out of the Jewish Closet: Facing the Hidden Secrets of Child Sex Abuse—and the Damage Done to Victims." In *Tempest in the Temple: Jewish Communities and Child Sex Scandals*, edited by A. Neustein, 77–104. Lebanon, NH: Brandeis University Press.

Simmel, G. 1908. "The Stranger." In *On the Individual and Social Forms*, edited by D. N. Levine, 143–149. Chicago: University of Chicago Press.

———. 1955. *Conflict and the Web of Group Affiliations*. Translated by K. H. Wolff and R. Bendix. New York: Free Press.

Simpson, J. H. 1997. "Leaving Religions: An Inventory of Some Elementary Concepts." In *Religion and the Social Order: Leaving Religion and Religious Life*, edited by D. Bromley, M. Bar-Lev, and W. Shaffir, 17–29. Greenwich, CT: JAI Press.

Singer, D. 2003. "The Rebbe, the Messiah, and the Heresy Hunter." *First Things* 133:42–49.

Skinazi, K.E.H. 2018. *Women of Valor: Orthodox Jewish Troll Fighters, Crime Writers, and Rock Stars in Contemporary Literature and Culture*. New Brunswick, NJ: Rutgers University Press.

Skonovd, N. L. 1981. "Apostasy: The Process of Defection from Religious Totalism." Ph.D. diss., University of California, Davis.

Smith, J. Z. 1982. *Imagining Religion: From Babylon to Jonestown*. Chicago: University of Chicago Press.

Sobczak, M. 2010. *American Attitudes toward Immigrants and Immigration Policy*. El Paso, TX: LFB Scholarly.

Sokol, S. 2015. "Former Hasidic Woman Who Committed Suicide Blasts Orthodox Community in Her Final Letter." *Jerusalem Post*, July 23. Available at http://www.jpost.com/Diaspora/Ex-hassidic-woman-who-jumped-off-roof-blasts-Orthodox-in-last-letter-410008.

Sontag, S. 1978. *Illness as Metaphor*. New York: Farrar, Straus and Giroux.

Stadler, N. 2009. *Yeshiva Fundamentalism: Piety, Gender, and Resistance in the Ultra-Orthodox World*. New York: New York University Press.

Steinsaltz, A. 2014. *My Rebbe*. New Milford, CT: Maggid.

Streib, H., R. W. Hood, B. Keller, R. M. Csöff, and C. F. Silver. 2009. *Deconversion: Qualitative and Quantitative Results from Cross-cultural Research in Germany and the United States of America*. Göttingen, Germany: Vandenhoeck and Ruprecht.

Student, G. 2002. *Can the Rebbe Be Moshiach? Proofs from Gemara, Midrash, and Rambam That the Rebbe Cannot Be Moshiach*. Irvine, CA: Universal.

Tabory, E., and S. Hazan-Stern. 2013. "Bonds of Silence: Parents and Children Cope with Dissonant Levels of Religiosity." *Contemporary Jewry* 33:171–192.

Tanny, B. 2012. *Freiing Out: Why People Go off the Derech and What We Can Do about It*. Jerusalem: Penina Press.

Tavory, I. 2010. "Off Melrose: Orthodox Life in a Secular Space." Ph.D. diss., University of California, Los Angeles.

Taylor, C. 2007. *A Secular Age*. Cambridge, MA: Belknap Press.

Teitelbaum, A. 2012. "Satmar Rebbe Epic Speech on the Internet." *YouTube*, April 26. Available at https://www.youtube.com/watch?v=dPNZV99C92M.

Teitelbaum, Y. 1961. *Vayoel Moshe*. Brooklyn, NY: Jerusalem.

Telushkin, J. 2014. *Rebbe: The Life and Teachings of Menachem M. Schneerson, the Most Influential Rabbi in Modern History*. New York: Harper Wave.

Tocqueville, A. 2000. *Democracy in America*. Translated by H. Mansfield and D. Winthrop. Chicago: University of Chicago Press.

Topel, M. F. 2012. *Jewish Orthodoxy and Its Discontents: Religious Dissidence in Contemporary Israel*. Lanham: MD: University Press of America.

Trencher, M. 2016. "Starting a Conversation: A Pioneering Survey of Those Who Have Left the Orthodox Community." Nishma Research, June 21. Available at http://nishmaresearch.com/assets/pdf/Press_Release_Survey_of_Those_Who_Left_Orthodoxy_Nishma_Research_June_2016.pdf.

Turner, V. 1967. *The Forest of Symbols: Aspects of Ndembu Ritual*. Ithaca, NY: Cornell University Press.

———. 1969. *The Ritual Process*. Chicago: Aldine.

Tversky, A., and D. Kahneman. 1973. "Availability: A Heuristic for Judging Frequency and Probability." *Cognitive Psychology* 5:207–232.

Vaughan, D. 1990. *Uncoupling: Turning Points in Intimate Relationships*. New York: Vintage Books.

Vincent, L. 2013. "The Post-Ultra-Orthodox Death Prophecy." *Zeek*, October 7. Available at http://zeek.forward.com/articles/117904.

Vizel, F. 2018. "The Truth about Hasidic Education." *Tablet*, April 16. Available at https://www.tabletmag.com/scroll/259976/the-truth-about-hasidic-education.

Waldron, J. 1992. "Minority Cultures and the Cosmopolitan Alternative." *University of Michigan Journal of Law Reform* 25 (3): 751–793.

Wallis, R. 1977. *The Road to Total Freedom: A Sociological Analysis of Scientology.* New York: Columbia University Press.

Waters, M. C. 1990. *Ethnic Options: Choosing Identities in America.* Berkeley: University of California Press.

Weber, M. 1978. *Economy and Society.* Edited by G. Roth and C. Wittich. Berkeley: University of California Press.

Western, B. 2018. *Homeward: Life in the Year after Prison.* New York: Russell Sage Foundation.

Wiener, M. 2006. *Hadras Ponim-Zokon.* New York: self-published.

Winston, H. 2005. *Unchosen: The Hidden Lives of Hasidic Rebels.* Boston: Beacon Press.

———. 2006. "Edgework: Boundary Crossing among the Hasidim." Ph.D. diss., City University of New York Graduate Center.

Wodzinski, M. 2018. *Historical Atlas of Hasidism.* Princeton, NJ: Princeton University Press.

Wolfson, E. 2009. *Open Secret: Postmessianic Messianism and the Mystical Revision of Menahem Mendel Schneerson.* New York: Columbia University Press.

Wonders and Miracles: Stories of the Lubavitcher Rebbe. 1993. Kfar Chabad, Israel: Maareches Ufaratzta.

Wright, S. A. 1984. "Post-involvement Attitudes of Voluntary Defectors from Controversial New Religious Movements." *Journal for the Scientific Study of Religion* 23 (2): 172–182.

———. 1987. *Leaving Cults: The Dynamics of Defection.* Indianapolis, IN: Society for Scientific Study of Religion.

———. 1991. "Reconceptualizing Cult Coercion and Withdrawal: A Comparative Analysis of Divorce and Apostasy." *Social Forces* 70 (1): 125–145.

———. 1998. "Exploring Factors That Shape the Apostate Role." In *The Politics of Apostasy: The Role of Apostates in the Transformation of Religious Movements*, edited by D. G. Bromley, 95–114. Westport, CT: Praeger.

Zablocki, B. 1980. *The Joyful Community: An Account of the Bruderhof, a Communal Movement Now in Its Third Generation.* Chicago: University of Chicago Press.

Zerubavel, E. 1991. *The Fine Line: Making Distinction in Everyday Life.* Chicago: University of Chicago Press.

———. 2006. *The Elephant in the Room: Silence and Denial in Everyday Life.* Oxford: Oxford University Press.

Zuckerman, P. 2012. *Faith No More: Why People Reject Religion.* Oxford: Oxford University Press.

Index

Schneur Zalman Newfield is an Assistant Professor of Sociology in the Department of Social Sciences, Human Services, and Criminal Justice, at the Borough of Manhattan Community College, City University of New York.